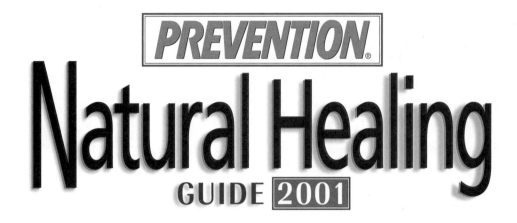

PREVENTION
Natural Healing
GUIDE 2001

Your Complete Resource
for Healthy Living from America's
#1 Health Magazine

from the Editors of **Prevention** Magazine

RODALE

Printed in the United States of America
Rodale Inc. makes every effort to use acid-free ♾ , recycled paper ♻

"Healing Spotlight" on page 54 is adapted from "Signing On for Good Health" by Jill Daniel, which appeared in *Prevention's Guide to Healing Foods* magazine, October 5, 1999.

"'One Size Fits All' Is *Not* a Smart Diet Plan" on page 59 is adapted from "Your Best Diet—At 30, 40, 50, 60+" by Elizabeth Somer, R.D., which appeared in *Prevention* magazine, July 1999.

"Healing Spotlight" on page 140 is adapted from "Natural Talent" by Jill Daniel, which appeared in *Prevention's Guide to Healing Herbs* magazine, July 27, 1999.

ISBN 1–57954–357–X   hardcover
ISBN 1–57954–393–6   paperback

2 4 6 8 10 9 7 5 3 1   hardcover
2 4 6 8 10 9 7 5 3 1   paperback

Visit us on the Web at www.preventionbookshelf.com, or call us toll-free at (800) 848-4735.

RODALE
WE INSPIRE AND ENABLE PEOPLE TO IMPROVE
THEIR LIVES AND THE WORLD AROUND THEM

About *Prevention* Health Books

The editors of *Prevention* Health Books are dedicated to providing you with authoritative, trustworthy, and innovative advice for a healthy, active lifestyle. In all of our books, our goal is to keep you thoroughly informed about the latest breakthroughs in natural healing, medical research, alternative health, herbs, nutrition, fitness, and weight loss. We cut through the confusion of today's conflicting health reports to deliver clear, concise, and definitive health information that you can trust. And we explain in practical terms what each new breakthrough means to you so that you can take immediate, practical steps to improve your health and well-being.

Every recommendation in *Prevention* Health Books is based upon reliable sources, including interviews with qualified health authorities. In addition, we retain top-level health practitioners who serve on the Rodale Books Board of Advisors to ensure that all of the health information is safe, practical, and up-to-date. *Prevention* Health Books are thoroughly fact-checked for accuracy, and we make every effort to verify recommendations, dosages, and cautions.

The advice in this book will help keep you well-informed about your personal choices in health care—to help you lead a happier, healthier, and longer life.

Notice

Prevention Natural Healing Guide 2001 Staff

EDITOR: Doug Hill

ASSISTANT EDITOR: Jennifer Bright

WRITERS: Anne Alexander; Sara Altshul; Alisa Bauman; Marla Bazar; Maureen Boland; Jennifer Bright; Michael Castleman; Jill Daniel; Jeff Davidson; Bridget Doherty; Doug Dollemore; James A. Duke, Ph.D.; Anne Egan; Julie Evans; Kelly Garrett; Laura Goldstein; Melissa Gotthardt; Bill Gottlieb; Sarí Harrar; Maria Mihalik Higgins; Doug Hill; Paula Hunt; David Joachim; Joely Johnson; Sherry Weiss Kiser; Diane Kozak; Nanci Kulig; Barbara Loecher; Gale Maleskey; Linda Marino; Jordan Matus; Jim McCommons; Holly McCord, R.D.; Gloria McVeigh; Christian Millman; Mary Jane Minkin, M.D.; P. Morgan; Kristine Napier; Lisa Pionegro; Linda Rao; Judith Springer Riddle; Tom Rinderle; Sarah Robertson; Michael F. Roizen, M.D.; Douglas Schar, DipPhyt; Elizabeth Somer, R.D.; Maggie Spilner; Elizabeth Anne Stephenson; Varro E. Tyler, Ph.D., Sc.D.; Mariska Van Aalst; Julia VanTine; Teri Walsh; Denise Webb; Jeff Weingrad; Judy West; Selene Yeager

COVER ART DIRECTOR: Darlene Schneck

INTERIOR ART DESIGNER: Richard Kershner

PHOTO EDITOR: James A. Gallucci

COVER DESIGNER: Christopher Rhoads

ASSISTANT RESEARCH MANAGER: Sandra Salera Lloyd

PRIMARY RESEARCH EDITOR: Anita C. Small

RESEARCH EDITOR: Jennifer Bright

SENIOR COPY EDITOR: Kathryn C. LeSage

EDITORIAL PRODUCTION MANAGER: Marilyn Hauptly

LAYOUT DESIGNER: Keith Biery

MANUFACTURING COORDINATORS: Brenda Miller, Jodi Schaffer, Patrick Smith

Rodale Healthy Living Books

EXECUTIVE EDITOR: Tammerly Booth

DIRECTOR OF SERIES DEVELOPMENT: Gary M. Krebs

EDITORIAL DIRECTOR: Michael Ward

VICE PRESIDENT AND MARKETING DIRECTOR: Karen Arbegast

PRODUCT MARKETING DIRECTOR: Guy Maake

BOOK MANUFACTURING DIRECTOR: Helen Clogston

MANUFACTURING MANAGER: Eileen Bauder

RESEARCH MANAGER: Ann Gossy Yermish

COPY MANAGER: Lisa D. Andruscavage

PRODUCTION MANAGER: Robert V. Anderson Jr.

DIGITAL PROCESSING GROUP MANAGERS: Leslie M. Keefe, Thomas P. Aczel

OFFICE MANAGER: Jacqueline Dornblaser

OFFICE STAFF: Susan B. Dorschutz, Julie Kehs Minnix, Catherine E. Strouse

CONTENTS

The RealAge Quiz
Find out how your
quality of life affects
your rate of aging
PAGE 6

Look Out!
Avoid natural
reactions
PAGE 12

PART TWO

The Supplement Story

Vitamin and mineral supplements can give your body the resources it needs to fight disease, fatigue, and even aging.

The Basics:
Anti-aging
starts here
PAGE 21

Limey's Legacy
The sailors who
discovered vitamin C
PAGE 27

THE PREVENTION LIST
Surprising Supplement Secrets
Lesser-known benefits of

Feed Your Head
What vitamin
cures migraines?
PAGE 40

Soy Story
A superfood for
super health
PAGE 56

Less Is More
Save your heart
with mini-meals
PAGE 63

The Easy Way
Getting an extra
serving of veggies
PAGE 66

PART THREE
Miracle Foods for Health and Healing

Food has the power to heal the body as well
as delight the senses. Use that power to address
the health problems that most concern you.

THE PREVENTION LIST
Spice Rack Therapy

PART FOUR
Triple Defense

When it comes to fighting disease, why not use all the weapons at your disposal?

PART FIVE
Delicious Recipes for Glorious Health

There's no reason that food can't be great tasting and good for you at the same time.

Backed by Science
What does the herb
research say?
PAGE 139

**The Herbal
Difference**
Why vitamins
aren't enough
PAGE 146

The King of Immunity
Get well 4 days
sooner
PAGE 151

PART SIX

The Healing Power of Herbs

Sure, herbs can be used to treat specific conditions. But they can also keep you feeling young, fit, and full of vitality.

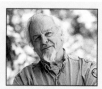

THE PREVENTION LIST
Dr Duke's Picks

PART SEVEN

Soul Survival

Modern life threatens to crush your spirit in a thousand ways. Don't let it.

THE PREVENTION LIST
Stress Busters

The Replacement Principle
Conquering the Clutter Monster
PAGE 169

When Anger Turns Violent
Female anger can be just as dangerous as male anger
PAGE 177

Evidence of Anger
Uncovering the true sources of your anger
PAGE 181

Dress for Success
Simple tips from
fashion pros
PAGE 197

Joyful Eating
Put zest in
your kitchen
PAGE 204

The Beginner
A basic get-started
walking plan that
will get you up to
speed safely
PAGE 216

PART EIGHT
No Fat, No Fuss

Lose weight the easy way.

THE PREVENTION LIST
Real-Life Weight-Loss Secrets
Advice from regular folks who fought
the weight-loss battle and won 223

In a High-Tech World, Celebrate the Gift of Natural Healing

Here we are in the year that film director Stanley Kubrick made famous more than 3 decades ago: 2001. As is often the case with science fiction, the gee-whiz factor in Kubrick's *2001: A Space Odyssey* was some-  what optimistic—passenger trips to the moon aren't routine just yet. Still, we are living in a time when technology is accomplishing miracles on a daily basis.

Nowhere is that more true than in health care. Not a day goes by, it seems, that we don't hear about another amazing medical breakthrough: new transplant successes, new wonder drugs, new microsurgery techniques, gene therapies, three-dimensional diagnostic imaging . . . the list is endless.

But even as we marvel at the feats that our technical expertise make possible, many of us have grown wary of relying too much on technology. HAL, the renegade computer of *2001*, runs a spaceship in the movie; today, he could just as easily run a major metropolitan hospital. In either place, your intuition tells you that he shouldn't be making all the decisions.

That intuition, as much as anything, has sparked the natural healing revolution. You know that by taking care of your health naturally, you avoid having to rely on technology to save your skin. Or your heart, or your bones, or any other part of you. Given a choice, it's obviously preferable to protect your health with herbs, vitamins, good food, and exercise, rather than having to submit to some needle-wielding technician who wants to fill test tubes with samples of your bodily fluids.

This guide is dedicated to putting the whole world of natural healing before you in one easy-to-use package. Its mission is to sort out the options and to suggest ways to make them work together. A universe as sprawling as natural health care can definitely use a little sorting and organizing.

One theme we've focused on this year is aging: how to slow it down and how to reverse it. Prompted by the huge wave of baby boomers chugging through middle age, healers of every sort have increasingly focused their attention on what makes us get older and what keeps us young. As a result, an astounding variety of natural, practical techniques for keeping the years at bay have emerged.

We've all been impressed when we've met someone who looks and acts 20 years younger than her age. By the same token, we've all met people who seem worn down and older than their years. If youthful exuberance is more your style, taking care of yourself naturally can help you get there, and stay there. It really *is* possible to feel more vital at 45 than you did when you were 25.

That's the spirit in which we bring the *Prevention Natural Healing Guide 2001* to you. We hope you enjoy it in good health.

Catherine M. Cassidy

Catherine M. Cassidy
Editor-in-Chief
Prevention magazine

Part One

You Look
Marvelous

Aging isn't as inevitable as it used to be. Learn why growing older doesn't necessarily mean growing old.

Chapter 1

Welcome to the World of Positive Aging

Have more vitality at middle age than you did as a teenager

You could say that the art of aging well is uncharted territory. On average, women are living 31 years longer than they did a century ago. Men are living 16 years longer.

That's great news, but living longer also brings a challenge: learning how to live longer well. After all, what's the point of having another 20 to 30 years to play with if you're too sick and frail to play? The goal is to maintain what the French call joie de vivre—the joy of living—as long and as fully as possible.

Millions of baby boomers are rising to this challenge with gusto. They're laying the foundation for a healthy, vital old age by living well right now. They're practitioners of a new art form called positive aging.

Onward and Upward

What does positive aging mean? It means that when you hit 60, you may be able to keep up with Deane Feetham.

Deane was in her mid-forties before she started strapping on her running shoes on a regular basis. Now, at 62, she has a shelf filled with triathlon trophies. For the uninitiated, a triathlon is a grueling, all-day sweatfest of running, bicycling, and swimming. It's no hobby for couch potatoes.

Deane sells supplies for a printing company for a living. She has two grown daughters who adore her, a wide circle of friends, and volunteer work she loves. (She's a facilitator for a breast cancer–survival group.) As if that weren't enough, she studies exercise science at the University of Alaska with the eventual goal of becoming a physical trainer for older women.

Clearly, Deane isn't ready for the bridge-game and shuffleboard circuit. She has a fire in her belly and a twinkle in her eye. She has joie de vivre.

Learn and Live

Positive aging is more than just a healthy attitude. It's health, period.

At the dawn of the 21st century, we know infinitely more than we did even a quarter-century ago about what causes our bodies to break down as we age. That knowledge, in turn, tells us what

HEALING SPOTLIGHT
Jacklyn Zeman

After 22 years playing Bobbie Spencer, loyal sister of Luke Spencer on the soap opera *General Hospital*, no one has to remind Jacklyn Zeman that life goes on and on. But the 47-year-old actress is not about to consider herself a senior citizen.

"I feel now as strong and as healthy as I've been, and as energetic," she says. "People used to dread turning 30. That's so not true anymore. Now, 30, 40, 50, 60, and beyond, people are staying fit and healthy. The life span, the vital life span, is just so increased."

Zeman's personal health regimen is strongly oriented toward consistency. She takes her vitamins every day, runs every day, and eats three healthy meals at regular times every day.

She also believes that the body and the mind are intimately connected. "I feel strongly that your immune system is closely related to your psyche, your spirit, your ambition, your motivation," she says. "It's all tied together."

we can do to slow down the aging process. It's no accident, then, that millions of us are eating healthier and exercising more or that millions have given up smoking cigarettes and drinking to excess. As a result, lots of Americans are healthier in middle age than they have been since they were children.

Those advances in healthy, intelligent living are matched by a generation's worth of advances in medical science. For example, doctors now have tests that can detect cancer earlier and more reliably than ever before. They also have better drugs and more successful surgeries to beat it. The same goes for heart disease, diabetes, and a dozen other serious illnesses.

Ongoing research is already paving the way for still further medical advances. This is especially true for women, whose health concerns are finally getting the attention they deserve from the research community. Take the Women's Health Initiative, for example. This long-term national health study is tracking the health patterns of some 160,000 women ages 50 and over and is expected to produce crucial information on such diseases as osteoporosis, breast cancer, and heart disease.

Knowledge Is Power

Another factor that is changing the face of health care for the better is information—tons and tons of information. From the morning news shows to the Internet, never has there been so much coverage of health. With more information, Americans are in a better position than ever be-

NATURALFACT

The baby boom consisted of more than 76 million boys and girls born between 1946 and 1964.

fore to make informed lifestyle and medical decisions.

This growing wealth of information is expanding the variety of health care resources upon which we can draw. The family doctor and prescription drugs are still there if and when we need them, but so are herbs and acupuncture, meditation and aromatherapy, Ayurveda and naturopathy. One study found that 4 of every 10 Americans used alternative therapies in 1997, including more than half of those who are between 30 and 50 years old.

Free at Last

One more key element of the positive-aging formula is wisdom. Living longer teaches lessons that begin to bear fruit in later years, when the drives, insecurities, and passions of youth have mellowed a bit. At midlife, many people develop a sense of comfort with who they are, which in turn leads to a renewed curiosity and openness to new experiences.

This is another trend that seems to benefit women in particular. "My research strongly supports the view that women are happier and more fulfilled as they age," says Mary Guindon, Ph.D., associate professor of counseling in the department of graduate education at Rider University in Lawrenceville, New Jersey. "They feel it's the best time of their lives."

That's what they mean when they talk about positive aging. That's also what they mean when they talk about joie de vivre.

Chapter 2

Are You Younger (or Older) Than You Think?

Here's how to determine your real age—and how to knock years off your total

We used to assume that every person of a given age was in roughly the same state of health. Today, that conventional wisdom is breaking down.

Doctors now believe that people age at different rates. For evidence supporting that theory, look around. It's not hard to see a guy who is 40 years old going on 65. Next to him is a woman who is 70 but acts and looks as if she were only 55.

What accounts for these differences? Michael F. Roizen, M.D., internist and preventive gerontologist at the University of Chicago, combined more than 25,000 studies on aging to find out. Then, he devised a concept that he calls RealAge and that can tell you the truth about how old you are, regardless of how many birthdays you've had.

You Have the Power

The wonderful news about Dr. Roizen's research is that he has found that the aging process is much more in your control than you probably thought.

Environment and behavior affect as much as 70 percent of how long and how well you live, he says. By comparison, the sorts of things you can't control—genetic factors such as how long your parents lived, for example—play a relatively minor role. Why? Because how you live and what you live through have everything to do with how quickly your years, in RealAge terms, mount up.

Almost everyone knows by now that poor health habits such as smoking cigarettes will make you older in real age than you are chronologically, and that positive health habits such as exercising regularly will make you younger. What surprised Dr. Roizen was how significant the less tangible quality-of-life issues turned out to be. "Living a balanced life helps slow aging," he says. "We are an integral part of our environment; and everything in that environment, from the food that we eat to the stress we're under to the friends we have, affects our biology—and our rate of aging."

Science is increasingly confirming that balanced lives are healthier lives, Dr. Roizen says. Stress, for example, can age you as much as any other single factor. Only high blood pressure comes close. (Not coincidentally, stress is a major cause of high blood pressure.) Having a happy marriage or long-term love relationship helps prevent aging. So do having lots of friends and a strong social network, regularly getting a good night's sleep, and owning a dog.

The RealAge Quiz

More than 144 health and lifestyle factors have been shown to affect how quickly or slowly you age. To see how the quality of your life is affecting your rate of aging, take the RealAge quiz, designed by preventive gerontologist Michael F. Roizen, M.D.

1. **Stress: How many major stressful events, such as a job change, a move, or the death or illness of a loved one, have you endured in the past year?**
   a. none
   b. one
   c. two
   d. three
2. **Marriage: Are you married?**
   a. yes, happily
   b. no, single
   c. no, widowed
   d. no, divorced
   e. no, but I am in a long-term, committed relationship
   f. I am in an unhappy marriage/ relationship
3. **Social Connections: How many friends and family members do you see more than twice a month, and how many social groups do you participate in more than twice a month?**
   a. more than six
   b. more than four
   c. between one and four
   d. none

4. Sleep: How much sleep do you get per night?

    a. less than 6.5 hours
    b. 6.5 to 7.5 hours
    c. 7.5 to 8.5 hours
    d. more than 8.5 hours

5. Pets: Do you have a pet?

    a. yes, a dog
    b. yes, another pet
    c. no

The positive or negative number assigned to each answer refers to the number of years added to or subtracted from your life. Add all the numbers. Take your chronological age and add or subtract that total. The result is your RealAge.

1. Stress

    a = 0
    b = +1
    c = +2
    d = +3

2. Marriage

    a = −0.5 for women; −1.5 for men
    b = 0 for women; +3 for men
    c = +1 for women; 0 for men
    d = +2 for women; +1 for men
    e = no research, but presumed
        similar to happy marriage (−0.5
        for women; −1.5 for men)
    f = no research, but presumed to
        accelerate aging

3. Social Connections

    a = −1.5
    b = −1
    c = 0
    d = +2

4. Sleep

    a = +1 for women; +1 for men
    b = −1 for women; +0.5 for men
    c = 0 for women; −0.5 for men
    d = +1.5 for women; +1.5 for men

5. Pets

    a = −1
    b = little research available
    c = 0

This quiz is based on the book *RealAge: Are You as Young as You Can Be?* by Dr. Roizen and Elizabeth Anne Stephenson, published by Cliff Street Books, 1999. For a more complete version of the test, see the book or go to Dr. Roizen's Web site at www.realage.com.

Start the Time Machine

If somebody told you that he could magically shave 10, 20, or 30 years off your age, you'd probably think that he was either a con artist or a witch doctor. Dr. Roizen is neither, but adding decades to your life expectancy is what he promises, if you can heed the following RealAge prescriptions. The number alongside each prescription estimates how many years younger you can grow if you follow the doctor's advice.

Reduce Stress

-32 When was the last time you had too much time on your hands? If you're like most Americans, you're overworked, harried, and pressured to accomplish far too many tasks in far too little time. In other words, you're stressed. A small amount of stress can actually improve performance, Dr. Roizen says, but too much stress ages you in any number of ways.

Stress weakens your arterial and immune systems, making you more prone to heart disease and just about every other form of illness. Men who have a lot of stress in their lives are less likely to recover from heart attacks. Women who can't handle stress succumb to cardiovascular disease sooner than women who can.

Stressful life events—the death of a spouse, for instance, or a major money crisis—have been shown to increase your risk of premature death. Take a 42-year-old woman who loses her job, for example. Until she recovers emotionally from the blow, she may have the same life expectancy as a 50-year-old. A person who undergoes three or more major events in a year can have a RealAge as much as *32 years* older than their chronological age, according to Dr. Roizen.

People who know how to manage their stress will undergo some aging but not as much as those who don't cope well with it. What's the key to managing stress? Exercise is one great way to reduce it. Studies have shown that people who exercise regularly are less likely to age needlessly as a result of stress than those who don't.

For both physical and mental health, Dr. Roizen recommends 30 minutes of exercise every day. If you're too busy to do it all at once, try to work out in 8- to 10-minute bursts. Relaxation techniques such as meditation or yoga can also reduce stress. (For more advice on fighting stress, see page 98.)

Hug Your Family

-6½ Perhaps the most effective stress buster of all is a loving family. Don't neglect yours. Studies show that people who are happily married tend to be physically and mentally healthier than people who are single, Dr. Roizen says. Married people can have a RealAge as much as 6½ years younger than people who remain single. (Although most studies haven't looked at people in long-term relationships who are not married, the benefits are most likely the same for all people in stable, committed relationships, married or not.)

The benefits of marriage are not just psychological but biological as well. Married people are more likely to have shorter hospital stays than unmarried patients, and they have lower mortality rates when in the hospital. Married people are more likely to make difficult changes to improve their health too. For example, people enrolled in drug and alcohol treatment programs are less likely to relapse if they're married.

This is not to say that all marriages are healthy. An unhappy or abusive relationship can make you older. If you're in an unhappy marriage or relationship, consider couples counseling to improve your situation. If a divorce or breakup is the only option, know that this will be a stressful, emotionally difficult route. If divorce is imminent, lean on friends, loved ones, and counselors during this difficult time to help minimize stress and needless aging.

People who know how to manage their stress undergo some aging, but not as much as those who don't cope well with it.

studies have shown the benefits of participating in other types of social groups.

Work to develop social contacts. Invite a neighbor to dinner. For an age-reduction double dip, exercise with a friend. Join a group or social activity that reflects your interests, whether it's participating in your church's Bible study group or taking guided nature walks at the local park. You may want to consider volunteering. Studies show that volunteers reap health benefits from giving to others. During extremely stressful periods, your friends can help prevent many years of needless aging.

Love Your Neighbor

-2 Don't limit your support network to just your family. Being part of a larger community can also add years to your life. Let's face it: Human beings are social animals. Being part of a group is as important to our survival as are eating and drinking. In the same way that having a great love relationship helps keep you young, so does friendship.

People who have lots of friends and social supports are more likely to keep the effects of aging at bay. They have less disease and live longer than people with no or few social supports. In a series of famous studies, people who attended church or participated in other religious groups were shown to live longer and healthier. Other

Get Enough Sleep

-3 You may think you don't have time to get adequate sleep, but the somber truth is that you don't have time not to, Dr. Roizen says. The symptoms of chronic sleep deprivation mimic the normal effects of aging. In other words, if you're not getting the sleep you need, you're actually getting older faster.

Regular, quality sleep is as important as exercise and diet in terms of your overall health and well-being. In the most well-known study of sleep patterns, men who regularly slept 7 to 8 hours per night and women who regularly slept 6 to 7 hours per night lived longer and stayed younger than those who got less sleep. Other studies have shown that chronic sleep deprivation contributes to cardiovascular disease and gastrointestinal disorders.

Women should aim for between 6 and 7 hours of sleep per night, and men should try to get between 7 and 8. If you're not getting enough sleep, find ways to sneak in an extra hour or two, or take a reinvigorating nap.

Walk Your Dog

-1 Do you have friends of the four-legged variety? They can help you fend off the effects of aging, says Dr. Roizen.

About half of all households in the United States have some kind of pet, and surveys show that many people view pets as family members. While more research needs to be done before the health benefits of pet ownership can be definitively proved, Dr. Roizen says, what research there is strongly suggests that pets can keep you young.

For example, a 1995 study of heart attack survivors showed that owning a dog significantly

> **NATURAL**FACT
>
> Studies have found that as many as 89 percent of Americans between the ages of 65 and 74 report having no serious disabilities.

improved their 1-year survival rates. (When translated into RealAge terms, heart attack survivors who own dogs can be as much as 3.25 years younger during their recovery period than those who don't own dogs.) A related study showed that dog owners over age 60 exercised more and had lower levels of triglycerides, a harmful blood fat, than people without dogs. In fact, the health benefits of dog ownership may be due in large part to the increased exercise that dog owners get.

But that's certainly not all there is to it. There are psychological gains from pet ownership that affect overall quality of life and, presumably, quantity of life. One study found that elderly people who owned pets had a better quality of life, based on their abilities to perform everyday tasks such as bathing and dressing. There have also been studies documenting the positive affects of using pet therapy in mental health treatment and rehabilitation.

A Dog's Life

Several studies have shown that having a pet can significantly improve your health—but only if you have the time, resources, and interest to take care of one. "If you can't walk the dog regularly or pay attention to the cat, it may just cause more stress," says Karen Allen, Ph.D., research scientist at the State University of New York at Buffalo.

Chapter 3

This Way to That Fresh, All-Natural Look

Give your skin a healthy glow with these five homemade age defiers

Walking through the cosmetics section of a major department store can be a lot like walking down the midway of a carnival. There are so many flashy temptations, so many salespeople waving you in their direction, smiling insincerely, hawking their wares like barkers. "Try this!" "You'll love this!" "Special sale!" "Free sample!"

The problem is that they all want your money, and if you give in to their sales pitches and believe their claims, they'll get it. All of it.

Relax. You don't need to walk through the cosmetics-counter gauntlet if you don't want to. Chances are that you have everything you need to make five fabulous skin creams right in your own kitchen. And they're all natural.

Tropical Fruit Mask

What it does: Smooths wrinkles and refreshes skin.

What's in it: 1 cup of fresh pineapple chunks, ½ cup of fresh papaya chunks (slightly green), 2 tablespoons of honey.

Why it works: Pineapple and papaya are natural sources of alpha hydroxy acids (AHAs), which dissolve dead skin cells, increase moisture, and stimulate the production of collagen (the stuff that gives your skin firmness). AHAs also smooth the skin's surface, which can even skin tone and make tiny lines less visible, says Leslie Baumann, M.D., director of cosmetic dermatology and assistant professor of clinical dermatology at the University of Miami. When AHAs are combined with honey, a natural humectant that hydrates your skin, the result is a soft, luminescent complexion.

Safety First

Just because a home remedy is natural and homemade doesn't mean that you can't have a bad reaction to it. Before you try any of these treatments, test each one by dabbing a dime-size drop on your inner arm. Leave it on for 20 minutes. Don't use the treatment if the area becomes red or itchy. And don't use any remedy with an ingredient that has caused you to have an allergic reaction in the past.

How to make it: Puree the pineapple and papaya in a food processor or blender. Add the honey and mix thoroughly.

How to use it: Wash your face, then spread the mixture over your skin, avoiding the eye area. Leave it on for no more than 5 minutes (less for sensitive skin; see "Safety First"), then rinse with cool water. Follow with a moisturizer. Don't use the mask more than once a week.

Milk-and-Honey Wrap

What it does: Refreshes and soothes dry skin.

What's in it: 1½ gallons of whole milk, 2 cups of honey.

Why it works: Milk has exfoliating properties because it contains lactic acid, an AHA. Honey is a natural humectant that retains moisture. The combination is a sure bet for softening and smoothing your skin, say Audra Senkus and Gabrielle Ophals, owners of Haven, a New York City day spa.

How to make it: Cut a twin-size sheet into 1-inch-wide strips. In a large pot over low heat, combine the milk and honey. Stir constantly until the first bubble breaks the surface. Remove from the heat and thoroughly immerse the sheet strips, being careful not to burn yourself. Cover the pot and let stand for 5 minutes.

How to use it: Set aside at least an hour for preparing and enjoying your wrap. The most comfortable way is to lie on a bed draped with a heavy plastic drop cloth or shower liner. But giving yourself a wrap can be a little messy, so if you don't want to risk dripping on the bed, create a sanctuary in your bathroom.

First, run hot water in the tub until the room is warm and steamy. Drain the tub, then lay warm towels and a bath pillow inside to make a comfortable nest. Place the pot in the bathroom sink or on a tiled floor. Remove the cover and check the temperature of the sheet strips. They should be warm but not hot.

Remove the strips and wring out any liquid. Wrap yourself tightly with the strips from your neck to your ankles, and lie down on the plastic-covered bed or in the tub. Cover yourself with a bathrobe or blanket and relax for 15 to 20 minutes, or until the strips cool. Then rinse thoroughly and moisturize with the Jojoba-Grapefruit Nighttime Body Moisturizer below.

Mother Nature's Beauty Supply

Most of the ingredients you need for homemade skin creams can be found at a grocery store, drugstore, or health food store. Or try contacting one of the following sources.

Aphrodisia
264 Bleecker Street
New York, NY 10014

Rainbow Meadow
www.rainbowmeadow.com

Jojoba-Grapefruit Nighttime Body Moisturizer

What it does: Soothes dry skin overnight.

What's in it: 3 tablespoons of jojoba oil, 3 drops of grapefruit essential oil, ½ cup of grated grapefruit peel.

Why it works: Grapefruit is another great source of AHAs, while jojoba oil lubricates the skin and keeps it smooth.

How to make it: In a medium bowl, combine the jojoba and grapefruit oils. Toss in the grapefruit peel to coat. Set aside to infuse for at least 24 hours. Remove the peel, squeeze it against a spoon to retain as much of the oil as possible, and discard. Pour the oil mixture into a storage container.

How to use it: Apply this refreshing body moisturizer before you go to bed—it works while you sleep. Be sure to wash it all off in the morning, however, because, like other citrus fruits, grapefruit is a photosensitizer that can cause skin to discolor in the sun.

Buttery Night Cream

What it does: Moisturizes dry throat skin, softening neck lines.

What's in it: 2 tablespoons of cocoa butter, 1 tablespoon of lanolin, 2 teaspoons of light olive oil, ½ teaspoon of vitamin E oil.

Why it works: Cocoa butter can be too heavy for daytime use, but it's fine at night. The lanolin and olive oil are easily absorbed by your skin and seal in moisture. The vitamin E oil naturally preserves the cream and adds its own moisture. The cream can be stored in a cool, dry place for up to 4 months.

Note: If your complexion is oily or blemish-prone, this recipe may be too rich for your skin.

How to make it: In a small microwaveable bowl, combine the cocoa butter, lanolin, olive oil, and vitamin E oil. Cover and microwave on high power for 45 seconds. Stir the mixture thoroughly and set aside to cool. Store in a jar with a tight-fitting lid.

How to use it: The best time to moisturize is right after a bath or shower, says Janice Cox, author of *Natural Beauty from the Garden.* That way, the moisturizer can form a barrier to keep water from evaporating out of your skin. Massage an amount the size of a quarter into your neck area every night.

"I think your whole life shows in your face, and you should be proud of that."

—Actress Lauren Bacall

Why it works: Green tea, which is obtained from the *Camellia sinensis* plant, is a marvelous and versatile remedy. A green tea bath is a delicious way to unwind and tone your skin after a stressful day, say Senkus and Ophals. Because of its starchy nature, oatmeal is a wonderful soother, especially for sensitive skin.

How to make it: Combine the tea leaves and oatmeal in a muslin or cheesecloth bag. Hang the bag from your bathtub spout with a long string or ribbon. Let the mixture steep as you fill the tub with warm water. Remove the bag from the tub spout and discard.

Green Tea Soak

What it does: Soothes sensitive skin.

What's in it: ½ cup of loose green tea leaves, ½ cup of rolled or instant oatmeal.

How to use it: Grab a book or magazine, a bath pillow, and a loofah. Climb into the tub and soak for 10 to 15 minutes. Then, rub your body gently with the loofah and rinse. Towel dry and moisturize lavishly. Make a fresh bag of Green Tea Soak each time.

THE PREVENTION LIST

Lighten Up!

Supposedly, the older you get, the stuffier you get; but a lot of people find that the opposite is true. It isn't until you get past 35 or so that you finally learn how to enjoy yourself. Here are 10 reasons why older is better, from Sue Patton Thoele, a licensed psychotherapist in Boulder, Colorado, and author of *Freedoms after 50*.

1. **You don't mind making a fool of yourself.** Laugh loudly in public, tell a spicy joke, give a friend a great big hug. At a certain point, you stop worrying about who's watching.

2. **You know you'll survive.** One of the benefits of aging is a deep, hard-earned trust in your ability to regain your equilibrium when you're knocked off-kilter.

3. **Your inner artist emerges.** You're likely to have more time as you get older, which gives you room to let your creative juices flow. And with nothing left to prove, you're not afraid to try.

4. **You can say no and mean it.** Being able to say that wonderfully assertive word without guilt, explanation, or remorse is to break free from the prison of obligation. You've earned the privilege.

5. **Sex becomes more spiritual.** There's a depth of feeling between you and your mate that makes sex less about performance and more about tenderness and sharing.

6. **You don't have to cook if you don't want to.** Grant yourself the freedom to assert the noncooking credo: "Forage, take out, or take me out."

7. **You can choose to snooze.** Pets are admirable nappers, able to doze off whenever the mood strikes. Now, you have time to follow their example.

8. **You can leave guilt alone.** For years, you found yourself chanting the "shoulda" mantra: "I shoulda done this; I shoulda done that." Eventually, you realize that at least half the stuff you "shoulda" done you didn't need to do.

9. **You get smarter.** With experience comes perspective—wisdom, even. You gain a deeper understanding of what *really* counts in life. (Hint: Having a bright red convertible probably isn't it.)

10. **You learn to let things be.** One of the joys of maturity is realizing that it's perfectly all right to give up trying to control everything, and accept what is. What a blessed relief.

Part Two

The
Supplement
Story

Vitamin and mineral supplements can give your body the resources it needs to fight disease, fatigue, and even aging.

Chapter 4

Can You Find Youth inside a Pill?

Try these five supplements from the cutting edge

If Ponce de León were to go looking for the fountain of youth today, you can bet he wouldn't be driving around the freeways of Florida. He'd be looking in a laboratory and having a lot better luck than he had in his own time.

A new breed of scientist is working in laboratories around the world, developing a field of research called longevity medicine. Among the hotter advances that these researchers are exploring are dietary supplements that can help prevent the breakdown of the body that results from time, age, and disease.

The potential of these supplements for prolonging life is extraordinary. Here are descriptions of five of the most exciting to become available so far.

Why They Work

One of the best things about these supplements is that they're designed to work with your body's natural systems of self-defense. Many are potent antioxidants. Antioxidants neutralize free radicals, the unstable oxygen molecules that punch holes in cell membranes, destroy vital enzymes, damage cellular DNA—and, ultimately, lead to the diseases of aging.

The antioxidant power of five of the supersupplements featured here is, in some cases, many times more powerful than better-known antioxidants such as vitamins C and E, says Ronald Klatz, M.D., D.O., author of *Brain Fitness* and president of the American Academy of Anti-Aging Medicine. Some actually recycle vitamins C and E, giving them new life in the war against free radicals. Still others dissolve in both fat and water, enabling them to neutralize free radicals wherever they occur, from your watery blood to your fatty brain.

You're most likely to find these five supplements in your local health food store or on the Internet. Remember that it's a good idea to check with your doctor before adding any supplement to your diet.

Alpha-Lipoic Acid (ALA)

What it is: An antioxidant made by the body, ALA helps break down food into the energy needed by your cells. It helps your body recycle and renew vitamins C and E, making them serviceable again. And unlike many other antiox-

Save Your Money

Expensive multivitamins aren't necessarily best. Look for any brand that has USP (for "United States Pharmacopeia") on the label. It should list 100 percent of the Daily Value (DV) for most essential vitamins and minerals—no supplement contains them all.

idants, which dissolve only in fat or only in water, ALA fights free radicals in both the fatty and watery parts of cells, protecting both from free radical damage.

"Lipoic acid can zip in and out of any cell in the body, even those in the brain," says Lester Packer, Ph.D., professor of molecular and cell biology at the University of California, Berkeley.

How it delays aging: Clinical studies suggest that ALA may help prevent the kind of nerve damage that frequently accompanies diabetes, damage that is caused by free radical attacks.

What you'll find: ALA comes in capsules and tablets, in dosages from 50 to 300 milligrams.

How much to take: The general recommended dose is 50 to 100 milligrams a day. In the treatment of diabetes, the recommended dosage is 300 to 600 milligrams a day, says Dr. Packer.

Be aware: If you have diabetes and are being treated for symptoms of nerve damage, Dr. Packer suggests that you talk to your doctor before taking ALA supplements.

‖ Bioflavonoids

What they are: Bioflavonoids are a group of plant pigments that give fruits and flowers some of their color. Some bioflavonoids act as powerful antioxidants, many of them more potent than vitamins C and E, says Shari Lieberman, Ph.D., a nutrition scientist and exercise physiologist in New York City.

How they delay aging: Bioflavonoids can help lower your risk of heart disease by preventing blood clots that can block your arteries. They also keep harmful low-density lipoprotein (LDL) cholesterol from oxidizing and sticking to artery walls. In 1996, a Finnish study found that women who ate the most flavonoids had 46 percent lower risks for heart disease than those who ate the least.

Bioflavonoids can also help stop cancer before it starts. For example, some laboratory studies suggest that a bioflavonoid called quercetin, found naturally in apples, red onions, and tea, may discourage the growth of tumors and prevent malignant cells from spreading. And rutin, found in buckwheat, helps reduce cancer risk through its action as an antioxidant.

What you'll find: You can get bioflavonoids by eating fruits and vegetables or by taking them in supplement form. Supplements may contain either a single bioflavonoid or several in combination, says Michael Janson, M.D., president of the American College for Advancement in Medicine and author of *Dr. Janson's New Vitamin Revolution*. They usually contain extracts of quercetin, hesperidin, rutin, and citrus bioflavonoids and come in 500- or 1,000-milligram doses.

How much to take: Dr. Janson recommends taking 1,000 milligrams once or twice a day. Powerful antioxidants themselves, bioflavonoids increase the absorption of vitamin C.

‖ Coenzyme Q_{10}

What it is: An antioxidant made by our bodies, coenzyme Q_{10} helps make adenosine triphosphate (ATP), the fuel that allows your cells to do their jobs. Every cell in your body contains this antioxidant, but it is most concentrated in heart muscle cells, which require the most fuel. We have plenty of coenzyme Q_{10} until we hit age 40. After that, our levels take a nosedive.

How it delays aging: Coenzyme Q_{10} is used to treat a variety of heart conditions, from heart pain (angina) to cardiomyopathy (any non-inflammatory disease of the heart muscle), says Peter Langsjoen, M.D., staff cardiologist at Mother Francis Hospital and the East Texas Medical Center in Tyler.

Research shows that people with various types of heart disease are deficient in coenzyme Q_{10} and that the more severe the heart disease, the lower the levels drop. This substance appears to improve the heart's ability to contract. And because it's a powerful antioxidant, coenzyme Q_{10} also helps prevent "bad" LDL cholesterol from sticking to the walls of arteries and clogging blood vessels.

Coenzyme Q_{10} also helps treat congestive heart failure, which occurs when the heart is too weak to pump blood through the body. In a large study conducted by Dr. Langsjoen, at least 86 percent of those taking coenzyme Q_{10} showed measurable improvement.

What you'll find: Coenzyme Q_{10} can be found in 10- to 200-milligram capsules. Dr.

Two Old Standbys

While it's great to keep up with the latest break-throughs, it wouldn't do to forget the foundations of any antiaging supplement regimen: vitamin C and vitamin E. After all, it wasn't so long ago that *they* were the hot new kids in town.

Vitamin C. The grandfather of all vitamin supplements, vitamin C is an antioxidant found in citrus fruits, strawberries, and broccoli, among other fruits and vegetables.

Studies suggest it can help lower rates of cancer, heart disease, and high blood pressure. There's also evidence that vitamin C supplements may help stave off cataracts.

You can find vitamin C just about anywhere these days, from capsules and tablets to powders. Whatever form you buy, don't waste your money on "natural" brands—there's no difference between synthetic and natural vitamin C, says Jeffrey Blumberg, Ph.D., chief of the antioxidants research laboratory at the USDA Human Nutrition Research Center on Aging at Tufts University in Boston.

The Daily Value recommended by the government is 60 milligrams, but researchers concede that that amount is too low to prevent disease. Aim for 200 to 500 milligrams a day, says Dr. Blumberg.

Vitamin E. An antioxidant nutrient, vitamin E is widely available in capsule and liquid form. It's found naturally in nuts, seeds, and vegetable oils.

Research suggests that vitamin E's antioxidant power may help prevent heart disease and cancer. It is also believed to boost the immune system, fight prostate cancer, slow the progression of Alzheimer's disease, and help normalize blood sugar levels in people with diabetes.

Our bodies appear to absorb the natural form of vitamin E (d-alpha tocopherol) more effectively than the synthetic kind (dl-alpha tocopherol). Take it with meals that contain a small amount of fat. The recommended Daily Value is 30 IU—not enough, suggests some research, to head off heart disease or other illnesses. Aim for 100 to 400 IU, recommends Dr. Blumberg.

If you are taking anticoagulant drugs, use vitamin E only with medical supervision.

Langsjoen prefers the soft-gel supplements prepared with oil, because they're better absorbed by the body.

How much to take: As a preventive measure, take 30 to 60 milligrams per day, says Dr. Langsjoen. He prescribes higher doses of 120 to 360 milligrams for people with heart problems.

Coenzyme Q_{10} dissolves only in the presence of fat, so if you aren't using it in gel form, take it with a meal or snack that contains a small amount of fat, says Dr. Langsjoen.

Be aware: Some medications deplete the body's supply of coenzyme Q_{10}. These include cholesterol-lowering drugs such as lovastatin (Mevacor). In rare occurrences, a slight decrease in the effectiveness of the blood thinner warfarin (Coumadin) has been observed. If you have heart disease, consult your doctor before taking coenzyme Q_{10}, Dr. Langsjoen says.

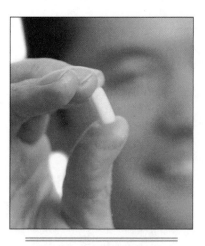

"It provides such dramatic improvement, it's unthinkable for me to practice medicine without it."

—Peter Langsjoen, M.D., staff cardiologist at Mother Francis Hospital and East Texas Medical Center in Tyler, on the benefits of coenzyme Q_{10}

‖ Melatonin

What it is: Melatonin is a natural hormone that helps regulate your sleep patterns.

How it delays aging: "Melatonin is one of the most powerful antioxidants there is," says Russel J. Reiter, Ph.D., cellular biologist at the University of Texas Health Science Center at San Antonio and author of *Melatonin: Your Body's Natural Wonder Drug*. Melatonin does what many antioxidants don't: It crosses what's called the blood-brain barrier. That allows melatonin's healing effects to penetrate the brain more easily than some other antioxidants do, says Dr. Reiter.

Evidence suggests that melatonin may also slow the progression of Alzheimer's disease. "Much of the dementia associated with aging, including Alzheimer's disease, is due to loss of neurons as a result of free radical damage," says Dr. Reiter.

In addition, studies have found that melatonin may help prevent the growth of cancer cells and slow the growth of some tumors.

What you'll find: Melatonin usually comes in 3-milligram capsules and tablets. You can find it in 1-milligram and 0.5-milligram (or 500-microgram) doses as well, though these are less common. Avoid so-called natural melatonin supplements, which probably don't contain enough of the hormone to be effective, says Dr. Reiter. The synthetic variety, which is probably what you will find, is fine.

How much to take: The generally recommended dose is 1 milligram, but you may need only half that—Dr. Reiter takes 0.5 milligram per day. He recommends that you take melatonin before bed and that you keep your bedroom dark. Darkness stimulates the production of melatonin.

Be aware: Since melatonin makes you drowsy, after taking it you shouldn't drive or engage in any other activity that requires you to be alert, says Dr. Reiter. Before you start using melatonin, talk with your doctor. Though rare, interactions with prescription medications can occur.

‖ Phosphatidylserine

What it is: This substance is a phospholipid, a kind of a fat concentrated in the nerve cells of the brain. In elderly people, low levels of phosphatidylserine have been linked with impaired mental functioning and depression.

How it delays aging: Phosphatidylserine improves memory and age-related brain changes, says Timothy Smith, M.D., an expert in antiaging medicine in Sebastopol, California, and author of *Renewal: The Anti-Aging Revolution*. It also helps regenerate damaged nerve cells so that they can send and receive their messages more effectively.

Researchers at Stanford University and at Vanderbilt University in Nashville studied the effects of phosphatidylserine in 149 people between the ages of 50 and 75 with normal age-related memory loss. The most memory-impaired people reversed an estimated 12-year decline in memory. In other words, the average scores attained by 64-year-olds rose to match the average scores of 52-year-olds.

What you'll find: Phosphatidylserine supplements are made from lecithin, a derivative of soy. In this country, it's available in 20- to 100-milligram capsules and tablets.

How much to take: Dr. Smith recommends taking 100 milligrams of phosphatidylserine two or three times a day. After a month, he says, switch to a maintenance dose of 100 to 200 milligrams a day.

Be aware: Phosphatidylserine appears to be safe with no serious side effects, according to Dr. Smith.

Chapter 5

Vitamins and Minerals from A to Z

The whole supplement story: what to take, when, and why

What's your nomination for the most confusing place on Earth?

Some would say a freeway interchange at rush hour. Others would say the Internet.

We'd nominate the vitamin-and-supplement aisle at the neighborhood pharmacy. The shelves there are lined with hundreds of bottles of

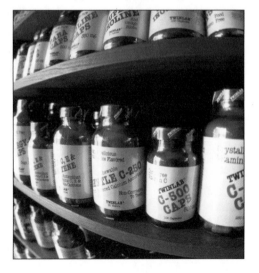

every size, shape, and color, most bearing labels that need to be translated by an M.D. and a team of lawyers.

That's where this A-to-Z guide comes in. We'll tell you what each vitamin or mineral does for you, how much of it you should take, and what you need to know before you take it.

Then you'll be able to devote your full attention to the freeway and the Internet.

‖ Vitamin A

Why you need it: Without enough vitamin A, your body is vulnerable to infections that can cause anything from measles to AIDS. Deficiencies can also increase your risks of cancer and blindness.

What you need: Most people in the United States get enough vitamin A from their diets, but deficiencies can occur in people who have cancer, tuberculosis, pneumonia, chronic nephritis, urinary tract infections, or prostate disease.

Daily Value: 5,000 IU.

Safe upper limit: 10,000 IU; 5,000 IU for pregnant women.

Good food sources: Beet greens, butternut squash, cantaloupe, carrot juice, carrots, dandelion greens, mangoes, pumpkins, spinach, sweet potatoes, tuna, turnip greens.

Helpful hints: Most doctors recommend that you get this important vitamin from fruits and vegetables. That's because the form in which they offer vitamin A—known as beta-carotene—has none of vitamin A's potentially toxic dangers.

Safety check: Although vitamin A is unquestionably essential, more is not necessarily better. In fact, more can be downright dangerous. Regular use of just 10 times the Daily Value (DV) can cause hair loss, weakness, headaches, and other problems. Pregnant women should never take daily supplements of 5,000 IU or more, and other women of childbearing age should check with their doctors before taking that much vitamin A. They should also check their multivitamin/mineral supplements to make sure they contain less than 5,000 IU of this helpful and yet potentially troublesome nutrient.

Through a Glass Darkly

Without adequate Vitamin A, you're unable to see in dim light. In Indonesia, where vitamin A deficiency is common, this condition is called chicken eyes because chickens can't see at night. That's part of why they go to sleep when the sun goes down—that, plus the roosters have to get up first thing in the morning.

‖ Vitamin B$_6$

Why you need it: Vitamin B$_6$ ensures that such basic biological processes as fat and protein metabolism take place as they should. It also helps create neurotransmitters, the chemicals that allow brain cells to communicate with one another. As a result, a lack of B$_6$ can impair memory. Shortages of the B vitamins can also lead to nerve damage in your hands and feet, which is why B$_6$ plays a role in treatment for carpal tunnel syndrome and diabetes.

What you need: Stock up on those foods richest in vitamin B$_6$. They provide barely a milligram of B$_6$, but that's half the DV.

Daily Value: 2 milligrams.

Safe upper limit: 100 milligrams.

Good food sources: Avocados, bananas, beef, brewer's yeast, brown rice, chicken, eggs, oats, peanuts, soybeans, walnuts, whole wheat.

Safety check: Too much vitamin B_6 has been linked to serious nerve disorders as well as to oversensitivity to sunlight, which can produce skin rashes and numbness. Experts suggest that you consult your doctor before taking more than 100 milligrams of B_6 a day. They also recommend getting this vitamin as part of a B-complex tablet that supplies the DVs of all of the B vitamins.

Vitamin B_{12}

Why you need it: Also called cobalamin, B_{12} is vital to the production of myelin, the fatty sheath that insulates nerve fibers, keeping electrical impulses moving through the body as they should.

Because of this important function, when B_{12} is in short supply a whole host of problems can arise, including memory loss, confusion, delusion, fatigue, loss of balance, decreased reflexes, impaired touch or pain perception, numbness and tingling in your arms and legs, tinnitus, and noise-induced hearing loss. Deficiencies of B_{12} have also been linked to multiple sclerosis–like symptoms and dementia.

B_{12} is a key ingredient in your body's production of red blood cells, and it may be fundamental in helping your body fight heart disease. Finally, it helps produce the nucleic acids that form the basic genetic material, DNA.

What you need: Unless you are a vegetarian who avoids all animal products, it's easy to get adequate amounts of vitamin B_{12} from

NATURALFACT

Higher blood concentrations of vitamin B_6 were associated with better performance on two tests of memory in a study at Tufts University in Medford, Massachusetts.

food sources, because you need very little of it. There's probably no need to take a supplement, therefore, unless you've been instructed to by your doctor. Vegans should look for B_{12}-fortified products or take a supplement.

Daily Value: 6 micrograms.

Safe upper limit: 3,000 micrograms.

Good food sources: Clams, ham, herring, king crab, oysters (cooked), salmon, tuna.

Helpful hints: As you age, you absorb B_{12} better from supplements than from food.

Safety check: Vitamin B_{12} supplements are considered extremely safe, though if you have any kind of infection, you should check with your doctor before using one.

Biotin

Why you need it: Biotin is a B-complex vitamin necessary for the processing of dietary proteins and fats—it helps your body turn food into energy. Certain fatty acids that your body uses to make hair and nails can't be utilized unless biotin is on hand.

What you need: Except for those of us who have brittle nails or a genetic inability to absorb biotin, most people get enough biotin from their diets. Crohn's disease, an intestinal disorder, may cause a deficiency because of a difficulty absorbing biotin from food. People with type 2 diabetes may have significantly lower levels of biotin than people without the disease. One study showed that when people with diabetes were given 9 milligrams of biotin daily for a month, their blood sugar levels were cut nearly in half.

Daily Value: 300 micrograms.

Safe upper limit: 2,500 micrograms.

Good food sources: Barley, brewer's yeast, cauliflower, cereals (fortified), corn, egg yolks, milk, molasses, peanuts, soybeans, walnuts.

Helpful hints: One study found that 2,500 micrograms a day of biotin helped to strengthen and thicken brittle fingernails.

Safety check: Biotin may be one of the safest of all vitamins. There are no reports of toxicity, even when it's taken in doses far above the DV of 300 micrograms.

‖ Vitamin C

Why you need it: Vitamin C is an antioxidant that helps your body resist free radicals, marauding molecules that damage cells. That protection lowers vulnerability to a variety of cancers, including those of the esophagus, mouth, stomach, pancreas, and possibly the cervix, rectum, and breast. Vitamin C keeps your immune system, gums, and capillaries healthy and may have a role in protecting against cardiovascular disease, HIV infection, cataracts, and other conditions.

What you need: As many as 20 percent of Americans may not be getting enough of this powerful nutrient. Early signs of vitamin C

A Lime a Day

During the days of Christopher Columbus, sailors who signed on for long sea voyages knew that they had only a 50 percent chance of coming home alive. The reason wasn't pirates or sea monsters but scurvy, a dread disease that causes bleeding gums, loose teeth, bruising, and ultimately death.

Though no one knew it at the time, scurvy was caused by a deficiency of vitamin C. Sailors developed the deficiency because ships' cooks used up their fresh fruits and vegetables first. After that, meals consisted of cereals and meats—and no vitamin C.

In 1747, a British physician named James Lind showed that oranges and lemons could prevent scurvy. Even so, it was another 50 years before the British navy mandated a daily ration of lime juice on all vessels (thus giving British sailors the traditional nickname "limeys"). It took nearly another 200 years before the component of citrus that protected against scurvy, vitamin C, was isolated. Its scientific name, ascorbic acid, reflects its anti-scurvy past.

depletion include weakness and lethargy, followed by delayed wound healing.

Daily Value: 60 milligrams.

Safe upper limit: 1,000 milligrams.

Good food sources: Broccoli, cantaloupe, kiwifruit, oranges, peppers, pineapple, pink grapefruit, strawberries.

Helpful hints: Because nicotine robs the body of vitamin C, the Food and Nutrition Board of the National Research Council recommends that smokers get 100 milligrams of vitamin C per day rather than the normal DV of 60 milligrams.

Safety check: High doses of vitamin C appear to be safe, although doses of 500 milligrams a day have been linked to kidney stones in people who are prone to them. Larger doses of vitamin C may also cause diarrhea, interfere with the results of certain diagnostic blood and urine

> **NATURALFACT**
>
> A 12-year study found that people low in vitamin C were twice as likely to develop coronary heart disease as those who got enough C.

tests, or inhibit the absorption of tricyclic antidepressants.

‖ Calcium

Why you need it: Calcium combines with phosphorus to help form the foundations of strong teeth and bones. When your diet is low in calcium, your body is forced to steal calcium from your bones and teeth to perform other vital functions. Although 99 percent of your body's calcium is stored in your skeleton, heart, and blood, every nerve and muscle cell in your body requires calcium to function properly.

What you need: Even though calcium is vital for bone growth and maintenance in everyone, some groups need more than others. Adults over 50 should have 1,500 milligrams per day to ensure strong bones and teeth and to guard against osteoporosis. For more information, see "How Much Calcium?"

Daily Value: 1,000 milligrams; age 50 and over: 1,500 milligrams.

Safe upper limit: 2,500 milligrams.

Good food sources: Broccoli, cheeses, collard greens, corn tortillas (processed with lime), kale, milk, mustard greens, orange juice (fortified), salmon with bones, sardines with bones, yogurt.

Helpful hints: Calcium is best absorbed when it's taken with food and at a dose not exceeding 500 milligrams. If you're taking supplements exceeding that amount, you should divide your doses during the day. Also avoid taking your calcium with high-fiber wheat-bran cereals, which can reduce absorption by 25 percent.

Open Wide

When you're shopping for a multivitamin, don't expect to find one that supplies 100 percent of the Daily Value for every vitamin and mineral. Putting 100 percent of the Daily Value of some minerals (calcium, magnesium, phosphorous, and potassium) into a single pill would make the multi too big to swallow.

How Much Calcium?

Even though calcium is vital for bone growth and maintenance in everyone, experts don't advise a one-size-fits-all intake. Here are daily intake levels as set by the Consensus Development Conference of the National Institutes of Health.

Age/Sex	Daily Intake (mg)
INFANTS UP TO AGE 6 MONTHS	400
INFANTS AGES 6–11 MONTHS	600
CHILDREN AGES 1–10 YEARS	800–1,200
ADOLESCENTS AND YOUNG ADULTS, AGES 11–24	1,200–1,500
MEN AGES 25–65	1,000
WOMEN AGES 25–50	1,000
PREGNANT AND NURSING WOMEN	1,200–1,500
WOMEN AT MENOPAUSE (AGES 51–65) WHO ARE TAKING ESTROGEN	1,000
WOMEN AT MENOPAUSE (AGES 51–65) WHO ARE NOT TAKING ESTROGEN	1,500
MEN AND WOMEN OVER AGE 65	1,500

Safety check: High calcium intake (more than 2,000 milligrams a day) may cause constipation and kidney stones and inhibit zinc and iron absorption. High levels of calcium in your blood can also cause your body to excrete the excess, which in turn triggers a loss of magnesium.

‖ Chromium

Why you need it: Chromium hooks up with insulin to help transport glucose across cell membranes and into cells, where it can be burned up for energy. It may also help raise "good" high-density lipoprotein (HDL) cholesterol and blood sugar levels in people with low blood sugar.

What you need: Even balanced diets designed by dietitians contain less than 50 micrograms of chromium—far less than the 120 micrograms that's the recommended DV. As a result, chromium deficiency can be quite common, and people who don't get enough chromium may develop "glucose intolerance," a condition that can lead to type 2 (non-insulin-dependent) diabetes.

Daily Value: 120 micrograms.

Safe upper limit: 200 micrograms.

Good food sources: Brewer's yeast, broccoli, grape juice, ham.

Helpful hints: Look for supplements labeled "chromium picolinate." This form of the mineral is more easily absorbed than those supplements labeled "GTF" (glucose tolerating

Chrome-Plated Muscles?

Promotions for chromium supplements often imply that chromium can help you lose fat and gain muscle. As usual, though, the truth is a little more complicated than that. Some studies have, in fact, shown that chromium supplements resulted in favorable changes in body composition—for serious bodybuilders. Even then, though, other studies showed no improvements.

Your best bet for getting in shape is still going to the gym, not taking a supplement. "Don't think that chromium alone is going to take you from a size 16 to a size 8," says Richard Anderson, Ph.D., a scientist for the USDA Human Nutrition Research Center.

factor) because GTF's composition varies greatly from product to product.

Safety check: The only reason to take more than 200 micrograms is to control blood glucose if you have diabetes. But you should do this only under a doctor's care, because your insulin dosage may need to be reduced as your blood sugar drops.

‖ Copper

Why you need it: Copper plays a role in your body's formation of strong, flexible connective tissue; in the production of neurochemicals; and in the functioning of your muscles, nerves, and immune system. Some experts suspect that low levels of copper could be connected to chronic diseases such as heart disease and osteoporosis. Copper also interacts with iron, so copper shortages can lead to iron deficiency and possible anemia.

What you need: Copper deficiency may be more prevalent than we think. Few people get more than 2 milligrams of copper a day (the recommended DV) from diet alone, and a fair number get less. Taking more than 100 mil-

ligrams of vitamin C at the same time as copper or eating large amounts of fructose, the type of sugar found in many different fruits and commercial products, could impair your body's ability to absorb the mineral.

Daily Value: 2 milligrams.

The Cholesterol Connection

Research has shown that copper plays a key role in cholesterol metabolism. "Over 20 independent laboratories around the world show that copper deficiency raises cholesterol levels in animals," says Leslie Klevay, M.D., research medical officer at the USDA Human Nutrition Research Center. When people are deprived of copper, their cholesterol levels shoot upward, which is similar to what happens in animals that are deprived of the mineral.

A Vital Link

If you examine a chain-link fence, you'll see that each strand of wire knits with the adjacent one, forming a strong mesh. In our bodies, copper helps link the long strands of proteins that make up the connective tissues throughout our bodies. It literally helps to hold us together.

Safe upper limit: 10 milligrams.

Good food sources: Beans, cocoa powder, mushrooms, nuts, seeds, shellfish (especially cooked oysters), whole grains.

Helpful hints: Zinc also limits copper absorption, so experts who recommend zinc supplements often suggest extra copper as well, generally in a ratio of 1 milligram of copper to 10 milligrams of zinc. For the DV of 15 milligrams of zinc, you need 1.5 milligrams of copper daily.

Safety check: Copper is toxic in large amounts (it causes vomiting), so avoid taking more than 3 milligrams a day. Be aware that water from pipes made of copper will also carry the mineral. People with Wilson's disease, an inherited disorder that makes copper accumulate in the liver, should not take copper supplements.

‖ Vitamin D

Why you need it: Vitamin D is responsible for getting calcium and phosphorus to the places in your body where they can keep bones strong. Mounting evidence suggests that vitamin D deficiency in elderly people is a silent epidemic that results in widespread bone loss and fractures.

Got Milk?

Vitamin D deficiency is a real problem in the United States, and it becomes increasingly likely in people age 50 and older, says Michael Holick, M.D., Ph.D., chief of the section on endocrinology, nutrition, and diabetes at Boston University Medical Center. People just don't get enough of the few foods that contain vitamin D—milk and fatty fish such as mackerel and salmon.

"In fact, milk may not be as reliable a source as people think it is," Dr. Holick says. In the United States, milk is generally fortified with 400 IU of vitamin D per quart. When Dr. Holick's laboratory analyzed samples of milk in all regions of the United States and western Canada, however, many samples didn't contain as much vitamin D as they were supposed to. Fat-free milk was worst: One out of every six samples contained no vitamin D at all.

What you need: During your time in the summer sun, you can store up quite a bit of vitamin D in your fat cells. If your diet is good, the D will probably last through the winter. People who wear sunscreen all the time or who have chronic intestinal absorption problems or chronic liver or kidney disease may be at risk for deficiency.

Daily Value: 400 IU; people over 50 may need up to 800 IU.

Safe upper limit: 800 IU.

Good food sources: Cereals (fortified), eggs, herring, milk (fortified), salmon, sardines.

Helpful hints: It's easy to get the vitamin D you need by eating cheese or yogurt or by drinking milk, but you don't have to rely on diet alone. Ten minutes of summer sun on your hands and face can provide your daily requirement, but make sure you're outside—glass will filter out the rays you need, so sitting next to a window doesn't count.

Safety check: Some vitamin D is good—essential, in fact—but more is not better. Because the nutrient is stored in fat cells, long-term high doses can cause calcium to be deposited in the soft tissues of your body, resulting in irreversible damage to your kidneys and cardiovascular system. Doses of 1,800 IU a day in infants and young children can cause stunted growth.

‖ Vitamin E

Why you need it: Vitamin E's key mechanism is its ability to neutralize free radicals.

> **NATURAL**FACT
>
> Olive oil is one of our richest sources of vitamin E, yet to get the recommended Daily Value, you'd need to drink more than 2 quarts daily.

Studies indicate that vitamin E fights heart disease, prevents cancer, alleviates respiratory problems, and boosts your immune system's ability to fight off infectious disease. It may also prevent some of the damage that diabetes does to the body, particularly the eyes.

What you need: As many as 69 to 80 percent of older adults may not be getting even the required DV of 30 IU. Certain drugs (anticonvulsants, cholesterol-lowering drugs, tuberculosis drugs, ulcer medications) can increase your body's need for vitamin E.

Daily Value: 30 IU.

Safe upper limit: 400 IU.

Good food sources: Oils (corn, olive, safflower, soybean), spinach, sunflower seeds, wheat germ, whole grains.

Helpful hints: Look for natural forms of vitamin E supplements, labeled "d-alpha-tocopherol," "d-alpha-tocopheryl acetate," or "d-alpha-tocopheryl acid succinate." They make more vitamin E available to your body than any other form. E loses its potency when exposed to air, heat, and light, so make sure to store it in a cool, dark place.

Safety check: Vitamin E appears to be relatively safe, even at higher doses. People who take anticoagulants (blood thinners) or aspirin should consult their doctors before taking vitamin E supplements; supplements can prevent normal blood clotting. It's also a good idea for people who have had strokes or bleeding problems to consult their doctors before taking supplements of E, because it can interfere with absorption of vitamin K, which is involved in blood coagulation.

‖ Folic Acid

Why you need it: Folic acid (folate is the naturally occurring form of folic acid) is essential for nerve functioning and the building of DNA for new cells. It may also help prevent heart disease and strokes by lowering the level of homocysteine in the blood. Deficiencies have been linked to birth defects in the brain and spine and to precancerous cell growth in the cervix, colon, and lungs.

What you need: Your diet will probably provide only about 200 micrograms of folic acid per day, but most standard multis provide at least 400 micrograms. The federal government recommends this amount for all women capable of bearing children, because folic acid has been proven to cut in half the chance of life-threatening nervous system birth defects.

Daily Value: 400 micrograms.

Safe upper limit: 1,000 micrograms.

Good food sources: Asparagus, beans (navy, pinto), broccoli, brussels sprouts, cereals (fortified), okra, orange juice (fortified), spinach.

Helpful hints: As much as 50 percent of folic acid is destroyed during food processing, storage, and preparation, so your best bet is to get folic acid from fresh, raw sources such as spinach. Fortified orange juice

"Folic acid actually helps to make the building blocks, called bases, that are strung together like pearls to form the DNA."

—Barry Shane, Ph.D., professor of nutrition and chair of the department of nutritional sciences at the University of California, Berkeley

and cereals are other good sources.

Safety check: Doses above 1,000 micrograms must be taken under medical supervision. Doses of more than 400 micrograms a day can also mask symptoms of pernicious anemia, a potentially fatal vitamin B_{12}–deficiency disease.

‖ Iron

Why you need it: Most of the iron that you consume helps red blood cells transport oxygen from your lungs to the rest of your body; the rest is stored in your bone marrow, liver, spleen, and other organs. Iron plays a key role in helping your immune system resist infection, so low levels can lead to colds and other infections. Other symptoms of iron deficiency include split nails, a sore tongue, cold hands and feet, and the condition called restless legs, which causes odd sensations of creeping, crawling, or tingling in the legs.

What you need: Roughly 20 percent of Americans are deficient in this mineral, with women of reproductive age the most likely to come up short. In children, low iron levels can cause stunted growth and impaired learning. Some experts even believe that minor gastrointestinal problems such as gas, belching, constipa-

Is Styrofoam Fattening?

If you don't get enough vitamin C, you might catch a cold. If you don't get enough iron, you might find yourself eating Styrofoam.

Iron deficiency has been identified as partially responsible for a bizarre disorder known as pica. The name comes from the same Latin root as magpie, the name of a bird known for its indiscriminate appetite. Over the years, doctors have reported cases of people with pica eating such unpalatable items as dirt, chalk, clay, library paste, laundry starch, paint chips, paper, cardboard, ice chips, and, yes, Styrofoam.

"Pica is a strange mix of the physical—usually an iron deficiency—influenced by psychological and even social settings," says William H. Crosby, M.D., a retired hematologist in Joplin, Missouri, who has a long-standing interest in pica. The condition tends to occur in pregnant women, who are often low in iron, and in some babies. The babies affected tend to be "milkaholics," meaning that they drink milk to the exclusion of other foods, thus lowering their intake of iron.

No one knows why iron deficiency would cause such strange behavior, but often, when the deficiency is corrected with iron supplements, eating habits return to normal, Dr. Crosby says.

tion, and diarrhea may be rooted in iron deficiency.

Daily Value: 18 milligrams; men and postmenopausal women shouldn't take more than 10 milligrams.

Safe upper limit: 25 milligrams.

Good food sources: Baked potatoes, beef, cereals (fortified), clams, pumpkin seeds, soybeans.

Helpful hints: Experts say that iron supplements made from ferrous sulfate are the best. If you experience constipation, try taking them with meals for maximum absorption.

Safety check: High levels of iron can be toxic, and nutritionists advise against taking an iron supplement unless your doctor recommends one.

‖ Vitamin K

Why you need it: Vitamin K's primary job is to help blood clot when you're injured. Deficiencies can cause blood to clot very slowly, which may lead to easy bruising, frequent nosebleeds, or cuts that won't stop bleeding. Vitamin K is also essential in making two proteins found in bone; a deficiency in K may play a role in the breakdown of bone after menopause.

What you need: Your body needs such tiny amounts that if your diet includes some green leafy vegetables, you probably get enough. Supplements are available, but doctors don't usually recommend them. Babies usually get a shot of vitamin K at birth, however, because their systems are unable to produce it on their own.

Daily Value: 80 micrograms.

Safe upper limit: 30,000 micrograms (30 milligrams).

Good food sources: Broccoli, cauliflower, leafy green vegetables, liver, soybean oil, wheat bran.

Helpful hints: Since your body can absorb vitamin K only when it's accompanied by dietary fat, it's best to eat your leafy greens with a food that contains at least some fat.

Safety check: If you are taking anticoagulants, always talk to your doctor before taking supplemental vitamin K. Patients on anticoagulants should try to keep their vitamin K consumptions at fairly constant levels each day—the amount probably doesn't matter, but the level should remain the same. Maintaining this constant level will allow your doctor to prescribe the right amount of anti-

NATURALFACT

Vitamin K was named by the Danish researchers who discovered it. The K stands for *koagulation*, the Danish version of *coagulation*.

coagulant to strike a very delicate balance between the two.

Lecithin and Choline

Why you need them: Lecithin eases digestion and helps your body absorb valuable nutrients. It also helps maintain the structural integrity of cells and is a source of the chemical messengers that control blood pressure and regulate insulin. One component of lecithin, choline, helps transmit nerve impulses in your brain and is a part of the process of controlling memory, heart rate, and sweating.

What you need: The average American diet provides 400 to 900 milligrams of choline a day, enough to meet your basic needs. Although there's no evidence that more would provide additional benefits, studies are under way to uncover lecithin and choline's possible connection with better brain functioning.

Daily Value: None specified.

Safe upper limit: 3.5 grams of choline.

Good food sources: Peanuts, soybeans, wheat germ; also available as an additive in cheese, chocolate, margarine, salad dressing.

Helpful hints: Because choline breaks down into a fishy-smelling compound in the small intestine, taking choline supplements can cause body odor. Lecithin doesn't cause an odor because it is absorbed before releasing choline. Excess choline can cause low blood pressure in some people.

A Fat Friend

Your body can't absorb vitamin K unless it's accompanied by dietary fat. A dollop of oil-based salad dressing on a bed of greens or even a serving of lettuce on a lean burger will make sure your vitamin K is there when you need it.

The Great Emulsifier

If you've ever frozen a chocolate bar, when you took it out of the freezer you may have noticed that the whole bar was tinged with white. What you're seeing is lecithin at work.

Derived from soybeans and egg yolks, lecithin is often added to foods such as chocolate, cheese, margarine, and salad dressings. That's because it acts as an emulsifier, which simply means that it helps mix fats with water and keeps them from separating.

When the chocolate bar is frozen, the lecithin-fat interaction falls apart. The fat rises to the surface, giving the candy that whitish tinge.

Safety check: Large doses of lecithin may cause stomach upset, sweating, salivation, loss of appetite, or low blood pressure. Do not take more than 3.5 grams of choline without medical supervision.

‖ Magnesium

Why you need it: An essential component in hundreds of biochemical reactions, magnesium helps turn food into energy and assists in the transmission of electrical impulses across nerves and muscles. It also eases premenstrual syndrome, cramps, high blood pressure, heart arrhythmia, asthma, and kidney stones, and it may help prevent heart attacks. Magnesium sulfate, otherwise known as Epsom salts, relieves aching feet by drawing water away from inflamed muscles and tissues.

What you need: No multivitamin has 100 percent of the DV of magnesium, so doctors suggest that you aim for 100 milligrams and try to eat lots of cooked dried beans, whole grains, and spinach. People with uncontrolled diabetes, severe stress, or alcoholism, or who rarely eat magnesium-rich foods, are at risk of deficiency.

Daily Value: 400 milligrams.

Safe upper limit: 350 milligrams from supplements (does not include food sources).

Good food sources: Avocados, baked potatoes, bananas, broccoli, brown rice, haddock, lima beans, navy beans, oatmeal, spinach, yogurt.

Helpful hints: Magnesium gluconate is absorbed more quickly and is easier on the stomach than either magnesium oxide or magnesium chloride.

Safety check: Don't take more than 350 milligrams in supplement form; higher amounts can cause diarrhea. If you take diuretics or have heart disease or arrhythmia, impaired kidney function, high blood pressure, or migraine headaches, consult your doctor before taking magnesium.

‖ Niacin (Vitamin B_3)

Why you need it: Niacin is a major player in the process of breaking down food into a form of energy that your cells can use. Like most of the other B vitamins, niacin assists enzymes, the catalysts that help spark chemical reactions. These enzymes play an important role in your body's handling of fat and cholesterol as well as in its production of hormones and other natural chemicals.

What you need: Don't take levels of niacin higher than the DV unless you're under a doctor's care.

Daily Value: 20 milligrams.

Safe upper limit: 35 milligrams, but only under a doctor's care.

Good food sources: Breads and cereals (fortified), chicken breast, tuna, veal.

Helpful hints: Niacin is tricky because it has several different chemical structures, which have different names. One of its forms,

"It's the only drug on the market that improves *all* the measures of cholesterol."

—Researcher William B. Parsons Jr., M.D., on the benefits of niacin

nicotinic acid, lowers harmful cholesterol and raises good cholesterol. But if used improperly, it can cause severe side effects, including liver damage.

Niacinamide, a form of niacin that's often included in vitamin supplements, doesn't reduce blood cholesterol levels. (It also lacks the side effects associated with nicotinic acid.)

Safety check: It's virtually impossible to get too much niacin by eating foods rich in the nutrient, but taking niacin supplements in the amounts needed to improve cholesterol levels can produce side effects (flushing, itching, nervousness, headaches, intestinal cramps, nausea, and diarrhea, to name a few). High doses of niacin, especially the slow-release form used to treat high cholesterol, can also cause liver damage.

A Successful Failure

In the 1950s, doctors hoped that high doses of niacin might help people with schizophrenia. The vitamin did nothing for the schizophrenia, but—quite unexpectedly—it did improve the patients' cholesterol levels.

Pantothenic Acid

Why you need it: Pantothenic acid helps to convert carbohydrates and fats to energy, and to break down and reassemble fats into new forms, some of which are used to make important hormones. Your body may also use coenzyme A, which contains pantothenic acid, to detoxify harmful compounds in herbicides, insecticides, and drugs. Signs of deficiency include the sensation of burning feet, loss of appetite, depression, fatigue, insomnia, vomiting, and muscular weakness or cramping.

What you need: It's hard not to get enough of this important nutrient in your diet, yet deficiencies can occur. Those at greatest risk are older folks (who tend to absorb nutrients poorly), alcoholics, and people who take cholesterol-lowering drugs.

Daily Value: 10 milligrams.

Safe upper limit: 1,000 milligrams.

Good food sources: Cereals (fortified), mushrooms, peanuts, salmon, whole grains.

Helpful hints: Up to 50 percent of the pantothenic acid in food is destroyed by processing, canning, or cooking. That's why the best food sources are unprocessed whole grains or enriched cereals to which the nutrient has been added. When sold as a supplement, pantothenic acid is sometimes labeled as vitamin B_5.

Safety check: Pantothenic acid has been taken in a wide range of doses all the way up to 10,000 milligrams a day (1,000 times the

DV) with no ill effects other than an occasional case of diarrhea.

‖ Potassium

Why you need it: Potassium is a key factor in keeping blood pressure at the right level for maximum cardiovascular health. It's widely known that potassium can lower blood pressure, and some scientists suspect that low dietary levels of the mineral may actually trigger high blood pressure in certain people. Symptoms of deficiency include heartbeat irregularities, muscle weakness, numbness and tingling in the lower extremities, nausea, vomiting, confusion, and irritability.

What you need: Most of us get about 2,650 milligrams of potassium every day, but that's not enough. You should probably add at least three more servings of potassium-rich fruits and vegetables to your daily diet. Supplements are not as well utilized as dietary sources of potassium, but they may be necessary for people on diuretics or the heart medicine digitalis (Digitoxin, Digoxin).

Smart Supplement Shopping

Vitamin supplements have a shelf life of about 3 years. Check the expiration dates on the labels, especially if you're buying large quantities.

Another way not to get snookered into spending more than you need to on supplements is to avoid vitamins and minerals that brag about having "natural" ingredients. In most cases (vitamin E is one exception), your body doesn't distinguish between a synthetic vitamin and a natural one.

Stop a Stroke

A long-term study from Harvard has found evidence that potassium can reduce your chances of developing blood clots and of having a stroke.

Doctors analyzed data from food questionnaires completed by nearly 44,000 healthy men ages 45 to 75. The study broke the men into two groups. Men in the high-potassium group consumed nine servings of fruits and vegetables a day. Men with diets that were lower in potassium ate only four servings of fruits and vegetables a day.

During the 8 years of follow-up, the doctors found that men in the first group had 38 percent lower risks of stroke than men in the low-potassium group. Remarkably, the greatest benefit was seen among men who had a history of high blood pressure and were taking potassium supplements along with diuretics. Their risk was slashed by a whopping 64 percent.

Daily Value: 3,500 milligrams.

Safe upper limit: 3,500 milligrams.

Good food sources: Apricots (dried), baked potatoes, bananas, cantaloupe, prunes, spinach.

Helpful hints: Dried apricots are a potassium powerhouse—a half-cup provides 1,790 milligrams of potassium and gets you more than halfway to your DV.

Safety check: Because of potential serious risks, take potassium supplements only under a doctor's care.

Riboflavin (Vitamin B$_2$)

Why you need it: Riboflavin is one of the essential B vitamins necessary for all sorts of chemical processes inside your body, such as turning food into energy. It also acts as an antioxidant, potentially helping to prevent cancer and heart disease.

What you need: Most people get all the riboflavin they need from their diets. Potential exceptions include people who drink alcohol and women who use oral contraceptives. Both seem to reduce the body's ability to absorb riboflavin.

Daily Value: 1.7 milligrams.

Safe upper limit: 200 milligrams.

Good food sources: Asparagus, broccoli, cereals (fortified), cheeses, fish, grains (fortified), milk, poultry, spinach, turnip greens, yogurt.

Safety check: There's no need to worry about a riboflavin overdose because any excess is excreted in the urine. (It's the riboflavin in supplements that turns your urine bright yellow.)

Feed Your Head

While it's unlikely to rival aspirin as a headache stopper, riboflavin seems to have the power to control migraines. In a study at the University of Oklahoma Health Sciences Center in Oklahoma City, people with migraines who took riboflavin showed 68 percent reductions in headache symptoms. A more rigorous study showed a slightly lower but still substantial improvement: 37 percent fewer migraines and less nausea and vomiting in people who took 400 milligrams of riboflavin a day.

"This improvement is similar to what can be achieved using conventional preventive migraine drugs," says researcher Marc Lenaerts, M.D., a neurologist at the center. He's hoping to do more studies to confirm this benefit of riboflavin and to determine if a lower dose might be just as helpful.

‖ Selenium

Why you need it: Selenium helps boost your immune system and protect cells from the damage caused by free radical molecules. Selenium also binds with toxic substances such as arsenic, cadmium, and mercury to make them less harmful. Selenium may play a pivotal role in determining whether some viruses in your body live harmlessly or turn into killer pathogens. Some studies suggest that a selenium deficiency could be the trigger that shifts the AIDS virus into overdrive.

What you need: Because pollution and excessive food processing may be depleting the amount of selenium we get from food, some experts have argued that the optimum amount of selenium may be much higher than the current DV. While the specific impact of selenium deficiency has not been proven, some research has suggested that an insufficient level of the mineral may play a role in the development of heart disease.

Daily Value: 70 micrograms.

Safe upper limit: 200 micrograms.

Good food sources: Brazil nuts, clams, crab, lobster, oysters (cooked), whole grains.

Sun Worshipers, Take Note

Overdoing riboflavin supplements can make you photosensitive. "If your body is saturated with riboflavin and you're sitting out in the sun, there is the possibility of injury to your skin or eyes," says Donald McCormick, Ph.D., chairman of the department of biochemistry at Emory University in Atlanta.

Helpful hints: When shopping for a selenium supplement, avoid those marked "sodium selenite;" they may react with vitamin C to block selenium absorption. Instead, choose supplements marked "l-selenomethionine." Another option is to eat one or two Brazil nuts. These selenium gold mines give you enough of the mineral to meet the DV.

Safety check: Ingesting too much selenium can cause a loss of hair and nails. Other side effects of excessive selenium intake include a persistent garlic odor on your breath and skin, a metallic taste in your mouth, dizziness, and nausea. Selenium supplements in excess of 200 micrograms should be taken only under medical supervision.

‖ Thiamin (Vitamin B₁)

Why you need it: Thanks to this water-soluble vitamin, your body is able to turn starches and sugars into energy. That affects your thinking and feeling as well as your ability to

> **NATURAL**FACT
>
> When a horse grazing in Kansas starts acting woozy, his owner knows he's eaten too much loco-weed—a plant rich in selenium.

keep running around, which is why thiamin deficiencies play a role in everything from mood changes and depression to memory loss.

What you need: If you eat baked goods or cereals, you needn't worry about B₁: It's been added to them. Check the products' nutritional labels.

Daily Value: 1.5 milligrams.

Safe upper limit: 50 milligrams.

Good food sources: Beans, beef, breads, ham, oatmeal and other cereals, oranges, pasta (enriched), peas (fresh), pork, rice bran, wheat germ.

Safety check: It's virtually impossible to take an overdose of thiamin, since your kidneys clear excess amounts from your system.

‖ Zinc

Why you need it: Zinc helps to produce new cells and is found in all organs and

A Cancer Crusader

Researchers believe that selenium may help the body defeat cancer by inducing a kind of suicide in malignant cells, according to Larry Clark, Ph.D., associate professor of epidemiology at the Arizona Cancer Center in Tucson. "In tumor cells grown in the laboratory, selenium stimulates programmed cell death, which is a very late effect in the cancer process. This makes us think that it is never too late to start taking selenium, because it may have effects on actual tumors as well as on premalignant cells."

tissues of your body. Zinc is also used for immune cells that fight infection; hormones that regulate growth, appetite, and sex drive; and neurotransmitters that allow your various body parts to communicate with each other. Several key enzymes that protect and preserve vision can't be formed without zinc. Signs of possible deficiency include impaired immunity, hair loss, depression, weight loss, bloating, loss of appetite, and rashes and other skin changes.

What you need: Since red meat is a rich source of zinc, people who are cutting back on meat in their diets may need to find another source of this valuable nutrient. Some vegetarian diets can interfere with zinc absorption, too, as can alcoholism, oral

NATURALFACT

Part of the mental deterioration associated with alcoholism is due to thiamin deficiency. Drinking depletes the body of this vitamin.

penicillin therapy, and diuretics. Increased calcium intake, recommended to prevent osteoporosis, also removes some zinc from the body.

Daily Value: 15 milligrams.

Safe upper limit: 20 milligrams.

Good food sources: Beef, eggs, lamb, nuts, oysters (cooked), whole grains, yogurt.

Helpful hints: Zinc can cause stomach upset, so take the mineral with food. Dairy products, bran products, and foods high in calcium and phosphorus may decrease zinc absorption. On the other hand, protein-rich foods such as lamb, beef, and eggs may enhance it.

Safety check: Excessive amounts of zinc can cause nausea, headaches, lethargy,

Save Your Money

When it comes to buying supplements, you don't necessarily get what you pay for. "Generally, supplements sold at health food stores cost more than brand names, while generic supplements from large supermarkets or drugstore chains are the cheapest," says Bonnie Liebman of the Center for Science in the Public Interest. Behind the label, however, the generic, brand name, and health food brands are often made by the same company. What you're paying for, in most cases, is the advertising that makes a brand name recognizable.

A Key to Your Nose

Colds have become a little less bothersome since the introduction of zinc gluconate lozenges in 1994. Why are these little pills, marketed under the name Cold-Eeze, so effective at taming sore throats and other cold symptoms?

There's a lock-and-key relationship between the rhinovirus that causes the cold and the cells in your mouth and nose, according to Sabrina Novick, Ph.D., assistant professor of chemistry at Hofstra University in Hempstead, New York. The two attract each other, and when they fit together, you get cold symptoms.

Zinc gluconate helps prevent that mutual attraction from being consummated, Dr. Novick says, because it contains a positively charged ion that temporarily blocks the virus from locking together with your cells.

irritability, stomach irritation, and vomiting. Taking between 30 and 150 milligrams of zinc daily for several weeks interferes with copper absorption and can cause copper deficiency. (Doctors often recommend that people using zinc supplements take additional copper, in a ratio of 1 milligram of copper to 10 milligrams of zinc.) More than 30 milligrams of zinc a day can also increase your risk of developing anemia, and such high doses have also been found to lower levels of HDL while raising levels of low-density lipoprotein (LDL), the "bad" cholesterol. (A doctor may, however, recommend amounts this high to treat Wilson's disease, a condition involving excess copper in the body.) Increased dietary zinc has been shown to markedly decrease mental functioning in people with Alzheimer's disease. Because of these risks, doctors recommend that zinc supplements in excess of the DV be taken only under medical supervision.

Chapter 6

Can Supplements Cure Cancer?

A *Prevention* investigation examines the claims of four leading contenders

I f vitamin supplements could actually do everything that their labels claim they can do, the world would be free from disease and probably from hunger and violence as well.

A lot of the hype has focused on supplements that supposedly fight cancer, especially breast cancer. Most of it claims that they are backed by impressive scientific research.

Most supplements are derived from everyday foods, so they can claim to be natural. But do they really work? Are they safe? Are they worth the money?

A *Prevention* investigation found that the answer to all three questions is sometimes yes, sometimes no. The leading researchers in the field of cancer prevention helped us sort through the evidence. Here's what we learned.

People Need People

The first thing our experts pointed out was that little of the research on which these products rest their claims has actually been conducted on humans. Some products have prevented or inhibited cancer in test-tube experiments, others in studies on lab rats, but that's it.

What's wrong with that? Test-tube and animal studies are important research tools, but only human studies can fully demonstrate whether an anti-cancer substance is truly safe and effective. Here are good reasons why.

Test tubes aren't bodies. "Test-tube studies can't take into account the full and complex metabolism of a human being," says Michael Wargovich, Ph.D., professor of pathology and director of basic research at the South Carolina Cancer Center at the University of South Carolina in Columbia.

Your chemistry is different than a rat's. Researchers induce tumor growth in lab animals with chemicals or by manipulating the animals' genes. In contrast, humans seem to develop cancer from long exposure to low levels of a carcinogen.

Dosages are different. Animals graze all day. That means they get a steady supply of any substance being studied. Humans, by contrast, usually eat three relatively big meals a day and may take a supplement once or twice a day. Those differences in dosage could be crucial.

Mice get megadoses. Researchers test anti-cancer substances in animals at dosages many times higher than a human would take.

Where's the Beef?

Let's take a hard look at the leading anti-cancer supplements to see what's known about their

Have Your Compound and Eat It, Too

Cancer-fighting compounds are available in foods as well as in supplements. Here's what to eat.

Garlic: Fresh

Calcium D-glucarate: Apples, grapefruit, broccoli and other cruciferous vegetables, and bean sprouts

Inositol hexaphosphate: Whole grains, including rice, oats, wheat, and corn; nuts, seeds, and beans

Resveratrol: Grape juice, red wine (smaller amounts in white and rosé wines), and other grape products such as raisins; mulberries; and peanuts

cancer-fighting abilities and what's not known.

Aged Garlic

The promise: Advertising states that aged garlic "may afford protection against cancer."

The evidence: Aged garlic contains two sulfur compounds, S-allylcysteine (SAC) and S-allylmercaptocysteine (SAMC), that slowed the growth of breast cancer cells in test-tube studies, says John Pinto, Ph.D., associate professor of biochemistry and cancer researcher at Memorial Sloan-Kettering Cancer Center in New York City.

In other test-tube and animal studies, garlic has inhibited the growth of tumors of the colon, rectum, prostate, esophagus, skin, and stomach. Meanwhile, population studies in China, Italy, and the United States have found lower rates of colon and stomach cancers among people who consume raw or cooked garlic on a regular basis.

But SAC and SAMC are just 2 of 10 to 15 active compounds in garlic that may play roles in reducing cancer risk, Dr. Pinto says. Researchers don't know which of these compounds or which combination of these compounds is most effective. There also may be other compounds involved that we haven't even discovered yet, says Dr. Pinto. In any event, it's certain that SAC and SAMC are not the whole story.

One reason that aged garlic has garnered all the headlines is that it's used more often in garlic research than fresh is. That's because aged garlic contains standard amounts of SAC and SAMC and because lab animals will tolerate it more easily than raw garlic. Researchers have also

> **NATURAL**FACT
>
> Let chopped or crushed garlic cloves sit for about 15 minutes before cooking. This "rest" gives cancer-battling compounds time to form.

studied this deodorized supplement because many consumers are put off by the taste and smell of the real thing.

The bottom line: Plenty of questions persist, but researchers are still enthusiastic about garlic.

"It's rare to come across a single food, such as garlic, that has proven to provide considerable protection against the development of gastric and colon cancers in two kinds of studies—basic research and population studies," says Dr. Wargovich. "I'd say it's important to get garlic and other vegetables from the allium family, such as onions and shallots, on a regular basis."

Consume some form of garlic every week or, better yet, every other day, Dr. Wargovich suggests. "We don't know how much is the right dosage, but population studies show that people who eat more garlic have more protection."

What kind of garlic? "Both fresh and deodorized aged garlic contain compounds that work against cancer in lab studies," says garlic researcher John Milner, Ph.D., head of the nutrition department at Pennsylvania State University in State College.

"If you want extra insurance or can't tolerate fresh garlic, take any deodorized garlic supplement," Dr. Pinto suggests.

Calcium D-Glucarate

The promise: This is the main ingredient in products advertised for women concerned with breast health and for former smokers. Marketing suggests that glucarate may help your body fight off breast cancer by regulating estrogen levels. There are also claims that glucarate may help prevent lung cancer by helping the body rid itself of carcinogens.

The evidence: While researchers at top cancer centers say glucarate may hold promise for reducing cancer risk, the evidence comes almost exclusively from test-tube and animal studies. It hasn't been supported by human studies so far.

In several studies conducted by biochemist Zbigniew Walaszek, Ph.D., at the University of Texas M.D. Anderson Cancer Center in Houston, rats were given a cancer-causing agent and then fed glucarate. These rats developed fewer breast cancer tumors than rats who didn't get glucarate. Some existing tumors also shrank. In other rat and mouse studies, glucarate inhibited the development and growth of colon, lung, and skin cancers. Glucarate slows the development of prostate cancer in animals as well, says Dr. Walaszek, now a scientist at the AMC Cancer Research Center in Denver.

Glucarate seems to work, in part, by inhibiting the release of cancer-promoting hormones such as estrogen and testosterone into the bloodstream. But so far, this effect has not been demonstrated in humans, according to Alexandra Simkovich Heerdt, M.D., director of a program at Memorial Sloan-Kettering that observes women who have a higher-than-average risk of

"Nearly two-thirds of cancer deaths in the United States can be linked to tobacco use, diet, and lack of exercise."

—Graham Colditz, Dr. P.H., associate professor of medicine at Harvard Medical School

developing breast cancer. In her study, women with a family history of breast cancer were given 10 grams of calcium D-glucarate a day. Dr. Heerdt had hoped to find that the women excreted higher amounts of estrogen in their urine, indicating that it had been flushed safely from their systems. But such was not the case.

Still, Dr. Heerdt feels that glucarate is promising; it just needs more research. "We may need a different form, a different dose, or a different way to deliver it," she says. Further research studies are in the works.

The bottom line: There simply isn't proof that glucarate will prevent breast cancer, at least not in the forms available now, Dr. Heerdt believes. And until the results from the other studies are in, no one really knows if it will help other cancers, either.

"I tell my patients to eat a low-fat diet rich in fruits and vegetables, including citrus, which contain calcium D-glucarate," Dr. Heerdt says. "This kind of diet may reduce cancer risk, and it can lower heart disease risk, so you can't go wrong."

Inositol Hexaphosphate

The promise: Advertising calls inositol hexaphosphate, known as IP6, a "natural cancer fighter" because it can increase the activity of the body's own killer cells. IP6's leading research proponent claims that it transforms cancer cells into normal ones.

The evidence: Test-tube and animal studies back up the supplement maker's claim. But so far, there have been no human cancer studies.

"In every cell line we tested, including breast, colon, lung, and liver cancers, IP6 showed that it can inhibit cancer," says lead IP6 investigator Abul Kalam M. Shamsuddin, M.D., professor of pathology at the University of Maryland School of Medicine in Baltimore.

In one study, only 10 percent of rats fed IP6 developed colon cancer, compared with 43 percent of rats who didn't get the supplement. The treated rats also showed smaller and fewer tumors than the untreated ones. "IP6 doesn't kill cancer cells—it tames them," says Dr. Shamsuddin, who also holds the patent for IP6's over-the-counter supplement formula. Human studies looking at IP6 and cancer are set to begin soon.

The bottom line: The potential of IP6 for humans is unknown until the results of those human studies are in. The safety of giving the supplement to humans also needs further testing.

Resveratrol

The promise: Advertised mainly to promote cardiovascular health, resveratrol's cancer-fighting potential is often mentioned in educational literature supplied with the supplements. One manufacturer calls its resveratrol product "a new cancer fighter."

The evidence: When researchers at the University of Illinois at Chicago tested hundreds of plants in search of new cancer-prevention compounds, resveratrol—a substance found in abundance in grape skins—came up the clear winner. But so far, studies have been limited to test tubes and lab animals, says lead resveratrol investigator John Pezzuto, Ph.D., director of the university's program for collaborative research in the pharmaceutical sciences.

Using resveratrol extracted from a Peruvian legume, and later a synthetic form, researchers have found that it inhibited the development or growth of skin and breast cancers in mice and defused colon cancer as well.

"Resveratrol seems to work at all stages of cancer development," Dr. Pezzuto says. "It also has an anti-inflammatory action, which may make it particularly effective against tumors of the gastrointestinal tract."

More laboratory studies of its effectiveness against breast, lung, and prostate cancers will take place soon, Dr. Pezzuto adds.

The bottom line: Promising as these results are, the efficacy of resveratrol remains unknown. Human studies are at least 2 years away. And there are no population studies linking the consumption of resveratrol-rich foods with lower rates of cancer. Studies to determine safe dosages are also needed.

For now, you're probably better off getting your resveratrol from food, says Bernard Levin, M.D., vice president for cancer prevention at the University of Texas M.D. Anderson Cancer Center.

THE PREVENTION LIST

Surprising Supplement Secrets

We've all heard Hollywood movie stars railing about being typecast. You know, Mr. Action-Movie Tough Guy makes a low-budget romance picture because he wants to demonstrate his emotional range, while Ms. Curvy Sexpot, hoping to gain a little respect, plays a floozy from the bowery.

Well, oddly enough, vitamins get typecast too. We all know that vitamin C helps beat back colds, for example. But did you know that it also fights stress?

Here are four amazing facts that we bet you didn't know about some of the best-known vitamins.

1. We already told you about vitamin C's secret antistress factor, which derives from the assistance it gives your adrenal glands in producing two stress-resisting hormones (epinephrine and norepinephrine).

Here's a bonus: Vitamin C also helps you fight fatigue. That's because your body needs it to synthesize a substance called carnitine. Carnitine transports fatty acids into your cells, where they're turned into energy. Without carnitine, no energy. Without vitamin C, no carnitine.

2. You know calcium as a bone builder, which it definitely is. But did you know it's also vitally important for your muscles?

The movement of calcium ions back and forth within cells allows your muscles to relax and contract. One muscle that especially depends on the right amount of calcium is your heart. Calcium interacts with potassium and sodium over and over again, in a carefully orchestrated sequence, to produce a heartbeat.

3. What two mystery vitamins help fight diabetes? One is vitamin D, which helps cells in your pancreas produce insulin. The other is vitamin B_6. Low levels of vitamin B_6 can lead to a blood condition called glycosylation, in which blood sugar sticks to proteins. The potential consequences of glycosylation are dire: They include kidney damage, nerve damage, and cataracts.

4. Most pregnant women know that folic acid helps prevent serious birth defects in their unborn babies. What they may not know is that folic acid also prevents cancer in adults.

Folic acid helps your body make the genetic material that enables cells to divide and multiply. Without it, abnormal cells can be produced, a condition that can in turn lead to cancer.

Part Three

Miracle Foods
for Health
and Healing

Food has the power to heal the body as well as delight the senses.
Use that power to address the health problems that most concern you.

Chapter 7

Put Youth on Your Table Tonight

Follow a longevity diet and stop the aging process in its tracks

There are plenty of ways to postpone getting older. Exercise. Plastic surgery. Magic spells. And then there's food.

Food?

That's right, food.

We've known for a long time that eating the right foods is one of the keys to preventing heart disease, cancer, and other age-related diseases. But now there's growing evidence that a healthy diet can actually delay—and, in some cases, even reverse—the aging process itself.

How can you take advantage of the antiaging properties of food to keep yourself as young as you can possibly be?

Simple. Follow a longevity diet, and keep age at bay with every bite.

‖ Youth Insurance

The right diet can encourage our bodies to produce youth hormones that control the ebb and flow of our antiaging mechanisms. The result is increased energy; stronger immunity; improvements in memory, vision, and hearing; more muscle; and denser bone. Eating right can also help our cells repair and replace themselves more quickly, transport energy, and get rid of waste and toxins more efficiently. Just as important, diet can help protect our DNA, the genetic blueprint that tells our bodies' 50 to 60 trillion cells how to do their jobs.

You can take maximum advantage of all these benefits by eating a longevity diet, says Vincent C. Giampapa, M.D., president of Longevity Institute, a company based in Montclair, New Jersey, that designs antiaging programs. A longevity diet works to return your body to youthful efficiency in three basic ways, Dr. Giampapa says.

1. It boosts youth hormones. Your pituitary gland and your adrenal glands make several hormones that carry chemical messages throughout your body. These messages help your cells and organs maintain and repair themselves, thereby keeping you young and healthy.

The problem is that your body's production of those hormones begins to slow down as you reach your twenties and gets steadily slower at a rate of about 10 percent every decade. This reduction begins to weigh on your body in any number of ways, says Dr. Giampapa, from loss of muscle and bone density to lowered immunity. Lowered immunity means greater vulnerability to a host of diseases, from colds to cancer.

But the situation isn't hopeless. "Increasing the body's production of these hormones can slow the aging process significantly," says Dr. Giampapa. "And it can be done primarily through diet."

2. It stems free radical damage. Your cells use oxygen to produce energy. In the process, they generate free radicals, unstable oxygen molecules that damage cells and DNA. Free radicals are also produced by pollution, the pesticides in our food supply, and poor diet.

Your body is good at fending off free radicals when you're young. But as you grow older, the damage caused by years of exposure starts to take its toll. Increasingly, you need help—the sort of help that a longevity diet provides.

3. It replenishes your "cellular soup." Each of your cells contains a substance called cytoplasm that makes energy and fights free radical damage, says Israel Kogan, M.D., director of the Anti-Aging Medical Center in Washington, D.C. Again, eating the wrong diet hurts; eating the right diet helps.

Put Your Diet into Rehab

The cleaner and more natural your diet, the more nutrients your cells get and the more efficiently they're likely to work, says Vincent C. Giampapa, M.D., president of Longevity Institute in Montclair, New Jersey.

Two key steps can help you detoxify your diet and keep you young, he says: (1) Eat organic fruits and vegetables whenever possible and (2) avoid white sugar.

The Longevity Diet

The longevity diet consists of several basic food strategies that, together, erect a defense shield against the onslaught of aging.

The first of these strategies is blood sugar balance. The idea is to eat the sort of foods that keep your blood sugar at a relatively even level, instead of eating foods that cause your blood sugar to soar into the stratosphere and then crash.

By maintaining a steady blood sugar balance, you assure that the hormones you need to remain youthful and energetic are released into your bloodstream on a steady, well-balanced basis. That means you have more energy and less stress.

Foods that send your blood sugar soaring are foods that rate high on Dr. Giampapa's glycemic

HEALING SPOTLIGHT
Marlee Matlin

Like many of us, Marlee Matlin grew up eating meat and potatoes, but she has since changed her ways. This versatile actress (who's been deaf since the age of two) has starred on both big screen and small. She won an Academy Award for her work in the film *Children of a Lesser God* and more recently has been a featured performer on NBC's hit White House drama, *The West Wing*. Matlin says she learned the basic principles of healthy eating by talking to nutritionists and reading; eventually, following those principles became second nature.

"Most of the time, when people think of eating healthfully, they think about what they shouldn't eat," Matlin says. "I prefer to focus on the many foods we *should* be eating to enhance our well-being. I mean, I could easily make myself miserable by always thinking, 'Okay, I have to limit this and that, and I can't ever eat that.' That's not a healthy or realistic diet. Once you find healthy foods that you enjoy, then you make an effort to always have them available. They'll be staples on your grocery list."

Staples on Matlin's grocery list include bottled water; fresh fruits; fish; vegetables, especially asparagus; and garlic—lots of garlic. A self-confessed garlic fanatic, Matlin credits the "stinking rose" with keeping her virtually free of colds.

index. These include things like pastries, corn-flakes, white potatoes, and white rice. Foods that score low to medium ratings on the glycemic index tend to be high in fiber and complex carbohydrates, as most fruits, vegetables, and whole grains are.

Here are four simple ways to build up the complex carbohydrates and fiber in your diet.

1. Have a whole grain. Choose whole-grain bread rather than white bread or even low-calorie whole-wheat bread, suggests nutrition scientist Shari Lieberman, Ph.D. The heavier, the better: Look for brands that contain at least 3 grams of dietary fiber per slice. Remember that while dense bread contains more calories, it also fills you up, leaving you more satisfied.

2. Pass on the puffs. Lightweight cereals like puffed wheat, puffed rice, and corn-flakes send blood sugar through the roof, according to Dr. Lieberman. Choose an unsweetened cereal that contains at least 3 grams of fiber per serving, such as Nabisco Shredded Wheat.

3. Believe in beans. Dried beans are great sources of both protein and fiber. While virtually all beans are fiber providers, the champs are black-eyed peas, chickpeas, kidney beans, lima beans, and black beans.

4. Mix it up. You can moderate the blood sugar spike of high-glycemic foods such as white rice by mixing them with a high-protein food, such as chicken.

Detour around Fat

Supermarket managers know what they're doing. They put temptation right in your path. That's

High-Test Oil

Cold-pressed, extra-virgin olive oil contains more antioxidants and phytochemicals than yellow olive oil, says nutrition scientist Shari Lieberman, Ph.D. That's because the oil is extracted from the olives by literally crushing them rather than by using heat and chemicals. It's more expensive, but it's worth it.

why the bakery section is always in a prominent location, a place you're sure to pass. It's hard not to linger and then buy, but you'll be younger if you don't.

Cutting back on foods that are high in saturated fat can help maintain or increase your levels of youth hormones. Conversely, a steady diet of saturated fat switches off production of those same hormones. "We don't know why saturated fat has this effect, but it does," says Dr. Kogan.

You can encourage your body's production of youth hormones by getting no more than 10 percent of your daily calories from saturated fat. In other words, if you consume 1,800 calories a day, no more than 180 of them (20 grams) should come from saturated fat.

As you trim the saturated fat from your diet, replace it with foods that are high in monounsaturated fats, such as canola, olive, and peanut oils. Monounsaturated fats tend to reduce the levels of "bad" low-density lipoprotein (LDL) cholesterol in your blood and raise your levels of "good" high-density lipoprotein (HDL) cholesterol. That's good for your youth hormones as well as for your heart.

Dance with Zorba

To get more monounsaturated fats into your diet, try eating like Zorba the Greek.

Like most people in Mediterranean countries, Zorba enjoyed a diet that was rich in fish, nuts, and olive oil. Do the same, and like Zorba, you'll be dancing down the beach to the sound of balalaikas.

Here are three ways.

1. Get oily. Olive oil is perhaps the best-known monounsaturated fat. Besides lowering LDL cholesterol, it contains several compounds that are powerful antioxidants.

2. Go nuts. You are what you eat, and as everyone knows, Zorba was a little nuts. Fortunately for him, nuts happen to be a great source of monounsaturated fats. You can easily add nuts to your diet by tossing a small handful of raw almonds, walnuts, or sunflower or pumpkin seeds on salads, rice dishes, or vegetables.

3. Eat with the fishes. Dr. Lieberman recommends that you eat fish such as salmon, tuna, cod, haddock, herring, perch, or snapper once or twice a week. These fish are rich in omega-3 fatty acids, substances that have been shown to raise HDL cholesterol. They also encourage your body to produce youthful hormones.

What about Meat?

When it comes to preserving youth, meat is a mixed blessing. It's an excellent source of protein, which our bodies need to make amino acids, substances that help regulate hormones; grow new tissue; and repair or replace worn-out tissue.

Soy Story

Ask any food expert to name his or her favorite antiaging foods, and soy will almost certainly appear high on the list.

"Soy is a superfood," says nutrition scientist Shari Lieberman, Ph.D. "You might even call it a youth food because it has such potential to stave off age-related conditions from menopausal symptoms to osteoporosis to breast cancer."

Skeptical? Consider our friends in Asia, where soy is a dietary staple. They have fewer heart attacks; are less likely to develop breast, colon, and prostate cancers; and suffer fewer hip fractures. Asian women going through menopause don't have as many hot flashes. And the Japanese, as a population, have the longest life expectancies in the world.

Is soy responsible for that? Scientists think it may be, at least partly. They point out that soy is packed with nutrients that older bodies need. In addition to protein, these include iron, calcium, and B vitamins like thiamin, riboflavin, and niacin. Perhaps

The downside of the picture is saturated fat. Meat is loaded with it.

The question is, can you get the best of both worlds, protein without saturated fat? The answer is an emphatic yes.

most important, soy is packed with natural protective compounds called isoflavones that scientists believe may be the key to soy's disease-fighting powers.

As the health benefits of soy have become more widely known, more supermarkets have begun stocking soy products. Here's a quick run-down of the basic ways to buy it.

Tofu. The mother of all soy foods comes in three varieties, one as versatile as the next. Firm tofu is solid, so it's often stir-fried, grilled, or added to soups and stews. Soft tofu, which has a creamy consistency, and silken tofu, which has a custardlike texture, can be mashed or pureed and added to blender drinks, dips, dressings, and puddings.

Don't be put off by the taste. Standing alone, tofu is bland, but it takes on the flavors of other foods with which it's mixed.

Tempeh. Pronounced "TEM-pay," this traditional Indonesian food is made of cooked, fermented whole soybeans. The result is a chunky, tender cake with a smoky or nutty flavor. Tempeh can be marinated

and grilled, just like a steak, or it can be added to soups, casseroles, or chilies.

Soy milk. This creamy liquid comes from soybeans that are soaked, finely ground, and strained. It's a good source of protein and B vitamins, and many brands are fortified with calcium. Lots of people pour it over their breakfast cereal or use it in cooking. And since soy milk comes in a variety of flavors, including vanilla and chocolate, it's easy to drink straight. Because it isn't dairy milk, look for "soy beverage" or "soy drink" on the labels.

A wide array of plant foods are excellent sources of protein. That doesn't mean you can't enjoy an occasional steak, Dr. Lieberman says. Your goal should simply be to get the majority of your protein from plant sources.

Here are three painless ways to accomplish that goal.

1. **Savor soy.** Soy is an excellent source of low-calorie, high-quality protein. But unlike the protein in animal foods such as meat, eggs, and milk, soy protein contains zero heart-damaging saturated fat and cholesterol.

2. Consume quinoa. The beadlike, ivory-color seeds of this plant are usually eaten like rice. But you can also cook this grain in fruit juice and eat it for breakfast, use it as a substitute for rice in pudding, or make a cold salad of quinoa, beans, and chopped vegetables. Its soft texture and somewhat bland flavor make it easy to add to other foods, such as soups and pasta dishes. You'll find quinoa in health food stores.

3. Wok at home. Using a wok can painlessly and deliciously cut down the amount of meat you consume. Simply add a small amount of steak or pork to a vegetable stir-fry.

The Toxic Avengers

The last piece of the longevity diet package takes direct aim at those free radicals that increasingly assault our bodies as we get older. Antioxidant vitamins such as C and E and minerals such as zinc and selenium neutralize free radicals. So do phytonutrients, a class of natural substances that occur in abundance in fruits, vegetables, and other plant foods.

Nutritionists believe that phytonutrients help our bodies fight a plethora of age-related diseases, from arthritis to cancer. To give just a few examples, ellagic acid, a compound found in berries (with strawberries and blackberries con-

NATURALFACT

Steaming vegetables locks in their antioxidants and phytonutrients. Boiling leaves their protective substances in the water.

taining the most), may help prevent cellular changes that can lead to cancer. Lutein, found in dark green vegetables like spinach and kale, has been found to cut by nearly half the risk of macular degeneration, the leading cause of irreversible vision loss in people over age 50. Indole-3-carbinol, found in broccoli, cabbage, and other cruciferous vegetables, may help prevent breast and cervical cancers.

Which foods provide the most antioxidant bang for the buck? Researchers at Tufts University in Boston analyzed 22 common vegetables and calculated the ability of each to neutralize free radicals. Among the winners were kale, beets, red bell peppers, brussels sprouts, broccoli, potatoes, sweet potatoes, and corn. Good fruit sources of antioxidants include strawberries, plums, oranges, red grapes, and kiwifruit.

Salad, Simply

No time to peel, slice, and dice salad fixings? Do it once a week. Every Sunday, prepare a huge bowl of dark green lettuce, carrots, peppers, and other vegetables. Store several servings separately in airtight plastic bags or containers to limit their exposure to oxygen.

Chapter 8

"One Size Fits All" Is *Not* a Smart Diet Plan

Learn how to tailor your menu to fit *your* special nutrition needs

D ifferent strokes for different folks."

That saying isn't as popular as it once was, but the sentiment it expresses still holds. All of us have different needs, and our needs change over time. This is true physically as well as psychologically. Your body requires different nutrients when you're 45 than it did when you were 35. Your nutritional needs shift again by the time you're 65.

Adjusting your diet according to the demands of your life cycle keeps you feeling great and slows aging. A diet that doesn't take your life cycle into account will do the opposite.

With this in mind, we've created the following decade-by-decade guide to women's nutrition concerns. Follow it, and you'll be at your nutritional peak, whatever your age.

Your Thirties

Everything seems to happen at once in your thirties—work, romance, family. It's all great stuff, but you need all the energy and strength you can get to pull it off. Here's how to maximize those resources.

Lift your iron. If your energy level is in perpetual low gear, your problem could be iron. As many as 20 percent of premenopausal women are low in iron but not low enough to be called anemic. The result is fatigue and poor concentration.

"Mild iron deficiency in women in their thirties goes unnoticed in many cases because routine blood tests screen only for anemia, a late stage of deficiency," says Robert Labbe, Ph.D., professor emeritus in the department of laboratory medicine at the University of Washington in Seattle.

What to do: Get a blood test called serum ferritin. If you are deficient in iron, include more iron-rich legumes, dark green leafy vegetables, and extra-lean meat in your daily menu.

Include a vitamin C–rich food such as orange juice with iron to boost absorption, and take a moderate-dose multivitamin/mineral supplement that contains the Daily Value (DV) for iron (18 milligrams).

Fight the blues. Women in their thirties often battle mood problems rooted in nutrition.

What to do: Eat foods that help you maintain a positive outlook, including the following:

• Milk. Getting three glasses of low-fat or fat-free milk (or its equivalent in yogurt or calcium-fortified OJ) a day may help you fight the mood swings of PMS. Researchers at St.

The ABCs of Supplements

Any vitamin you take should support—not substitute for—a healthy diet. Whatever your age, what to take is as simple as ABC.

A) The Multi: Select a broad-range multiple vitamin and mineral supplement that provides approximately 100 percent of the Daily Value for a wide variety of nutrients, including vitamin A or beta-carotene, vitamin B_6, vitamin D, copper, and zinc.

Premenopausal women with low blood levels of iron should take a multi that contains 18 milligrams of iron. All other women should take one with 0 to 9 milligrams of iron. Men should take supplements with no iron.

B) Calcium: Take 500 milligrams if you're under 50, 1,000 milligrams if you're 50-plus.

C) The Antioxidants: Consider separate supplements of 100 to 500 milligrams of vitamin C and 100 to 400 IU of vitamin E, unless your multi already contains these levels.

Luke's–Roosevelt Hospital Center in New York City report that women who have PMS find relief when they increase their intakes of calcium.

• Bananas. Birth control pills lower blood levels of vitamin B$_6$, a vitamin that helps manufacture the mood-elevating nerve chemical serotonin. Low B$_6$ could explain why some women on the Pill report feeling moody, grumpy, and irritable. Include B$_6$-rich bananas, extra-lean meat, and tofu in your daily menu.

• Salmon. Women are twice as likely to be depressed as men, and their thirties are when depression often crops up. Some researchers suggest that eating foods rich in omega-3 fatty acids, such as salmon and canned white tuna, may make you less vulnerable to depression.

Get ready for baby. Consuming less than 1 milligram (the weight of a small paper clip) of folic acid each day could be all it takes to prevent a serious type of birth defect called a neural tube defect.

What to do: Take a multi supplement that includes the DV for folic acid (400 micrograms) and eat two foods rich in folate (the naturally occurring form of folic acid) daily. Candidates include spinach, kidney beans, and orange juice.

"Women need to be taking a multiple that contains folic acid *before* they conceive," warns Meir Stampfer, Ph.D., Dr. P.H., professor of nu-

"Women need to be taking a multiple that contains folic acid *before* they conceive."

—Nutrition and epidemiology professor Meir Stampfer, Ph.D., Dr. P.H.

trition and epidemiology at Harvard School of Public Health. If you don't start supplementing until the pregnancy test comes back positive, it could be too late. During your pregnancy, switch to a supplement with 600 micrograms of folic acid.

Your Forties

Many women hit their strides in their forties, with careers and families going strong. But it's also the decade when you start noticing the effects of the approximately 1 to 2 percent yearly loss of muscle mass that began in your thirties. You'll probably also enter perimenopause, the period of fluctuating estrogen levels prior to menopause.

Here's what to focus on to keep your health robust.

Adjust your diet. As your metabolism slows, you'll burn fewer calories. Unless you adopt new habits, you're likely to gain weight—especially around the middle, where it is harder to lose and has a greater negative effect on blood sugar, cholesterol levels, and blood pressure.

What to do: Eat breakfast. If you're a breakfast skipper, make this your first new weight-control habit. Researchers at Vanderbilt University in Nashville found that women who ate breakfast had an easier time controlling cravings. Compared to breakfast skippers, they also consumed less fat throughout the day.

Wayne Callaway, M.D., weight-loss expert at George Washington University in Washington, D.C., recommends establishing a consistent pattern of eating three meals at regular times, which over the course of a few weeks will help reprogram your body's appetite and hunger clock.

Make every bite count. Your nutritional needs are high, but your calorie needs are starting to drop. That means that every forkful should be packed with nutrients.

What to do: Cut back on processed foods, which are typically lower in vitamins, minerals, and fiber than whole foods, and also higher in fat and sugar. Choose the oatmeal, not the granola bar; the potato, not the chips; the whole-wheat bread, not the white bread; the fresh fruit, not the fruit punch.

An added benefit is that this high-fiber diet helps balance the female hormone estrogen, which can reduce your risk of breast cancer.

Prepare for change. Don't be surprised if you notice an occasional hot flash, memory lapse, or sleepless night. Perimenopause can begin up to 10 years before your last menstrual period, bringing with it many of the same symptoms that are linked to menopause. That's where diet comes in. Evidence shows that estrogen-like compounds called isoflavones, found in soybeans, can help offset the drop in your natural estrogen.

What to do: Add a daily serving of soy foods to your menu, providing 30 to 50 milligrams of isoflavones. (A serving equals ½ cup of

> **NATURAL**FACT
>
> Moderate alcohol consumption has been shown to lower the risk of heart disease in women over age 55.

tofu, 1 cup of soy milk, or 3 tablespoons of roasted soy nuts.) One report showed a reduction in hot flashes of up to 40 percent when women added soy to their diets.

Your Fifties

Whoever said that 50 was old had it wrong. If you're meeting the special nutritional needs of menopause, you can help make your fifties the years when you reach your prime. Here are your special concerns.

Be bone smart. Your risk of osteoporosis rises after menopause, but consuming enough calcium can help keep your bones strong. After age 50, your calcium requirement rises from 1,000 to 1,500 milligrams a day. Yet Robert P. Heaney, M.D., a calcium expert at Creighton University in Omaha, Nebraska, estimates that 95 percent of women don't get enough of the calcium they need from their normal diets.

What to do: Eat three servings daily of calcium-rich foods, such as 1 cup of nonfat milk or yogurt, 1 ounce of low-fat cheese, 1 cup of calcium-fortified citrus juice, or 1 cup of calcium-fortified soy milk. Plus, take a calcium supplement.

Be heart smart. Heart disease is the number one cause of death after women reach menopause, but the right diet will reduce your risk significantly.

What to do: If you haven't already done so, adopt a low-fat, high-fiber diet. Your staples should be fruits and vegetables, whole-grain breads and cereals, legumes, soy foods, and nonfat dairy products. Make sure your multi supplement includes 100 percent of the DV for vitamin B_{12} (6 micrograms). After age 50, your body needs help absorbing this vital nutrient to help fight heart disease.

You can also fight heart disease by savoring an occasional glass of wine. "After age 55, consuming alcohol in moderation shows some benefit in lowering heart disease risk in women," says Dr. Stampfer.

Beat middle-age spread. After menopause, you'll find that it's easier to put weight on and harder to take it off.

What to do: Switch from three square meals to five to seven nutritious mini-meals of about 250 calories each, spaced throughout the day. After age 50, women who eat larger meals instead of mini-meals may burn off 60 fewer calories a day, suggests research from Tufts University in Boston. That means that switching to mini-meals could save you from gaining 6 pounds a year.

Researchers at the University of Michigan in Ann Arbor found that mini-meals help women lower their levels of body fat too.

‖ Sixty Plus

With some intelligent care, you can slow your body's aging process to a crawl and make your golden years truly shine. Put these concerns at the top of your agenda.

Obliterate free radicals. Free radicals are marauding molecules that attack your cells, making you more vulnerable to heart disease, cancer, cataracts, and a host of other diseases. As you age, your body needs more help fighting the free radical assault, and antioxidants, including vitamins E and C, are part of the answer. So are the phytonutrients found in many fruits and vegetables.

What to do: Bathe your cells in antioxidants by including at least eight fruits and vegetables in your menu each day. Vivid color in

Less Is More

Studies have shown that older women's insulin levels tend to stay high for up to 5 hours after even moderate-size meals (500 to 1,000 calories). In younger women, insulin levels quickly return to normal after such meals.

Since high blood sugar may set the stage for heart disease and other problems, including cataracts and wrinkles, women past age 50 or so should consider shifting to the mini-meal plan. Instead of eating three meals a day, eat five to seven, each consisting of about 250 calories, throughout the day.

Blueberry Thrill

The blueberry has emerged as nature's number one source of antioxidants among fresh fruits and vegetables. In tests at Tufts University in Boston, blueberries beat out 39 other common fruits and vegetables in antioxidant power—even such heavyweights as kale, strawberries, spinach, and broccoli.

produce often indicates high levels of phytonutrients, so choose carrots, sweet potatoes, spinach, broccoli, blueberries, strawberries, kiwifruit, and oranges, to name a few.

You won't be able to get all the vitamin E you need from food alone, though. It takes 27 cups of spinach or 1 cup of safflower oil to get 100 IU, the amount many experts recommend. Therefore, take a vitamin E supplement. Extra vitamin C makes sense too.

Go for quality. Your nutritional needs are higher than ever, while your calorie needs are still dropping. More than ever before, you need to make every bite count.

What to do: Make a decision to choose whole grains, beans, low-fat dairy foods, fruits and vegetables, and small amounts of extra-lean meats. Save empty-calorie foods such as cookies and sweetened sodas for just every once in a while. Take a good multi supplement to make doubly sure that you don't fall short.

Never miss your vitamin X. Vitamin X stands for exercise. Okay, it's not a food. But we're including it here because, now more than ever, it's critical that you get moving. With daily physical activity, seniors can not only slow the aging process—they may even be able to reverse it.

What to do: Develop a routine that combines daily weight-bearing exercise, such as walking or jogging, with two or three weekly sessions of weight lifting. Then, just do it—come rain or shine.

It's never too late to begin. Even people in their nineties have seen up to 200 percent improvements in strength within just a few weeks of starting exercise programs.

Chapter 9

Breast Cancer Special Report

Here are 25 fabulous foods that can prevent and fight this deadly disease

When it comes to cancer prevention, food is powerful medicine. Study after study shows that a healthful diet can vastly—repeat, *vastly*—reduce the risk of cancer.

The reason for that is simple: There are compounds in certain foods that prevent and fight cancer at the cellular level. By loading your diet with those foods, you can stack the odds in your favor.

The 25 foods we've lined up here will help you do just that—stack the odds in your favor. Not every one of these has been definitively proved to be a breast cancer beater, but all have shown definite promise, and all are healthy for plenty of other reasons.

Since they're all simple and delicious, why not go for it? You have nothing to lose and everything to gain.

1. Sweetest Carrot Juice

Eating foods high in beta-carotene has been linked in many studies to lower rates of breast cancer. One 8-ounce glass of Odwalla Carrot Juice gives you pressed carrot juice and nothing else. It has 700 percent of the daily recommendation for beta-carotene and only 70 calories. It can be found in health food stores, the natural food section of your supermarket, delis, or gourmet shops.

Bonus: It tastes fantastic.

2. Spicy Radish Sticks

The daikon radish is one of broccoli's spicier cousins. It looks like a huge white carrot, and you can peel it and cut it into sticks. Like all in the broccoli clan, daikon contains compounds that help sweep up cancer-causing substances—a dangerous type of estrogen, in this case—before they have a chance to do harm. For a double-barreled treat, dip your radish stick in Spinach Dip.

3. Spinach Dip

Women in one study who ate a serving of spinach at least twice a week had half the rate of breast cancer of women who avoided it. Use frozen spinach to make a luscious dip. Combine a 10-ounce package of thawed and drained frozen spinach with ¼ cup of reduced-fat mayonnaise, ¾ cup of fat-free sour cream, and 2 tablespoons of grated Parmesan or Romano cheese. Add several tablespoons of 1% milk, as needed, to make a thick dipping consistency. Chill for at least 1 hour. A ¼-cup serving has 70 calories, 2 grams of fat, and 1 gram of fiber.

4. Rye Crispbread

Eating refined grains may promote breast cancer, at least according to one study. So go in the opposite direction by eating crispbread made from 100 percent whole-rye flour. May we add that this is another perfect partner for Spinach Dip?

The Easy Way

You know that the best way to prevent breast cancer is to eat lots of fruits and vegetables, yet working them into your diet sometimes seems a pain. There's an easy solution to this problem, says Cheryl Rock, Ph.D., R.D., a cancer researcher at the University of California, San Diego: Drink up. Getting an extra serving of veggies is easy with vegetable juice—carrot, tomato, or vegetable juice cocktail.

5. A Mug of 1% Milk

Warm a mug of 1% milk, add ¼ teaspoon of almond extract, and enjoy it at bedtime. Why aren't we suggesting fat-free milk? There's an intriguing compound in milk fat, conjugated linoleic acid, that fights breast cancer cells in laboratory tests.

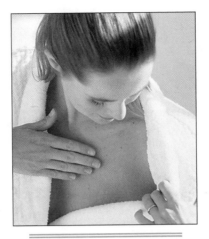

"Scientific research overwhelmingly supports annual mammography screening beginning at age 40."

—Daniel B. Kopans, M.D., associate professor of radiology at Harvard Medical School

6. Tomato Juice with a Kick

Diets high in lycopene are linked to lower rates of breast cancer, and Spicy Hot V8 will give you a zesty dose.

7. BroccoSprout Pitas

BroccoSprouts are a brand of broccoli sprouts with megalevels of SGS, a compound that has been shown to fight mammary tumors in animal experiments. To make a tasty BroccoSprout Pita, spread 1 tablespoon of fat-free cream cheese inside half of a 6-inch, whole-wheat pita. Add 1 chopped tomato, ½ cup of BroccoSprouts, and 1 tablespoon of crumbled low-fat feta cheese. There are 180 calories, 3 grams of fat, and 5 grams of fiber per ½ pita.

8. Concord Spritzer

Having more than one alcoholic drink a day increases your risk of breast cancer, so having a nonalcoholic drink as a substitute is a great idea. This bracing spritzer fits the bill deliciously, and Concord grape juice just happens to have the most cancer-fighting antioxidant power of any juice. Just mix ⅔ cup of Concord grape juice, ⅓ cup of club soda, ice, and a dash of lime juice. Each serving has 103 calories, no fat, and no fiber.

9. Salmon

Order salmon whenever you find it on a restaurant menu. Salmon is ultra-rich in omega-3 fats, and research suggests that women with higher levels of omega-3's in their tissues have lower rates of breast cancer.

10. A Daily Multi

Okay, technically a multivitamin isn't a food, but you *do* put it in your mouth, and it *is* important. Women whose diets are higher in vitamin D have less breast cancer. To ensure that you get the recommended level, nutrition experts advise adding a daily multivitamin to a healthy diet. The recommended Daily Value for vitamin D is 400 IU, though people over 50 may need up to 800 IU. Don't take more than 2,000 IU daily.

studies have shown that limonoids may inhibit breast cancer. But does commercial OJ have any limonoids in it? The answer is yes. The manufacturing process is vigorous enough that some of the peel gets in.

11. Pineapple-Carrot Smoothie

The secret weapon here is baby-food carrots, because the beta-carotene they contain is super-absorbable. Put one 4-ounce jar of chilled baby-food carrots and one 6-ounce can of chilled pineapple juice in a covered jar and shake well for 10 seconds. This makes about 1 cup, with 129 total calories.

12. Chilled Cherries

Cherries are a top source of perillyl alcohol, a compound that has shown promise as a breast cancer fighter in animal tests. Look for the Just Cherries brand of freeze-dried cherries in health food stores, the natural food section of your supermarket, delis, or gourmet shops. They're tangy, sweet, and crunchy, and a 1-ounce pack has less than a gram of fat.

13. Good Old Orange Juice

The peel and white membrane of oranges contain compounds called limonoids. Laboratory

14. Bran, Your Way

Women who ate one serving a day of a cereal high in wheat bran lowered their levels of breast cancer–promoting estrogen. If you're not ready for plain wheat-bran cereal, mix your favorite cereal half and half with one of the two highest wheat-bran varieties, All Bran Extra Fiber and Fiber One.

15. White Tuna Salad

Tuna is another source of those cancer-fighting omega-3 fats. You'll get more of them if you make your tuna salad from water-packed, canned white tuna rather than light tuna.

16. 8th Wonder Fat Free Fries

Most french fries, both frozen and fast-food, are a top source of trans fatty acids. One study suggests that a diet higher in trans fatty acids may increase the risk of breast cancer. But at last, the Holy Grail has been discovered: a truly great frozen french fry with no trans fatty acids. In fact, these babies have no fat, period. Look for 8th Wonder Fat Free Fries, made with Yukon Gold potatoes for buttery flavor and color. A 3-ounce serving (16 fries) has 70 calories.

17. A "Cuppa" Green

Green tea is rich in EGCG, a compound that inhibits breast cancer cells in mice. Try a flavored green tea, such as Celestial Seasonings Honey Lemon Ginseng Green Tea, to introduce yourself to this brew.

18. Iced Tea for Grown-Ups

Most bottled green teas are loaded with either tons of sugar or artificial sweetener. Honest Tea Moroccan Mint Green Tea with Peppermint is a delightful exception. A touch of white clover honey mellows the flavor but adds only 34 calories per 16-ounce bottle. Look for the tea in health food stores, the natural food section of your supermarket, delis, or gourmet shops.

19. Olive Oil Dressing

Studies show that Mediterranean women have low rates of breast cancer, which may be because olive oil is a staple of their diet. Unfortunately, most of the "olive oil" dressings we buy here in the United States are actually made with a mix-

> **NATURAL**FACT
>
> The *British Medical Journal* recently reported that as many as 80 percent of breast cancers may be diet-related.

ture of oils. Avoid this mongrel approach by making your own easy dressing using half olive oil, half balsamic vinegar. It's a delicious and healthy combination.

20. Easy-Going Garlic

Lab experiments have shown that garlic kills breast cancer cells, and a more flavor-packed medicine you'll never find. Make sure that you give your garlic a chance to "rest" before you cook it, though. Putting it in the pan right after you've peeled and chopped it doesn't allow its cancer-fighting compounds to form. Let it sit for 10 to 15 minutes before heating.

21. Crackers That Count

Old Stone Mill Whole Wheat Wafers give you the benefit of whole-grain wheat without any trans fatty acids. In eight crackers, you get 3 grams of fiber from wheat bran (a probable breast cancer fighter), 120 calories, and only ½ gram of fat. They're available in health food stores, the natural food section of your supermarket, delis, or gourmet shops.

22. Veggie Patties and Links

Women who eat lots of red meat, especially meat that's very well done, seem to get more breast cancer. That may be because of the cancer-causing compounds that form when meat is cooked. Veggie burgers and veggie sausage don't have that problem, and they taste great.

23. Anchovy Pizza

Order pizza with anchovies, or add them at home. Anchovies are rich in omega-3 fats.

24. Trans-Free Margarine

Make it a point to choose a trans-free margarine as your regular spread, since trans fatty acids may increase your risk of breast cancer. Smart Balance, Smart Beat, and the Promise lines of margarine are among the trans-free brands.

25. No-Bake Cranberry Flaxseed Bars

A compound called lignan precursors has shown potential as a breast cancer fighter, and flaxseed is your best source of it. In fact, flax has 75 times more lignan precursors than any other food.

Some people aren't wild about the taste of these cranberry bars, but others are. To make them, simmer ½ cup of frozen cherry juice concentrate and 2 cups of dried cranberries in a covered pan over medium-high heat for 5 minutes. In a food processor, blend the juice and cranberries with 1¾ cups of ground flaxseed until the mixture forms a ball. Press the dough into a 9- by 9-inch nonstick pan, cut into eight bars, and refrigerate. Each bar has 185 calories, 9 grams of fat, and 9 grams of fiber.

Note: You can buy ground flaxseed in health food stores, the natural food section of your supermarket, delis, or gourmet shops.

THE PREVENTION LIST

Spice Rack Therapy

The last thing you want to do when you're feeling lousy is drive all the way to the pharmacy. Relax—you don't have to. The exact medicine you need may be sitting in your kitchen spice rack, innocently disguised as a cooking ingredient. Here are our favorite spice rack remedies.

1. **Peppermint tea for bad breath.** The aromatic oil that gives peppermint its distinctive smell is a potent antiseptic that will kill the germs that cause bad breath. Use 1 tablespoon of whole dried peppermint leaves, 2 tablespoons of fresh leaves, or a tea bag per cup of hot water. Steep for 10 minutes.

2. **Turmeric for heartburn.** Bitter herbs help stimulate the flow of digestive juices, moving food along and preventing acid buildup. So spice up your food with the bitter herb turmeric, which is the base of most Indian curries.

3. **Ginger for indigestion.** For best results, grate fresh ginger and mix 1 teaspoon to 1 tablespoon in 1 cup of hot water. Steep for 10 to 15 minutes, then strain (or use a tea ball).

4. **Rosemary for migraines.** Dilating blood vessels helps relieve migraines, and rosemary will do the trick. Use 1 teaspoon of rosemary per cup of hot water.

5. **Thyme for a cough.** Thyme acts as both an expectorant and an antiseptic, and it relieves bronchial spasms. To prepare the tea, steep 1 to 2 teaspoons of dried thyme leaves in 1 cup of boiling water for 10 minutes. Drink up to three times a day when you're sick.

6. **Horseradish for congestion.** Anyone who has ever inhaled the potent vapors of horseradish will understand why it can break up congestion. Eating a teaspoonful on some crackers should clear you up.

7. **Parsley for urinary tract problems.** Parsley contains myristicin and apiol, compounds that are thought to help increase the output of urine by increasing the flow of blood to the kidneys. To make a tea, pour boiling water over a few sprigs of crushed fresh parsley or 1 teaspoon of dried parsley. Let it steep for 10 minutes, then strain and drink.

8. **Sage for a sore throat.** Cover 1 teaspoon of sage with boiling water. Let it steep, covered, for 10 minutes, strain, and gargle.

Part Four

Triple
Defense

When it comes to fighting disease,
why not use all the weapons at your disposal?

Chapter 10

For Optimum Health, Use a Triple Defense

Combine food, herbs, and vitamins to protect youself against illness

A core concept in natural healing is the idea of approaching health from a holistic point of view. Holistic health care recognizes that nothing in nature is isolated. Physical well-being derives from a harmonious interplay of elements.

This brings us to the program we call triple defense. In order to prevent disease and to get rid of illness you already have, it makes sense to bring to bear on a given problem a holistic range of natural healing approaches: healthy foods, healthy herbs, and healthy vitamins and minerals.

This section presents a triple-defense approach to 20 of the most common illnesses and complaints, from colds to cancer. Use this approach, and the odds are excellent that you'll be healthier than you would be if you were to use a single remedy alone.

‖ **Arthritis**

Arthritis, which causes pain, stiffness, and swelling in and around the joints, isn't just one disease, but many. The most common form of arthritis is osteoarthritis, which is caused by wear and tear on cartilage, the shock-absorbing material between your joints. When cartilage wears away, bone grinds against bone, causing pain and stiffness in your fingers, knees, hips, and back.

See a doctor if the pain, stiffness, or swelling in a joint persists for more than 2 weeks.

Fish. Arthritis is one of the many illnesses that are made worse by a diet high in saturated fats, so it's a good idea to cut back on those fats. Replace them with omega-3 fatty acids. This type of fat, found primarily in cold-water fish like mackerel, trout, and salmon, reduces the body's production of prostaglandins and leukotrienes, both substances that contribute to inflammation. To get the healing benefits from fish, eat it two or three times a week.

Omega-3 Scorecard

Fish and other ocean-living critters are our best sources of the omega-3 fatty acids that doctors think help ward off arthritis as well as fatal heart attacks and possibly depression, breast cancer, and severe menstrual cramps. Doctors and nutritionists recommend that you aim to consume 3.5 grams of omega-3's a week.

Here's how America's most popular seafoods, listed in order of popularity, stack up as sources of omega-3's. The figures represent the omega-3's in a 3-ounce serving, which is roughly the size of a deck of playing cards.

Seafood	Omega-3's (g)
TUNA, WHITE, CANNED IN WATER	0.7
TUNA, LIGHT, CANNED IN WATER	0.2
SHRIMP	0.3
POLLOCK (FREQUENTLY USED IN FISH STICKS, IMITATION CRAB, FAST-FOOD FISH)	0.5
SALMON (FARM-BRED, ATLANTIC), COD	0.1
CATFISH (FARM-BRED)	0.2
CLAMS	0.2
CRAB (KING)	0.4
FLOUNDER, SOLE	0.4
HALIBUT	0.4

Boswellia (*Boswellia serrata*). The bark of the frankincense tree is cut to collect aromatic gum resin that's used to make a standardized extract. The extract has been shown to improve blood supply to the joints and prevent the breakdown of tissues affected by all types of arthritis. To ease chronic pain, take 450 milligrams of boswellia in capsule form, four times a day.

Glucosamine and chondroitin. These are big names for simple stuff. Glucosamine comes from crab, lobster, or shrimp shells. Chondroitin comes most often from cattle trachea. Your body, too, makes both of these substances to help build and protect cartilage.

Scientists believe that glucosamine somehow stimulates the cartilage cells to product two important compounds that are the building blocks of cartilage. Once you have taken it for 8 weeks, the supplement seems to provide pain relief comparable to that of ibuprofen, but without side effects. Experts aren't quite as sure how chondroitin works, but they think that it inhibits the enzyme that breaks down cartilage. With your doctor's approval, take 1,500 milligrams of glucosamine and 1,200 milligrams of chondroitin sulfate daily.

‖ Bladder Infections

Bladder and urinary tract infections, commonly called UTIs, occur when bacteria take up residence in your bladder or urethra (the tube through which urine flows), causing painful or frequent urination. More common among

> **NATURAL**FACT
>
> According to one study, almost half of all women have had urinary tract infections at some point in their lives. Four of five women who have had UTIs have had repeat infections within 18 months.

women than among men, UTIs are usually treated with antibiotics, which can clear up the problem in a few days.

Cranberry juice. Research suggests that drinking cranberry juice can prevent and speed recovery from UTIs. They believe that women prone to UTIs may have "stickier" cells in their urethras and bladder, making it easier for bacteria to hold on. It appears that cranberries contain a substance, which hasn't been identified yet, that acts like a non-stick coating for those cells, making bacteria more likely to slip away. Doctors recommend that women who frequently get UTIs drink 10 ounces of unsweetened cranberry juice every day.

Goldenrod (*Solidago virgaurea*). Goldenrod, a feathery roadside flower that puts on quite a show at summer's end, is the number one urinary herb in Europe. A tea made from the yellow flowering tops of this perennial herb is a mildly astringent antiseptic to promote healing of inflammation in the urinary tract. Steep 1 well-rounded teaspoon in 1 cup of hot water for 5 to 10 minutes, then strain. Drink 3 to 4 cups a day until the burning and pain are gone.

Vitamin C. Building up your overall immunity will help fight a bladder infection, and taking a high-potency multivitamin each day is a good step in the right direction. When you have a UTI, add some extra vitamin C. Taking 500 milligrams every 2 hours can help improve immune function by boosting white blood cell counts, a sign of better defenses. While this much C probably isn't needed on a daily basis, the body seems to require additional amounts of this nutrient in times of infection. Cut back if you start having diarrhea.

‖ Cancer

Even while you sleep, there's a battle being waged inside you at the cellular level. Every day, your cells are attacked again and again by a barrage of harmful molecules called free radicals. These are oxygen molecules that have each lost an electron, and they careen around your body looking for replacement electrons. In the process of pilfering electrons, they damage healthy cells, possibly kicking off the cancer process.

Fruits and vegetables. Compounds in food called antioxidants stop the formation of free radicals or disable them before they do harm. Three of the best-studied and most powerful antioxidants are beta-carotene and vitamins C and E.

Beta-carotene is the pigment that gives many fruits and vegetables their deep orange to red hues. Dozens of studies have shown that people who get a lot of beta-carotene in their diets can reduce their risks of certain cancers. Evidence suggests that getting 15 to 30 milligrams a day—the amount in one to two large carrots—is probably all it takes.

Other studies have shown that people who consume the most vitamin C have the lowest risks of cancer. The Daily Value (DV) for vitamin C is 60 milligrams. That's an easy amount to get in foods: One green bell pepper has 66 milligrams and a half-cup of broccoli has 41 milligrams.

Vitamin E, the third powerhouse antioxidant, not only blocks free radicals but also fends off cancer by stimulating the immune system. Plus, it actually prevents the formation of cancer-causing compounds in the body. Vitamin E is difficult to get from foods. The easiest way is through wheat germ. A little less than 2 tablespoons of wheat germ contains about 4 IU of vitamin E, about 13 percent of the DV. Whole grains, legumes, nuts, and seeds are also good sources of vitamin E.

Garlic (*Allium sativum*). In addition to antioxidants, plant foods also contain substances collectively known as phytonutrients that have the ability to stop cancer. One food that is particularly rich in phytonutrients is

In Your Dairy Case

According to a study published in the *Journal of the American Medical Association*, low-fat dairy products may help protect against colon cancer. When people at high risk for the disease added low-fat dairy products to their daily diets, colon cells that may have been precancerous started acting like healthy cells.

The dairy products in question added about 1,200 milligrams of calcium to the daily diet.

HEALING SPOTLIGHT
Katie Couric

There are some things that all the healthy foods, healthy herbs, and healthy vitamins in the world won't do for you. Detecting cancer in its early, treatable stages is one of them.

Katie Couric, coanchor of NBC's *Today*, knows this all too well: Her husband, Jay Monahan, died from colon cancer at the age of 42. "Even those with the healthiest lifestyles can still be diagnosed with the disease," Couric says. That's why she considers regular screenings for colon cancer "critically important."

As dear as this issue is to Couric's heart, she knows that many people don't like talking to their *spouses* about their colons, much less to their doctors. That's why she's mounted a determined public-awareness campaign to get the whole subject out in the open. Estimates are that colon cancer deaths, which stand now at some 56,000 a year in the United States, could be cut in half if people made screenings part of their checkup routines. The National Colorectal Cancer Research Alliance, which Couric cofounded, recommends that anyone over 50 receive regular preventive screenings for colorectal cancer. People who have personal or family histories of colon problems should talk to their doctors about testing even earlier.

"We're trying to encourage a dialogue between physicians and patients," Couric says. "For too long, it's been a subject that people felt squeamish about—it's having to do with that part of our bodies and those functions. We're trying to make it as natural as talking about breast cancer is today. We just need to be very matter-of-fact about it. We always say we don't want anyone to die of embarrassment."

garlic, which has a long tradition as a healing herb. Some of the most impressive phytonutrients are allyl sulfides, which appear to help destroy cancer-causing substances in the body. One study found that women who ate more than one serving of garlic—either one fresh clove or a shake of powder—a week were 35 percent less likely to get colon cancer than those who ate no garlic.

Selenium. The essential trace mineral selenium has been connected with protection against cancer since the late 1960s. Researchers continue to gather evidence that selenium seems to have anti-cancer effects, though they're still unsure why this is the case.

Selenium supplements appear to encourage the death of potentially cancerous cells grown in lab dishes. They also seem to inhibit tumor

Further Support for a Healthy Diet

Confirmation that a healthy lifestyle prevents cancer comes from the Breast Cancer Demonstration Project, a huge research study comparing the food habits of more than 41,000 women over a period of more than 5 years. The study found that women who ate the most servings of fruits, vegetables, whole grains, low-fat dairy products, and lean meats had the lowest mortality rates of the group.

growth. Both these properties suggest that taking supplemental selenium may deliver cancer protection soon after you start taking it.

Fruits and vegetables that have been grown in selenium-rich soil are more likely to contain the mineral, but it's hard to know from looking at them in the supermarket where they've been grown. For that reason, supplements are the surest way to make sure that you get enough selenium. People who showed an increased resistance to cancer in one study were taking 200 micrograms a day. Experts say that's an effective amount to include in your anti-cancer supplement program.

Carpal Tunnel Syndrome

Just as highways go through tunnels in order to get around or under obstacles, some structures in your body, such as nerves and ligaments, also use tunnels to get where they're going. One of the busiest bodily tunnels is the carpal tunnel, which allows a nerve, blood vessels, and ligaments to pass through your wrist and into your fingers.

Usually there's a lot of room inside the carpal tunnel. But when you use your hands and wrists a lot while typing, sewing, or doing other repetitive motions, tissues inside the tunnel may become inflamed and swollen, which causes

them to press against the nerve. This can cause pain in your wrists as well as tingling or numbness in your fingers.

See your doctor if you have any symptoms of carpal tunnel syndrome (CTS)—numbness, pain, or tingling—that cause discomfort as you go about your daily activities.

Flaxseed. Flaxseed contains a compound called alpha-linolenic acid that has been shown to reduce levels of prostaglandins, chemicals in the body that contribute to inflammation. It also contains compounds called lignan precursors that have antioxidant properties that can block the effects of free radicals. This is important because free radicals are produced in large amounts whenever there's inflammation, and un-

Buy It Processed

Many people sprinkle whole flaxseed on salads or fresh-baked breads. That's not the best way to get its protective benefits, though, because your body can't crack open the hard shells. The cracked or milled forms will more readily yield the nutritious goodness that is packed inside.

less they're stopped, they make the inflammation even worse.

Some evidence suggests that getting about 3 tablespoons of ground flaxseed or 1 to 3 tablespoons of flaxseed oil might be enough to help ease the symptoms.

Turmeric (*Curcuma domestica*). Mix 2 tablespoons of turmeric powder with enough warm water to form a paste. Sandwich the paste between two layers of gauze, wrap it around your sore wrist, and hold it in place with a bandage. Leave the bandage on all day. It's safe to do this periodically, but for no longer than 3 to 4 days at a time.

If that's too messy a proposition for you, you can take an extract of a substance called curcumin. Believed to be one of the most active components in turmeric, curcumin has been shown to be as effective as cortisone in reducing inflammation. Take 400 to 600 milligrams of curcumin extract three times a day on an empty stomach until your symptoms subside.

Vitamin B$_6$. Vitamin B$_6$, also called pyridoxine, also seems to help relieve the symptoms of CTS. Doctors aren't sure why the supplement works, but some speculate that CTS is actually

> **NATURAL**FACT
>
> Carpal tunnel syndrome is most common among women ages 30 to 60.

caused by a deficiency. Although you can get vitamin B$_6$ pretty easily from foods, the average diet doesn't provide the DV of 2 milligrams.

Vitamin B$_6$ seems to work best on mild to moderate cases of CTS. Take 50 milligrams each day, and give it time to work. It usually takes 12 weeks to get the full benefit.

Colds and Flu

With more than 200 cold viruses floating around and a new strain of flu cropping up each year, it seems almost impossible to not get sick. Conventional medicine can offer only symptom squelchers such as pain relievers, decongestants, and expectorants, but alternative medicine can aid your body's natural healing powers while easing the accompanying discomforts of these illnesses.

See a doctor if your cold or flu doesn't improve within 7 days, if you have green or yellow phlegm, if you have trouble breathing, or if your temperature tops 102°F. Also, see your doctor if

Got Possum?

Granny Clampett, whom you may remember from the *Beverly Hillbillies* TV clan, guaranteed that if you took her homemade concoction of ground possum innards, you'd be cured of a cold within a week. The joke, of course, was that the only "cure" for the common cold is to let it run its course, which it will usually do within a week, with or without possum innards.

you have vomiting, dizziness, or generalized weakness for more than 1 to 2 days.

Tea and chicken soup. When you're hit hard by a cold, you may feel that the only thing you really want to do is curl up under the covers with a cup of hot tea or a bowl of chicken soup. Trust that instinct. Research has shown that these two traditional home remedies are among the most potent available. Both of these foods contain compounds that can relieve congestion and pump up your immune system.

Tea, for example, contains a compound called theophylline that helps break up congestion. Tea also contains quercetin, a compound that may help prevent viruses from multiplying.

Chicken soup is one of the best ways to relieve stuffiness and other cold and flu symptoms. In lab studies, researchers found that chicken soup was able to prevent white blood cells from causing inflammation and congestion in the airways. Strangely, you need to eat homemade chicken soup. Doctors aren't sure why, but canned chicken soup doesn't work as well as homemade, and broth made from bouillon doesn't work at all.

Echinacea (*Echinacea angusti-folia, E. purpurea, E. pallida*). Also known as purple cornflower, Kansas snakeroot, and black Sampson, echinacea is a famously effective remedy for any respiratory tract infection. It works because it strengthens your immune system by increasing your body's production of white blood cells, which attack viruses. It also activates the killer cells that destroy virus-infected cells.

Since echinacea doesn't work as well once a cold is full-blown, use it at the first hint that you're getting sick. Take 1 teaspoon of echinacea

NATURALFACT

The 12th-century physician and philosopher Maimonides recommended chicken soup for a fever and cough.

tincture mixed in ½ cup of water five times a day. Look for a tincture made with one part echinacea to five parts alcohol. For children and for those who want to avoid alcohol, look for a tincture made from glycerin.

Zinc. Of all the trace minerals, zinc is probably the most important for keeping your immunity strong. It generates new white blood cells and prepares them to battle viruses. If you have too little zinc, your production of white blood cells may drop, which can increase your risk of catching a cold or the flu.

While it's best to get zinc from foods, like oysters, beef, lamb, eggs, and whole grains, you can get what you need from supplements. Be careful not to take too much, though, because more is not necessarily better. Doctors recommend taking no more than 20 milligrams a day. You could also try zinc gluconate lozenges, which have been found to shorten the duration of colds. Check with your doctor first, and don't take them for longer than a week. After that, they can actually weaken your immune system.

Also, don't forget the original cold supplement, vitamin C. Studies show that vitamin C can shorten the duration of common colds and flu and even prevent them. At the first sign of a cold, take 500 milligrams of vitamin C with bioflavonoids or rose hips four to six times a day. Cut back if the vitamin C gives you diarrhea.

Constipation

Like so many other things, constipation means different things to different people—everything from stools that are too hard, too small, or too difficult to pass to those that are too infrequent or incomplete. The good news is that it's usually easily remedied.

See a doctor if your constipation lingers for more than 2 weeks, with fewer than one bowel movement every 3 days, and if it is accompanied by abdominal pain or blood in the stool.

Fruits, vegetables, legumes, and whole grains. For most people, getting enough fiber and fluids can banish constipation for good. Fiber acts like a sponge in your intestines. It absorbs water and makes stools fuller and easier to pass. Fruits, vegetables, legumes, and whole-grain foods all contain healthful amounts of fiber.

Both types of fiber, soluble and insoluble, help. Soluble fiber, found in prunes, apples, legumes, and oats, turns into a kind of gel in your intestines. The insoluble kind, found in bran, wheat, and vegetables like celery, carrots, and spinach, helps to sweep your system clean. Within a few days of getting your daily 25 grams of fiber, you should notice a difference.

> **NATURALFACT**
>
> On average, Americans get about 11 grams of fiber a day, far less than the Daily Value of 25 grams.

It's important to add fiber to your diet slowly because when your body isn't used to the added fiber, you may have cramping and gas. To get the benefits without the pain, gradually add fiber to your diet over a period of several months.

While you're adding fiber, it's also crucial that you add water. When stools don't get enough fluid, they become hard, sluggish, and more difficult to pass. This is especially true if you eat more fiber. Drink at least eight 8-ounce glasses of water a day. If you exercise or drink caffeinated beverages that make you urinate a lot, you should drink 12 glasses a day.

Cascara sagrada (*Rhamnus purshianus*). Probably the world's most popular laxative, cascara sagrada can help your bowels get moving right away. This herb contains compounds called anthraquinones that stimulate the intestines to contract. Take 15 to 20 drops of tincture once daily. Don't use this powerful herb for more than 2 weeks.

Psyllium. You may not have heard of psyllium, but you have probably heard of the brand name Metamucil. This seed-derived herbal

A Traveler's Best Friend

When 16th-century Spanish explorers came ashore in northern California, they weren't feeling so well. They were constipated, most likely because their traveling diet lacked adequate amounts of fruits and vegetables.

The local Native Americans offered the Spaniards an effective remedy for constipation: tea made from dried bark. It worked so well that the Spaniards named the herb *cascara sagrada*, which means "sacred bark."

product introduces bulk and fiber to your digestive tract. It also absorbs a lot of water as it passes through your body, which is why it's important to drink lots of fluids when taking psyllium.

You may find psyllium in more than one form at the store, so follow label instructions. It should start to work within 12 to 72 hours.

Depression

Everyone gets the blues on occasion. That sad, leave-me-alone feeling is usually caused by stressful situations, such as work or relationship troubles. Nutritional deficiencies, certain prescription drugs, food allergies, and health problems like thyroid disorders can also be causes.

You should see a doctor if the blues linger for more than a few weeks or if they interfere with your personal or professional life. Also seek help if you have any of these signs of clinical depression: feelings of hopelessness, loss of pleasure or interest in favorite activities, changes in appetite or sleep habits, fatigue, feelings of worthlessness and guilt, difficulty thinking, or thoughts of death or suicide.

Breads, pasta, and potatoes. Diets high in carbohydrate-rich foods like bagels and pasta have been shown to increase brain concentrations of the amino acid tryptophan. Your body then converts tryptophan into serotonin, the same mood-making chemical that many antidepressants are intended to increase.

This could explain why, for many people,

NATURALFACT

About 17 percent of Americans will have a bout of severe, lingering depression at some point in their lives.

comfort foods that are high in carbohydrates can ease feelings of depression, anxiety, and fatigue. Of course, some people can eat breads, pasta, and potatoes by the bagful without noticing a difference. But for others, known as carbohydrate cravers, the effects can be quite pronounced. It may be that carbohydrate cravings are the body's attempt to counteract low serotonin levels.

Food should not be used as a remedy for depression on a long-term basis, especially because overeating high-carbohydrate foods can lead to obesity, heart disease, and other problems.

St. John's wort (Hypericum perforatum). More than 20 studies have found that St. John's wort can help ease the blues with fewer side effects than prescription drugs. The herb's active ingredients include hyperforin, flavonoids, and other compounds that work in concert to increase serotonin levels in the brain.

If you'd like to take capsules, look for a formula that's standardized to 0.3 percent hypericin. Take 300 milligrams before or between meals three times a day. Like prescription antidepressants, St. John's wort takes a few weeks to reach its full effect. If you're already taking a prescription antidepressant, check with your doctor before adding the herb.

SAM-e. Used in Europe since the 1970s, SAM-e—pronounced "Sammy"—is now available in the United States as an over-the-counter supplement. Although it is a natural substance that your body makes from protein, you need supplements to get enough. In clinical studies, 400 to 1,600 milligrams of SAM-e were as effective at reducing depression as prescription anti-depressants.

Like many antidepressants, SAM-e supplements are believed to work by boosting production of brain chemicals such as serotonin. The bonus of SAM-e is that it works within 4 to 10 days. Take 1,600 milligrams a day.

‖ Diabetes

The most difficult thing about this disorder is that it can wreak havoc on your entire body. Here's why: The fuel that keeps your body running is glucose, or blood sugar. Soon after you eat, glucose pours into your bloodstream and is carried to individual cells throughout your body. Before it can enter the cells, it requires the presence of a hormone called insulin. In people with diabetes, either not enough insulin is produced or the insulin that is produced doesn't work efficiently. So the glucose can't enter their cells. It lingers in their bloodstreams and builds up over time. The cells go hungry, which can cause fatigue, dizziness, and other problems. But all that concentrated glucose becomes toxic and dam-

aging to the eyes, kidneys, nerves, immune system, heart, and blood vessels.

Diabetes is a serious condition that requires a doctor's care. It's critical that people with diabetes eat right, control their weight, and exercise regularly.

High-fiber diet. Research shows that a high-fiber diet can play a powerful role in controlling blood sugar. Of the two types of fiber, soluble and insoluble, it's soluble that helps stabilize blood sugar. It works by forming a gummy gel in the intestine that helps prevent glucose from being absorbed into the blood too quickly. This in turn helps keep blood sugar levels from rising too fast or dipping too drastically. Soluble fiber also seems to increase cells' sensitivity to insulin so more sugar can move from the blood into the cells.

It's easy to increase your intake of soluble fiber. Just eat more fruits, legumes, oat bran, and oatmeal.

Asian ginseng (*Panax ginseng*). Known as a feel-good herb to boost vitality, Asian ginseng can help stabilize blood sugar levels. It's been used for centuries in Traditional Chinese Medicine. In a study in Finland, re-

Beach Time Helps Too

One of the more delicious diet approaches to diabetes comes from Terry Shintani, M.D., director of preventive medicine at the Wainae Coast Comprehensive Health Center in Hawaii. He puts some of his patients on a traditional diet that is native to the islands. It consists mainly of high-fiber, high-carbohydrate foods such as taro, poi, greens, and fruits, plus plenty of fish.

This regimen was so effective in many cases, Dr. Shintani says, that many people no longer needed to take insulin.

A Word of Caution

The remedies in this section are available at grocery stores, health food stores, or pharmacies. They are natural and generally safe and gentle to use. For specific safety precautions, see the Safe Use Guides beginning on page 224.

searchers found that a daily dose of 200 milligrams of ginseng for 8 weeks improved mood, diet, and activity, which reduced weight and helped lower blood sugar levels. Take a daily dose of 200 milligrams in capsule form.

Chromium. Studies of people with diabetes have shown that supplementing with chromium can lower blood sugar levels, improve glucose tolerance, and reduce insulin levels. In studies where chromium proved helpful, patients were usually getting it in a form called chromium picolinate, in doses of at least 200 micrograms a day. Most multivitamin/mineral supplements contain a less absorbable form called chromium chloride. Thus, you'll probably need a chromium picolinate supplement to get an adequate amount, but be sure to talk with your doctor before you start taking one.

Caution is in order for several reasons. Since chromium makes the insulin that you have work better, the timing of when you take it is important. You also need to be careful because chromium can cause low blood sugar until your insulin levels stabilize. Your doctor will want to keep a close watch on your blood sugar levels until that occurs. In any event, don't take more than 200 micrograms.

‖ Diarrhea

For most people, diarrhea is not a serious problem but rather an embarrassing dilemma for a day or two. Usually, it goes away on its own, unless it's a symptom of a more serious problem such as food poisoning, Crohn's disease, ulcerative colitis, or an adverse drug reaction.

See a doctor if your diarrhea doesn't go away within 3 days or if there's blood in the stool. If you begin having signs of dehydration from diarrhea, such as thirst, dry skin, dry mouth, fatigue, and lightheadedness, see a doctor immediately.

Bland diet. Until diarrhea has run its course, it's a good idea to eat bland foods. Wise choices are noodles, white bread, bananas, and applesauce. These bland foods won't further irritate your cranky colon. Plus, they contain fiber. Fiber acts like a water-absorbing sponge in your colon and helps dry things up a bit.

It's also important to replace the fluids that you're rapidly losing. Drink vegetable or chicken broth and clear juices, diluted with water, to avoid dehydration, a potentially dangerous result of diarrhea.

When you have diarrhea, what you don't eat could be more important than what you do eat. For the first 48 hours, steer clear of solid food, milk products, and foods that are greasy or very sweet. Also avoid very high fiber foods, such as beans and high-fiber cereals.

Cinnamon (*Cinnamomum zeylanicum*). If your diarrhea is so severe that you risk dehydration and need to quickly dry up the flow, prepare some cinnamon tea. A natural astringent, cinnamon will dry up your bowel. Add 1 teaspoon of powdered cinnamon to 1 cup of

In the Nick of Time

When you're miles away from the nearest bathroom, a bout of diarrhea can be inconvenient, to say the least. When you're miles away from the nearest town, it's even worse. Cathryn Flanagan, N.D., used to work for the U.S. Forest Service in Colorado's Rocky Mountains, identifying plant species. One morning, she developed the telltale symptoms of a stomach in turmoil.

Dr. Flanagan remembered reading about cinquefoil, a readily available plant that's supposed to be good for treating diarrhea. She searched the ground, spotted a plant, and added a sprig to her tea.

Within minutes of sipping, her stomach's rumblings subsided. "It was very satisfying to find a cure literally at my feet," Dr. Flanagan said.

---

boiling water. Steep for 10 to 15 minutes. Pour the tea through a paper towel to strain out the cinnamon, then drink.

Glutamine. With severe diarrhea or a bout that lasts for several days, your intestines may remain inflamed. Try glutamine, an amino acid supplement frequently used by naturopathic physicians for gastrointestinal problems. Glutamine encourages the quick turnover or production of cells along the walls of your stomach and small intestine, helping you heal faster.

Take 500 milligrams of glutamine three times a day. Continue this dosage for about 2 weeks or until you have no more discomfort.

‖ Headache

Nearly 90 percent of men and 95 percent of women have had at least one headache in the past year. More than 90 percent of those headaches are tension headaches, which are caused by stress, poor posture, tiredness, and eyestrain.

Another type of headache, which includes migraines, is called vascular headache. Such a headache is caused by the expansion and contraction of blood vessels in your face, head, and neck. Vascular headaches can be extremely painful or even disabling, as anyone who gets migraines can attest. While the pulsating throb of a migraine headache is less common than the duller and more generalized pain of a tension headache, it's more likely to send you to the doctor in search of relief.

If you have a sudden onset of severe head pain that's different from any headache you've previously experienced or if your headache is accompanied by any other symptoms that are strange or unusual for you, see a doctor right away.

Magnesium-rich foods. While the underlying reasons aren't yet clear, certain minerals, particularly magnesium, appear to play a role in both preventing and easing migraine and tension headaches. People who suffer from migraines often have low levels of magnesium in their brain cells. Studies suggest that correcting a magnesium deficiency may help relieve migraine.

Ready-to-eat breakfast cereals are good sources of magnesium. Nuts, seeds, and leafy green vegetables are also rich in magnesium.

Feverfew (*Tanacetum parthenium*). Anyone who's prone to getting headaches can appreciate the notion that it's better to avoid them altogether than to worry about curing them once they've started. Preventing all types of headaches is the strong suit of feverfew, a cousin of dandelion and marigold. In order to get the benefit of its protective powers, you need to take 125 milligrams of feverfew every day for 6 to 8 weeks.

Riboflavin. Riboflavin is a B vitamin. In super-high doses, it can help ward off a migraine attack by helping your brain cells utilize energy. In a Belgian study of 49 people who frequently got migraines, researchers found good results with daily doses of 400 milligrams of riboflavin. At that dose, about half of the people in the study became migraine-free. Among the others, the intensity of pain was reduced by about 70 percent.

One expert puts all of his migraine patients on 200 milligrams of riboflavin for a week. Then,

> **NATURAL**FACT
>
> Americans spend more than $8 billion per year on over-the-counter and prescription pain relief.

A Feverfew Testimonial

One of the biggest fans of taking the herb feverfew for headache is James A. Duke, Ph.D., botanical consultant and former ethnobotanist at the USDA. In his book *The Green Pharmacy*, Dr. Duke describes how feverfew helped both his sister-in-law and his secretary's sister beat migraines. This personal experience is backed by the medical literature on feverfew, he adds: It works for about two-thirds of those who use it consistently.

"If we assume," Dr. Duke writes, "that the estimated 25 million Americans who suffer from migraines on a regular basis spend in the same way that my sister-in-law did"—some $200 a year on headache medications—"that would be an incredible $5 billion a year for migraine medication. I don't think the purveyors of modern pharmaceuticals would be pleased to see feverfew replace the many profitable drugs that are now prescribed for treating migraine."

he raises the dose to 400 milligrams. If that causes nausea, which it does in some people, they return to the 200-milligram dose.

‖ Heartburn

If you've ever had heartburn, you know that the name is appropriate. It feels as though a fire were raging in your chest. The pain can be so intense, in fact, that some people rush to their doctors because they think they're having heart attacks.

In fact, heartburn has nothing to do with your heart. It occurs when acid-laden digestive juices in your stomach surge upward into your esophagus. Normally, a tight little muscle at the base of your esophagus, called the lower esophageal sphincter, prevents juices from escaping. But when the muscle relaxes at the wrong times, juices splash upward, literally scorching tender tissues in your esophagus. This is what causes the burn. Your mucous membranes become painfully inflamed and irritated.

See a doctor if you have heartburn on a daily basis. Also, if your heartburn becomes more

NATURALFACT

Researchers estimate that up to 25 million Americans get heartburn every day.

of a blaze than in the past, have it checked out. Increased pain often signifies that something else is wrong.

Gum. Okay, we know it's not exactly a food, but food is probably what's causing your heartburn anyway. Chewing gum can provide temporary relief of heartburn. It stimulates the flow of saliva, which neutralizes acid and helps push digestive juices back where they belong. Sucking on a piece of hard candy will work in the same way. Just steer clear of anything peppermint-flavored. Peppermint makes heartburn worse because it lowers the pressure in the lower esophageal sphincter and allows acid reflux into the esophagus.

Licorice (*Glycyrrhiza glabra*). Licorice root lozenges have compounds that put a damper on the fire down below. Licorice can raise blood pressure. If your blood pressure is normally fine, you can use plain licorice tablets. If high blood pressure is a problem for you, look for deglycyrrhizinated licorice, or DGL. It's a modified form that has none of the compounds in the regular root that can raise your blood pressure. Whichever kind you take, it's important

Push Away

Overeating is a major cause of the acid reflux that creates heartburn, says Malcolm Robinson, M.D., gastroenterologist at the University of Oklahoma Health Sciences Center in Oklahoma City. "The stomach is a very adaptable organ and will relax and expand to accommodate what's in it. If you eat a lot more than you usually do, however, it will have difficulty expanding that quickly."

to chew the tablets slowly to mix them with saliva. That puts more of the active ingredients to work.

Glutamine. An amino acid that's available as a nutritional supplement, glutamine heals damaged mucous membranes. It encourages the turnover or disposal of damaged cells, and it increases the production of new cells along your gastrointestinal walls. Glutamine is also a potent antioxidant, helping to protect cells from the damage caused by free radical molecules. All of these actions cause faster healing.

Take one 500-milligram capsule four times a day until you're feeling better, but not for more than a month.

High Blood Pressure

A blood pressure reading is one of the simplest and most available medical tests around. That's why it's ironic that one in three people with high blood pressure (also called hypertension) doesn't even know he or she has it. Yet it's one of the leading causes of stroke, heart attack, congestive heart failure, kidney failure, and premature death.

Simply put, blood pressure is the force exerted on your artery walls by your blood as it's pumped through your body. When your arteries are clogged and hardened by cholesterol deposits, your heart has to work harder, and your blood pressure rises.

You should have your blood pressure checked at least once every 2 years. If it's higher than 140/90, which is defined as mild or Stage 1 high blood pressure, your doctor will probably want to monitor it more often.

Learn and Live

You've heard that what you don't know can't hurt you? Don't buy it. Most of us are aware that heart disease is the number one killer of men. Most of us *don't* know that heart disease is also the number one killer of women. In fact, women die far more frequently from heart attacks than they do from breast cancer.

The DASH diet. Doctors generally agree that if your blood pressure is too high, you should eat healthier foods, reduce your intake of sodium, avoid being overweight, and get regular exercise. A great way to cover the food, salt, and weight portions of that prescription is the DASH diet, which stands for Dietary Approaches to Stop Hypertension. It's a super-healthy eating plan based on fruits, vegetables, and low-fat dairy foods. In one very large study, the DASH diet helped people lower their blood pressures as effectively as some prescription drugs did. You may find that it can do the same for you, but always consult your doctor when treating high blood pressure.

For a rundown of the DASH diet, see "The DASH Pyramid," page 90.

Hawthorn (*Crataegus oxycantha, C. laevigata, C. monogyna*). Just as hawthorn benefits other heart problems, it can help lower elevated blood pressure. In fact, hawthorn is one of the most commonly used herbs for high blood pressure. Powerful but gentle, it works a lot like prescription medications. Look for hawthorn standardized for a specific flavonoid known as vitexin. Take two 500-milligram cap-

The DASH Pyramid

Food Group	Servings	Serving Sizes
MEAT, FISH, AND POULTRY	2 or fewer a day	3 oz, cooked
NUTS, SEEDS, AND LEGUMES	4–5 a week	⅓ cup nuts, 2 Tbsp seeds, ½ cup cooked legumes
GRAINS AND GRAIN PRODUCTS	7–8 a day	1 slice bread, ½ cup dry cereal, ½ cup cooked rice, pasta, cereal
LOW-FAT OR NONFAT DAIRY	2–3 a day	8 oz milk, 1 cup yogurt, 1 oz cheese
FRUITS AND VEGETABLES	8–10 a day	1 cup raw leafy vegetables, ½ cup cooked vegetables, 6 oz vegetable juice, ¼ cup dried fruit, 1 medium fruit, 6 oz fruit juice, ½ cup fresh, frozen, canned fruit

Foods below are **essential** to the DASH diet

Source: National Heart, Lung, and Blood Institute

sules or 1 teaspoon of tincture three times a day. When your blood pressure starts to come down, take one 500-milligram capsule or ½ teaspoon of tincture three times a day, then reduce the dosage to twice a day.

If you've been diagnosed with high blood pressure or other cardiovascular conditions, you should not take hawthorn regularly for more than a few weeks without medical supervision. You should also have your blood pressure checked at least every 2 weeks.

Magnesium. This mineral helps to relax the smooth muscles in blood vessels, which allows them to dilate. When blood vessels relax, blood pressure tends to go down. One study found just how effective magnesium can be at reducing blood pressure. For a 2-month period, researchers continually monitored the blood pressures of 60 people with hypertension. For half that time, they were given 480 milligrams of magnesium a day. The researchers then compared each person's blood pressure level with and without magnesium supplementation. They saw a small but significant drop in the overall pressures of the participants.

Aim for 350 milligrams of supplemental magnesium per day through a multivitamin plus a supplement.

‖ High Cholesterol

High cholesterol isn't a disease at all. It's actually a symptom. Your cholesterol levels tell you something about your risk of developing heart disease, the life-threatening condition that occurs when the arteries to your heart become clogged with cholesterol. The higher your blood levels of the "bad" kind of cholesterol—low-density lipoprotein, or LDL for short—the greater your risk of developing heart disease.

Two other kinds of fats also affect your arterial health: triglycerides and the "good" kind of cholesterol, called high-density lipoprotein, or HDL, cholesterol. Triglycerides are simply partners in crime with LDL, and when your blood profile shows high triglycerides, there's reason for concern. Elevated levels of triglycerides and LDL are what people generally mean when they use the term *high cholesterol*.

HDL cholesterol, on the other hand, is a fat that helps keep your blood flowing smoothly, which is exactly the opposite of the effect that LDL cholesterol has. In fact, HDL helps shepherd bad cholesterol out of your blood vessels. Therefore, the higher your HDL levels, the lower your risk of heart disease.

High cholesterol is a silent symptom, so it's important to have your levels checked in case yours are in the danger zone.

Asian diet. Eating a low-fat diet is an efficient way to reduce the amount of cholesterol in your blood. Here's an example. Among Chinese people who eat a traditional Chinese diet, the average overall cholesterol level is a healthy 127. Among Americans, the average is 100 points higher. If you're concerned about cholesterol, therefore, it makes sense to eat less like the average American and more like the average Asian. That means eating lots of fresh vegetables, fruits, and grains and relatively few red meats and dairy foods.

Garlic. Since HDL cholesterol helps flush excess LDL cholesterol out of your body, it's a

NATURALFACT

The National Cholesterol Education program recommends that your total cholesterol level remain below 200 milligrams per deciliter of blood. More than half of American adults have cholesterol levels higher than that.

good idea to build up the level of HDL in your blood. Garlic does just that, and plenty of studies show that regular consumption of the herb lowers overall levels of cholesterol in your bloodstream. Eat a clove or more a day, raw or cooked.

Vitamin E. Cholesterol doesn't hurt you as long as it's just floating around in your blood. It's when the fatty substance clings to your artery walls that it becomes a serious threat. Before it can stick to your artery walls, it has to be oxidized. To prevent the chain of events that leads to oxidation, you need a good dose of antioxidants that disarm free radicals, the free-roaming, unstable molecules that do the damage. One powerhouse antioxidant is vitamin E. Taking 400 IU of vitamin E can help to lessen the potential harmful effects of high cholesterol levels. Look for natural vitamin E; the body uses it twice as effectively as it uses synthetic.

‖ Insomnia

Few things are more miserable than lying awake, frustrated and tired, when everyone else is sleeping soundly. Insomnia is usually temporary, caused by too much coffee, perhaps, or anxiety about tomorrow's work. But sometimes, insomnia really sticks around, not just for days but for weeks, months, even years. After a few nights of staring at the ceiling, you may feel as if you'll never rest again.

See a doctor if lack of sleep is causing daytime sleepiness and impaired performance.

Milk. Mom was right: A glass of warm milk just might help you drift off to sleep. That's because milk, as well as cheese, turkey, and chicken, are high in an amino acid called tryptophan that has been shown to affect the part of your brain that governs sleep.

Your body converts tryptophan into serotonin, which it then converts into melatonin. Both serotonin and melatonin make you feel relaxed and sleepy. Tryptophan may be so effective, in fact, that for a long time, doctors recommended tryptophan supplements to help people sleep. Even though the pills were eventually banned (due to a tainted batch imported from Japan), doctors believe that the tryptophan found in foods is safe and effective as a sleep aid.

Valerian (*Valeriana officinalis*). Long before over-the-counter and prescription sleeping pills became available, herbal sedatives were widely used. One of nature's more popular herbal sedatives, used centuries ago and today, is valerian.

Valerian is particularly helpful for the kind of sleeplessness that comes from anxiety, muscle tension, or muscle spasms. Take 400 to 425 milligrams of valerian root 1 hour before bedtime.

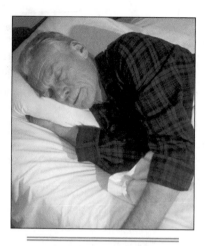

"I believe the greatest asset a head of state can have is the ability to get a good night's sleep."

—Sir Harold Wilson,
20th-century British politician

Melatonin. Trumpeted as a panacea for jet lag, cancer, and depression, melatonin has been widely accepted for treating insomnia. This hormone is secreted by the pineal gland, a pea-size gland in your brain that helps control periods of sleepiness and wakefulness.

The pineal gland releases melatonin into your bloodstream—less when your body detects light, more when it's dark. Production hits a peak between 2:00 and 4:00 A.M.

Before taking supplemental melatonin, have your doctor check your natural levels. If they are low, take up to 1 milligram at least 2 hours before you go to bed. If you don't respond to this dosage, 2 to 3 milligrams may do the trick. This supplement is for short-term use only.

Low Energy

Given the pace that most of us are trying to maintain these days, who wouldn't be tired? For just that reason, though, you need all the energy you can get. Food, herbs, and supplements can definitely help. Don't avoid getting medical attention when you really need it, though. If fatigue habitually turns simple tasks into chores or makes it difficult to concentrate in important situations, see your physician.

Protein-rich foods. To a large extent, your energy level is controlled by neurons, nerve cells in your brain that communicate with the help of chemical messengers called neurotransmitters. Studies have shown that changes in the levels of neurotransmitters such as dopamine and norepinephrine can dramatically affect your energy level, which is why these neurotransmitters are sometimes called wake-up chemicals. Studies show that people tend to think more quickly and feel more motivated and energetic when their brains are producing large amounts of these chemicals.

Your diet provides the raw materials needed for the production of these neurotransmitters. What you eat or don't eat can play a large role in how you feel.

NATURALFACT

Half of all adults who seek medical treatment complain of fatigue.

The building block for dopamine and norepinephrine, for example, is the amino acid tyrosine. Tyrosine levels are elevated when you eat high-protein foods such as fish, chicken, or low-fat yogurt. You don't have to eat huge amounts of protein to get tyrosine's energizing effects. Eating just 3 to 4 ounces of protein-rich food, like a broiled chicken breast or a hard-boiled egg, is enough to get the dopamine and norepinephrine flowing.

Gotu kola (*Centella asiatica*). This Indian herb contains no caffeine but has other stimulant properties that make it an effective treatment for fatigue. In addition to simply providing an energy boost, gotu kola may help lift your spirits—fatigue and depression are

No Quick Fixes

When you're tired, it's tempting to look for a quick fix. But many times, that's just the sort of thinking that got you tired in the first place.

"Fatigue and energy drain are symptoms," says Patricia Howell, a professional member of the American Herbalist Guild and director of the Living with Herbs Institute in Atlanta. "To treat people effectively, you have to alter things at a constitutional level, in terms of both lifestyle and body function."

Toward that end, if you're having energy problems, it makes sense to ask yourself a few questions before you look for a cure, suggests Donald J. Brown, N.D., a naturopathic doctor in Seattle and author of *Herbal Prescriptions for Better Health*. Chief among those questions are: Have you been tired for a long time? Have you been under stress for a long time?

If the answers to these questions are yes, go for a checkup, Dr. Brown suggests. "I'm adamant about getting to the root of a person's fatigue by taking a thorough medical history and recommending a few standard medical tests to rule out thyroid problems, anemia, or other conditions."

closely linked. Take 60 to 100 milligrams in capsule form each day. (For more on using herbs to combat low energy, see chapter 12.)

Vitamin C. Research has shown that having low levels of this vitamin is associated with fatigue. Vitamin C helps your body make a substance called carnitine that your muscles need in order to burn fat as fuel for energy. The good news is that vitamin C depletion and the fatigue it causes can be reversed quickly. Take 500 to 1,000 milligrams of vitamin C each day, in addition to eating a diet rich in fruits and vegetables.

Memory Problems

The words of a loved one, the beauty of a landscape, the joy of a celebration—most of the time, we want to remember as much about these things as we can. Yet many of us are frustrated that we seem to remember less than we'd like.

Some degree of memory loss is a normal part of aging. Stress, too, can cause us to lose track of details. See a doctor if you or those close to you notice consistent lapses in memory for which there seems to be no obvious cause. Otherwise, a triple-defense strategy can help you hold on to the memories of a lifetime—and keep track of daily details too.

Olive oil. An Italian study of nearly 300 people ages 65 to 84 showed that those who consumed 17.6 percent of their total calories from monounsaturated fats (much of which came from olive oil) scored better on memory, concentration, and language tests than those whose diets contained less of this brain-boosting fat. The reason for this benefit, researchers believe, is that olive oil increases the incorporation of omega-3 fatty acids in cell membranes, which in turn enhances cell-to-cell communication. As a result, the brain works more effectively.

Use monounsaturated fats such as olive oil in place of—not in addition to—other high-fat foods in your diet. If you just add them instead of

A Nation Confused

"Stress acts like poison to the brain," says Dharma Singh Khalsa, M.D., director of the Alzheimer's Prevention Foundation in Tucson and author of *Brain Longevity*. When stimulated by stress, your adrenal glands release cortisol, a powerful hormone that helps get you through sudden emergencies, such as swerving to avoid a truck. Over time, though, frequent or unrelenting stress can gradually kill or injure billions of brain cells. If stress continues unchecked, it can eventually interfere with your ability to think.

How the Monos Stack Up

People in Mediterranean countries get most of their monounsaturated fats from olive oil. Not so in the United States: We get about one-third of ours from meat, which means that we also get artery-clogging saturated fat at the same time. We need less meat and more monos from heart-healthy sources. Here are a few of your best mono choices.

Food	Monos (g)	Calories
PECANS, DRY-ROASTED, 2 TBSP	11	187
OLIVE OIL, 1 TBSP	10	119
PISTACHIOS, DRIED, 2 TBSP	9	167
ALMONDS, TOASTED, 2 TBSP	9	164
CANOLA OIL, 1 TBSP	8	124
PEANUT BUTTER, CHUNKY, 2 TBSP	7	188
CASHEWS, DRY-ROASTED, 2 TBSP	5	98
PEANUTS, DRY-ROASTED, 2 TBSP	4	107
OLIVES, EXTRA-LARGE, 6	3	42

replacing other fats with them, you'll gain weight. Shoot for a minimum of 15 percent of your total calories from monos. For a 1,800-calorie diet, that translates to at least 30 grams of monos a day.

Ginkgo (*Ginkgo biloba*). One of the best researched of all the medicinal herbs, ginkgo stimulates bloodflow to the brain. Evidence suggests that it also has the ability to boost brain function and protect nerve cells.

Take 60 to 120 milligrams of ginkgo extract in capsule form twice a day. Look for capsules that are standardized to contain 24 percent ginkgo flavone glycosides and 6 percent terpene lactones.

PS (phosphatidylserine). This brain chemical regulates neurotransmitters. Some studies have suggested that PS might help healthy people stave off normal age-related memory loss. For example, do you ever have trouble remembering names? In one study, PS made it easier for people to recall names right after an introduction as well as 1 hour later. Take 300 milligrams daily for 1 month and then a maintenance dose of 100 to 200 milligrams daily.

‖ Osteoporosis

Osteoporosis is a silent disease. People who have it don't usually know it, but their bones are gradually growing thinner and weaker.

Healthy bones are constantly replenished with new tissue. If you have osteoporosis, however, that process is disrupted, and bone tissue is lost faster than it's made. Without a bone density test, you'd never know this was going on.

Everyone is at risk for bone loss as they age, but women are hit the hardest. That's because estrogen helps bone absorb and keep calcium. When estrogen levels fall during menopause, bones often become weaker. In fact, the highest rate of bone loss occurs in the first 5 to 7 years after menopause.

That's not inevitable, however. Taking preventive measures now can help keep your bones strong and healthy in the years ahead.

Dairy foods. Calcium is the essential nutrient for keeping bones strong, and dairy foods (preferably low-fat dairy foods) like milk and cheese are the best ways to get it. Women need 1,000 to 1,500 milligrams of calcium each day to ward off osteoporosis. That's pretty easy to get through foods. A glass of fortified fat-free milk has 352 milligrams. Even if you're not a milk drinker, you can still get plenty of calcium by adding nonfat dry milk to cereals or baked goods, like muffins and cakes. A half-cup of nonfat dry milk contains almost 420 milligrams of calcium and has little effect on the taste of foods.

Horsetail (*Equisetum* spp.). Like tree branches, your bones need to be flexible as well as strong. Otherwise, they'll snap under pressure, rather than bend. Horsetail is a natural source of silicon, one of the minerals that give bones flexibility as well as strength. Take

NATURALFACT

Women have a 50 percent chance of experiencing an osteoporosis-related bone fracture in their lifetimes.

two droppers of liquid horsetail extract in 1 cup of water. Take it on an empty stomach, if possible, in the morning and evening. If you prefer capsules, take 700 to 800 milligrams twice a day.

Calcium, vitamin D, vitamin K, and magnesium. Supplements of all these vitamins and minerals can be key allies in your defense against osteoporosis. Calcium remains the key nutrient. Although it's possible to get the calcium you need from food, most people don't. Most women get only about 500 milligrams a day, far less than the 1,000 (for women under age 50) to 1,500 (for women age 50 and older) they need. Experts recommend supplements to bring you to the proper level. Women under 50 should take 500 milligrams each day and women over 50 should take 1,000 milligrams.

When it comes to keeping bones strong, calcium may be the star, but it isn't the whole show. Other vitamins and minerals might play supporting roles: vitamin D, vitamin K, and magnesium.

Vitamin D helps your body absorb calcium. A deficiency of D can lead to soft bones, which in turn could lead to fractures. Take 400 IU a day.

Vitamin K is also very important for maintaining bone health. It helps reduce the amount of calcium you lose through urine and is crucial to the formation of osteocalcin, a protein that is the matrix upon which calcium is put into bone. The DV for vitamin K is 80 micrograms. Since this vitamin is abundant in green leafy vegetables and whole grains, a diet rich in these foods may supply you with your daily quota.

Magnesium is important because it transports calcium to your bones. It also helps convert vitamin D to its active form in the body. To figure out how much magnesium you need, take your calcium dose and divide it in half.

Stomach Problems

One of life's ironies is that the rich foods we like best—creamy chocolate eclairs come to mind, or mashed potatoes with plenty of gravy—are often the foods that give our stomachs the most trouble, especially since we tend to eat more of them at a sitting than we should.

See a doctor if you're nauseated for several days or if your stomach is upset following a nasty knock on the head. Nausea can be a sign of problems more serious than simple indigestion.

Bland foods. When your stomach is upset, it makes sense to lay off food for a few hours. After you start to feel better, ease back into eating. Start with water, then move to toast, broth, bland soup, or soft-boiled eggs. Avoid hard-to-digest foods like ice cream and fried chicken.

Ginger (*Zingiber officinale*). One of the most popular remedies for an upset

"It's good food and not fine words that keeps me alive."

—Molière, 17th-century French playwright and poet

stomach is also one of the oldest. Studies have shown that ginger can be even more effective than antinausea drugs.

You can buy ginger tea bags at health food stores and some grocery stores. Just put a tea bag in a mug, pour boiling water over it, and steep for at least 5 minutes.

Perhaps best of all is real ginger ale, if you can find it. Not only will the ginger help but also the carbonation can help. Don't bother with Schweppes or Canada Dry, though—the mass-market ginger ales don't contain any ginger. Instead, look in health food or specialty stores for products that contain real gingerroot or its extract.

Enzymes. Digestion begins in your mouth, where enzymes in saliva begin the breakdown of starch as you chew. There are also digestive enzymes that break down carbohydrates, fats, and proteins as food moves through your digestive system. If enzymes aren't doing all of their work, an excess of undigested food may make it into your large intestine, making it more likely that bacteria can feed upon the food. The result may be bloating, gas, and intestinal pain.

Folks who are deficient in some types of digestive enzymes can benefit by taking digestive enzyme supplements. There are many products on the market, some containing up to 10 different enzymes. Look for one that contains amylase, lipase, and protease enzymes.

‖ Stress

One way to deal with stress is to not take yourself so seriously. Laughter is indeed good medicine. Nonetheless, stress itself is no laughing matter. Whenever you're filled with tension and anxiety, your adrenal glands, located above your kidneys, pump out stress hormones such as adrenaline and cortisol. This gives your body that burst of energy it needs to escape disaster—or used to need, back in the days when your ancestors were running from furry predators. Long-term stress causes chronically high levels of stress hormones, which can weaken your immune system, tax your heart and blood vessels, tire you out, and make you more susceptible to illness.

"In this world without quiet corners, there can be no easy escape from history, from hullabaloo, from terrible, unquiet fuss."

—Salman Rushdie, Anglo-Indian novelist

brain quickly uses up its supply of serotonin. When serotonin levels fall, negative feelings tend to rise. Eating foods that are high in carbohydrates, like pasta, bagels, or baked potatoes, can quickly raise low serotonin levels, making you feel less stressed and more relaxed. Be careful that you don't fall into a compulsive eating pattern, though; eating comfort foods should not be considered a long-term remedy for stress.

Chamomile (*Matricaria recutita*). Calming and exceptionally safe, chamomile is a good choice for taking the edge off stress. To brew a calming cup of chamomile tea, buy dried chamomile flowers that are yellow and white. If they're straw-colored, they're too old. Add 2 teaspoons of bulk flowers or 1 teaspoon of finely ground flowers to a mug, pour in 8 ounces of boiling water, cover, steep for 15 minutes, and strain. (For more on using herbs to combat the effects of stress, see chapter 12.)

See a doctor or counselor if you're under so much stress that it's keeping you up night after night, interfering with your ability to work, or damaging your relationships.

Comfort foods. Mashed potatoes. Fresh-baked bread. A steaming plate of pasta. These are just a few of the comfort foods that many of us instinctively turn to in times of stress. As it turns out, our instincts are dead-on. Researchers have found that foods high in carbohydrates produce changes in the brain that can take the edge off stress.

During emotionally trying times, your

B vitamins. The B-complex vitamins, including pantothenic acid and vitamins B_6 and B_{12}, are a treasure trove of stress relief. They can give you more energy, strip away fatigue, and manufacture brain chemicals that help keep you alert and cheerful. To combat stress, talk with your doctor about taking a daily high-potency B-complex vitamin formula that includes 100 to

500 milligrams of pantothenic acid, 50 to 75 milligrams of vitamin B_6, and 500 micrograms of B_{12}.

Yeast Infections

If you are a woman who's ever had a yeast infection, you know that you never want to have another one. Infection with an overgrowth of the yeast organism known as *Candida albicans* causes vaginal itching and burning, plus a thick-textured, bready-smelling discharge. It's not a pretty picture for that most private of places.

Unfortunately, yeast infections are fairly common. If you think you have one, but you haven't been diagnosed with a yeast infection before, see a doctor. Ditto if you are pregnant or have diabetes. You should also see a doctor if

NATURALFACT

More than one million American women are diagnosed with yeast infections each year.

your symptoms don't improve after using home remedies for 2 weeks.

Yogurt. For years, women have been recommending yogurt to one another as a great remedy for yeast infections, but doctors remained skeptical. One study, though, may change their minds. At Long Island Jewish Medical Center in New York, women who got frequent yeast infections were given 1 cup of yogurt every day for 6 months. At the end of the study, researchers found that the rate of yeast infections had dropped by 75 percent.

The yogurt used in the study contained live cultures of bacteria called *Lactobacillus acidophilus*, which are friendly bacteria that help control the growth of yeast in the intestines and vagina. Eating yogurt helps restore the vagina's natural environment, so yeast infections are much less likely to recur.

Name That Condition

If you think you have a yeast infection but you're not sure, it's probably a good idea to be checked out by a doctor. A study reported in the *Journal of Family Practice* tested the ability of about 550 women to accurately diagnose yeast infections and choose proper treatment. More than 350 of those women had been previously diagnosed with yeast infections.

Women who had been previously diagnosed with the condition were slightly better at diagnosing yeast infections than those who hadn't. Still, as a whole, few women were able to correctly diagnose the condition. In addition, they were likely to use over-the-counter antifungal treatments inappropriately, treating gynecological conditions that are similar to yeast infections but potentially more severe, such as pelvic inflammatory disease and bacterial vaginosis.

For most women, the amount used in the study, 1 cup daily, is plenty. Since yogurt sold at the supermarket generally has too low a concentration of bacteria—or even none at all—to be effective, your best bet is to buy it from a health food store.

Echinacea. Echinacea helps your body battle colds by boosting levels of white blood cells, which are your body's first line of defense against infection. That same effect can help defeat the candida fungus that causes yeast infections.

Take one dropper of echinacea tincture in ½ cup of water up to four times daily. Since echinacea becomes less effective the longer you take it, you should discontinue this herbal treatment after 2 weeks.

Acidophilus. The good bacteria found in yogurt, *Lactobacillus acidophilus,* also comes in supplement form. These capsules can help keep candida in check. Take them only when you have an active yeast infection or are having problems with recurring infections.

Look for acidophilus capsules that are refrigerated and contain at least one billion organisms per capsule. Stomach acid can inactivate the bacteria, so take the capsules between meals.

NATURALFACT

A good-quality echinacea tincture will cause a tingling sensation on your tongue.

THE PREVENTION LIST

1-Minute Lifesavers

Got a minute? Good—that's all you need. Here are eight ways to save your life in, literally, a minute or less.

1. **Floss your teeth.** If you have gum disease, you may be giving bacteria an open pathway to your bloodstream, which can increase your risk of heart disease.

2. **Take a multivitamin.** Multivitamins help prevent a whole range of health problems, from heart disease to osteoporosis. To cite just one example of how they can save your life: A 15-year study of almost 90,000 women showed that those who took a multivitamin daily had 75 percent less chance of developing colon cancer than those who didn't pop one.

3. **Buckle your seat belt.** A no-brainer? Maybe, but about 30 percent of Americans don't do it. They should. It's estimated that wearing seat belts saved more than 100,000 lives from 1975 to 1997.

4. **Change the batteries in your smoke alarm.** Some 93 percent of American homes have smoke alarms, but 20 percent of those alarms aren't working. The death rate from fires in homes without working smoke alarms is 50 to 60 percent higher than it is in homes with functioning alarms.

5. **Order the salmon.** In a study of more than 20,000 male doctors, researchers found that eating 4 to 6 ounces of fish just once a week reduces by 52 percent your risk of dying from a heart attack within an hour of the onset of symptoms.

6. **Wash your hands.** The Centers for Disease Control calls hand washing "the most important means of preventing the spread of infection"—and infectious diseases are a leading cause of death in the United States.

7. **Get a flu shot.** The flu vaccine is nearly 90 percent effective in preventing flu types A and B, which kill as many as 50,000 Americans a year. And contrary to what you might think, not all of those deaths are among the extremely elderly. A significant number of the fatalities are people between the ages of 50 and 64 who had other health problems.

8. **Check your bread and pasta labels.** In a study of almost 40,000 women, scientists at the University of Minnesota in Minneapolis found that those who ate the most unrefined grains (whole-wheat bread and whole-wheat pasta, for example) had 15 to 20 percent lower risks of death over a 9-year period than those who consumed the fewest.

Part Five

Delicious Recipes
for Glorious Health

*There's no reason that food can't be great tasting
and good for you at the same time.*

Chapter 11

Don't Let the Great Taste Fool You

All of these delicious recipes are packed with healthy, disease-fighting ingredients

Healthy food desperately needs a public relations makeover. Somewhere along the line, millions of Americans came to believe that good-tasting food is bad for you and that healthful food tastes lousy. Nothing, of course, could be further from the truth.

To be fair, in the early days of the organic movement, there was some justification for the stereotype. There were too many zucchini casseroles with the texture of Astroturf and the flavor of soggy cardboard. That made it easy for the burger and fried chicken outlets to claim that when you wanted something truly delicious, more grease was required.

A lot more grease.

We're here to do our part to reverse this great injustice.

So Long, Cholesterol King

Contrary to its lousy image, food can be both good for you and very good to eat, and the 25 recipes on the following pages prove it. In fact, as you probably know already, healthy food can be better tasting by far than the heart attack special they'll sell you at the local Cholesterol King restaurant.

"We've found that food with less fat allows people to more fully enjoy the experience of eating," says John La Puma, M.D., director of the CHEF (Cooking, Healthy Eating, and Fitness) pilot study at Alexian Brothers Medical Center in Elk Grove, Illinois. (For a detailed description of the CHEF plan, see chapter 22). "It's almost as if fats formed a layer over your palate, preventing an appreciation of food's other flavors and textures."

The recipes we've chosen here were not selected solely because they're low in saturated fats, which they are. Rather, we chose them for two main reasons: 1) because they provide one or more key ingredients of a healthy diet (antioxidants, fiber, omega-3 fatty acids, protein, or calcium) and 2) because they're delicious. Each section begins with a brief reminder of why the specific ingredients featured in that section benefit your health. That way, if you have specific health goals (say, for example, you have a genetic predisposition to breast cancer and want to do everything you can to build up your body's resistance to the disease), you can select the dishes that will help you achieve those goals.

What's in It for Me?

Healthy food has more benefits than you may realize, most of them having to do with cutting back on saturated fat. Here are some of the biggest payoffs you can expect.

You can eat more. Hallelujah! When you cut back on fat, you can actually eat a greater amount of food. That's because fatty foods are a denser source of calories than healthier, carbohydrate-rich and protein-rich foods.

You'll save money. Premium meats and processed foods usually cost more than healthy foods like chicken, vegetables, fruits, and grains. When you buy fewer high-fat items, you automatically lower food costs.

You'll lose weight. Want to lose a few pounds? Experts agree that one of the best ways to do it is with a better diet. Study after study shows that eating fewer calories (which comes naturally from eating less fat) can help you lose weight.

You'll cut heart attack risk. It's clear that eating healthfully can help prevent disease. But it can also help reverse it. Eating naturally low-fat foods like grains, vegetables, fruits, and lean proteins can actually help reverse the buildup of deposits (plaque) in the blood vessels and reduce your risk of heart attack. That's pretty powerful. If you think that you can't make up for a lifetime of overindulgence, think again. It's never too late.

‖ Antioxidants

Research suggests that the antioxidant vitamins C and E and beta-carotene (which the body converts to vitamin A) may play a significant role in the body's defenses against heart disease and cancer.

The primary job of antioxidants is to whisk away free radicals, unstable oxygen by-products that are produced by normal bodily functions as well as exposure to cigarette smoke, sunlight, and pollution. Free radicals are dangerous because they are chemically unstable. They carry an unmatched electron, unlike stable molecules, which carry a matched pair of electrons. To try to be-

come stable again, free radicals steal electrons from neighboring molecules, which in turn creates more free radicals. This process damages cells, which paves the way for disease.

Antioxidants neutralize these potentially harmful free radicals by binding to them and restoring their balance. The best way to get these antioxidant vitamins is in foods, since nutrients that come from foods provide more benefits when they are consumed in combination with each other.

The recipes that follow all provide healthful portions of antioxidants, among other important nutrients.

Cranberry-Orange Coffee Cake

Cranberries contain two potent antioxidants: ellagic acid, which has been shown to fight cancer, and flavonoids, which help fight both cancer and heart disease.

Streusel

¾ cup unbleached or
  all-purpose flour
⅔ cup packed brown sugar
1 teaspoon ground cinnamon
1 tablespoon butter or margarine, cut into small pieces
2 tablespoons frozen orange
  juice concentrate
¼ cup chopped toasted
  almonds

Cake

2¼ cups unbleached or
  all-purpose flour
1 cup sugar
1 teaspoon baking powder
1 teaspoon baking soda
½ teaspoon salt
¼ cup butter or margarine,
  softened
1 egg
1 egg white
2 teaspoons vanilla extract
1 cup (8 ounces) fat-free sour
  cream
2 cups cranberries

To make the streusel: In a small bowl, combine the flour, brown sugar, and cinnamon. Stir with a fork until no lumps remain. Add the butter or margarine. Press with the fork to work into the dry ingredients. Add the orange juice concentrate and almonds. Toss until coarse crumbs form. Set aside.

To make the cake: Preheat the oven to 350°F. Coat a 9" round cake pan with cooking spray. Line the bottom with a round of waxed paper. Coat lightly with cooking spray.

In a medium bowl, combine the flour, ½ cup of the sugar, and the baking powder, baking soda, and salt.

In another medium bowl, combine the butter or margarine and the remaining ½ cup of sugar. With an electric mixer on medium speed, beat until creamy. Add the egg, egg white, and vanilla extract. Beat until smooth. Add the flour mixture and the sour cream alternately to the batter, beating on low speed just until blended.

Spread half of the batter into the prepared cake pan. Sprinkle evenly with one-third of the streusel. Spread evenly with the remaining batter. Sprinkle with the cranberries and the remaining streusel.

Bake for 40 minutes, or until a wooden pick inserted in the center comes out clean. Cool in the pan on a rack for 5 minutes. Run a knife around the sides of the pan. Turn onto the rack. Remove and discard the waxed paper. Place a plate on the cake and turn it right side up.

Makes 12 servings

Per serving: 336 calories, 6 g protein, 63 g carbohydrates, 7 g fat, 18 mg cholesterol, 2 g fiber, 252 mg sodium

Italian Salsa and Chips

Tomatoes are a source of a red pigment called lycopene that some studies suggest may be twice as potent an antioxidant as its better-known cousin, beta-carotene.

Salsa

   5 plum tomatoes, chopped
   1 small onion, chopped
   ¾ cup chopped fresh basil
   3 tablespoons balsamic or wine vinegar
   2 tablespoons chopped kalamata olives
   1 tablespoon olive oil
   2 cloves garlic, chopped
   ¼ teaspoon salt
   ¼ teaspoon ground black pepper

Chips

   1 package (10 ounces) pitas (6" diameter)
   ¼ cup (1 ounce) grated Parmesan cheese
   1½ teaspoons Italian seasoning

To make the salsa: In a medium bowl, combine the tomatoes, onion, basil, vinegar, olives, oil, garlic, salt, and pepper. Serve with the chips.

To make the chips: Preheat the oven to 375°F. Cover a baking sheet with foil.

Cut the pitas into quarters. Separate each wedge into 2 pieces. Place on the baking sheet. Lightly coat the pitas with cooking spray.

In a small bowl, combine the cheese and Italian seasoning. Sprinkle over the pitas. Bake for 8 to 10 minutes, or until golden and crisp. Transfer to a platter or serving basket.

Makes 6 servings

Per serving: 210 calories, 7 g protein, 33 g carbohydrates, 6 g fat, 3 mg cholesterol, 2 g fiber, 498 mg sodium

Isle of Capri Pasta

Roasted peppers and peas give you a day's worth of vitamin C. Spinach is a rich source of cartonoids, a potent antioxidant.

1½ cups packed fresh spinach, stemmed and washed
⅔ cup packed fresh basil
¼ cup packed fresh Italian parsley
3 tablespoons grated Parmesan cheese
6 tablespoons fat-free, reduced-sodium chicken broth
5 teaspoons olive oil
1 clove garlic, chopped
⅛ teaspoon crushed red-pepper flakes
Salt and ground black pepper
12 ounces penne
2 roasted red bell peppers, chopped
1 package (10 ounces) frozen baby peas, thawed

In a food processor or blender, combine the spinach, basil, parsley, cheese, broth, oil, garlic, red-pepper flakes, salt, and black pepper. Process for 2 to 3 minutes, or until the mixture is smooth and creamy. Stop occasionally to scrape down the sides of the bowl.

Cook the penne in a large pot of boiling water according to the package directions. Drain and place in a large serving bowl. Add the spinach-basil pesto and toss to coat well. Add the roasted peppers and peas. Toss to mix.

Makes 6 servings

Per serving: 294 calories, 15 g protein, 46 g carbohydrates, 7 g fat, 5 mg cholesterol, 5 g fiber, 204 mg sodium

Any short, shaped pasta works well with this recipe. Try ziti, rotini, or medium shells.

Vegetable Paella

Almost every ingredient in this recipe is a cancer fighter, with the squash, pepper, peas, and tomatoes, in particular, providing a potent antioxidant quadruple-team.

1 tablespoon olive oil
1 onion, chopped
3 cloves garlic, chopped
1 cup basmati or long-grain white rice
1 yellow squash, cut into ½" cubes
1 red bell pepper, cut into ½" pieces
1 can (15 ounces) diced tomatoes
1 can (14½ ounces) reduced-sodium vegetable broth
1 cup water
1 bay leaf
¼ teaspoon salt
1 can (15 ounces) cannellini or great Northern beans, rinsed and drained
1 cup frozen peas, thawed

Warm the oil in a Dutch oven over medium heat. Add the onion and garlic. Cook, stirring, for 3 minutes, or until lightly browned. Add the rice, squash, and pepper. Cook, stirring occasionally, for 5 minutes, or until the pepper starts to soften. Add the tomatoes (with juice), broth, water, bay leaf, and salt. Reduce the heat to medium-low.

Cover and simmer for 20 minutes, or until the rice is tender. Add the beans and peas. Cook, stirring gently, for 3 to 5 minutes, or until heated through. Remove and discard the bay leaf.

Makes 6 servings

Per serving: 247 calories, 9 g protein, 45 g carbohydrates, 3 g fat, 0 mg cholesterol, 8 g fiber, 319 mg sodium

Chocolate Soufflé Cake

Chocolate contains flavonoids, antioxidants that help prevent heart attacks.

½ teaspoon + 1 tablespoon unbleached or all-purpose flour
2 ounces semisweet chocolate, chopped
1 cup granulated sugar
2 tablespoons butter or margarine, softened
5 tablespoons (2½ ounces) fat-free sour cream
1 egg yolk
¼ teaspoon vanilla extract
3 tablespoons cocoa powder
4 egg whites, at room temperature
⅛ teaspoon cream of tartar
2 tablespoons confectioners' sugar

Preheat the oven to 350°F. Coat an 8" springform pan with cooking spray. Dust with ½ teaspoon of the flour.

Place the chocolate in a microwaveable bowl. Microwave on high power for 1 minute. Stir until smooth. Add ¾ cup of the granulated sugar and the butter or margarine, sour cream, egg yolk, and vanilla extract. Stir until well-blended. Add the cocoa and the remaining 1 tablespoon of flour. Stir until smooth.

In a large bowl, combine the egg whites and cream of tartar. With an electric mixer on medium speed, beat until soft peaks form. Increase the speed to high. Beat, gradually adding the remaining ¼ cup of granulated sugar, until stiff peaks form. Fold about one-third of the egg-white mixture into the chocolate mixture. Gently fold in the remaining egg-white mixture in 2 additions. Spoon the batter into the prepared pan. Smooth the top.

Bake for 30 to 35 minutes, or until a wooden pick inserted in the middle comes out with just a few moist crumbs. Remove to a rack to cool. The cake will fall as it cools, leaving a raised edge. Gently press down on the edge as it cools.

To serve, remove the pan sides. Transfer the cake to a serving plate. Sift the confectioners' sugar over the top of the cake.

Makes 10 servings

Per serving: 160 calories, 3 g protein, 28 g carbohydrates, 5 g fat, 21 mg cholesterol, 1 g fiber, 29 mg sodium

‖ Fiber

Fiber comes only from plant foods, including fruits, vegetables, and grains. It is the structural part of a plant that actually passes through the human body undigested.

Two types of fiber, soluble and insoluble, promote health in different ways. Soluble fiber, found in foods such as beans, oats, barley, and apples, can help lower cholesterol by forming a gel in the intestine that traps cholesterol and escorts it out of the body. Insoluble fiber, which is found in wheat bran and most cereals, can help prevent certain types of cancers by moving potentially harmful substances through the intestine more quickly.

Another benefit to eating high-fiber foods is that they automatically help you cut back on calories and lower your fat intake because they are naturally low in fat and calories and offer plenty of appetite satisfaction.

Because most fiber-rich foods contain a combination of soluble and insoluble fiber, it is wise to eat a variety of plant foods daily. Choose whole-grain foods such as whole-wheat breads, brown rice, bulgur, and barley to get the highest amount of fiber. Leaving the peels on vegetables and fruits can also boost fiber.

When you start to increase your fiber intake, drink more water and other fluids, which will help your body manage the extra fiber comfortably. Acquaint yourself with high-fiber foods and find ways to work them into your day's meals and snacks.

As a rule, try to eat between 25 and 35 grams of fiber a day. A ½-cup serving of butter, navy, or kidney beans—an easy addition to a salad—contributes nearly 7 grams of dietary fiber. Ready-to-eat breakfast cereals can also be excellent sources of fiber. Some all-bran cereals, for example, contain nearly 14 grams of fiber in just ½ cup.

Menu Madness

Weight-conscious dieters who eat out need to know how a restaurant's dishes are prepared. One way to find out, of course, is to ask the waiter. But there are often clues on the menu as well. Here are some cooking methods to watch for.

- "Sautéed," "pan-fried," "pan-seared," and "fried" are all cooking methods that require additional fat. Request that the chef use just a touch of oil in your dish.
- "Light" can be a very misleading term. A light cream sauce can be laden with fat, and "lightly fried" is at least partially immersed in oil. Ask to find out what you're getting.
- "Au gratin," "Alfredo," "in cheese sauce," and "parmigiana" are typically high-fat dishes.
- "Fresh," "baked," "roasted," "broiled," "grilled," "seared," "braised," "poached," and "steamed" indicate the healthiest choices.

Creamy Black Bean Enchiladas

Black beans are an excellent source of soluble fiber. This fiber can help keep cholesterol in check while filling you up, delightfully.

⅔ cup white rice

¾ cup (6 ounces) fat-free sour cream

3 ounces reduced-fat cream cheese, softened

3 scallions, finely chopped

1 jar (4 ounces) chopped green chile peppers, drained

½ teaspoon ground cumin

1 can (15 ounces) black beans, rinsed and drained

6 corn or flour tortillas (6" diameter)

1 cup (4 ounces) shredded low-fat Monterey Jack or Cheddar cheese

½ cup mild red taco sauce

Preheat the oven to 375°F. Coat a 13" × 9" baking dish with cooking spray.

Cook the rice according to the package directions.

Meanwhile, in a medium bowl, combine the sour cream, cream cheese, scallions, chile peppers, and cumin. Stir until well-blended. Add the beans and rice. Stir gently to mix.

Place the tortillas on a work surface. Spoon some of the bean filling down the center of each tortilla. Sprinkle with Monterey Jack or Cheddar. Roll into cylinders. Place, seam side down, in the prepared baking dish. Drizzle with the taco sauce.

Bake for 12 to 15 minutes, or until heated through.

Makes 6

Per enchilada: 353 calories, 18 g protein, 54 g carbohydrates, 7 g fat, 21 mg cholesterol, 9 g fiber, 586 mg sodium

Mushroom-Barley Soup

Barley is loaded with a soluble fiber called beta-glucan. It also contains two powerful antioxidant compounds, ligands and tocotrienols.

1 ounce dried mushrooms
3 cups water
1 large onion, chopped
2 carrots, chopped
1 rib celery, chopped
12 ounces cremini or button mushrooms, stems removed, sliced
1½ teaspoons dried oregano
2 cans (14½ ounces each) fat-free, reduced-sodium chicken broth
½ cup barley
¼ teaspoon salt

In a small saucepan, bring the dried mushrooms and water to a boil. Remove and let stand for 15 minutes.

Meanwhile, coat a Dutch oven with cooking spray. Add the onion, carrots, and celery. Coat lightly with cooking spray. Set over medium heat. Cook, stirring occasionally, for 3 minutes. Add the sliced mushrooms and oregano. Cook, stirring occasionally, for 6 to 8 minutes, or until all the vegetables are soft. Add the broth, barley, and salt. Cook for 10 minutes.

Line a fine mesh sieve with a coffee filter or paper towel. Strain the dried mushroom water into the Dutch oven. Remove and discard the filter or paper towel. Rinse the dried mushrooms under running water to remove any grit. Chop and add to the Dutch oven.

Cook for 10 to 15 minutes, or until the barley is tender.
Makes 6 servings
Per serving: 148 calories, 10 g protein, 24 g carbohydrates, 1 g fat, 0 mg cholesterol, 6 g fiber, 294 mg sodium

Stuffed Acorn Squash

This recipe is chock-full of fiber sources, including squash and barley.

3 acorn squash, cut in half lengthwise, seeds removed
2 teaspoons vegetable oil
1 small onion, chopped
1 rib celery, chopped
1 clove garlic, chopped
3 ounces mushrooms, sliced
¼ cup chopped parsley
1 cup coarse fresh bread crumbs
⅔ cup dried cranberries
1 teaspoon grated lemon peel
¼ teaspoon salt
⅔ cup quick-cooking barley, cooked
¼–½ cup vegetable broth or apple juice

Preheat the oven to 400°F. Place the squash, cut sides up, on a baking sheet. Lightly coat the cut sides with cooking spray. Bake for 30 minutes, or until fork-tender.

Meanwhile, warm the oil in a medium nonstick skillet set over medium heat. Add the onion, celery, and garlic. Cook for 2 minutes. Add the mushrooms and parsley. Cook for 4 minutes, or until the mushrooms are soft. Remove from the heat. Add the bread crumbs, cranberries, lemon peel, salt, and barley. Stir to mix. Add up to ½ cup of the broth or juice to moisten and bind the stuffing.

Reduce the oven temperature to 350°F. Spoon the stuffing into the squash halves. Bake for 10 to 12 minutes, or until heated through.

Makes 6 servings

Per serving: 309 calories, 6 g protein, 68 g carbohydrates, 3 g fat, 0 mg cholesterol, 8 g fiber, 284 mg sodium

Five-Star Vegetable Chili

This chili is packed with beans, and therefore packed with fiber.

1   teaspoon olive oil
1   onion, chopped
1   green bell pepper, chopped
2   cloves garlic, minced
1   jalapeño chile pepper,
    minced (wear plastic gloves
    when handling)
1   tablespoon dried oregano
2   teaspoons chili powder
1   teaspoon ground cumin
1   teaspoon ground coriander
¼   teaspoon ground red pepper
1   can (28 ounces) no-salt-
    added chopped tomatoes
1   can (15 ounces)
    no-salt-added tomato sauce
2   cups water
2   teaspoons sugar
½   cup bulgur
1   can (14 ounces) cannellini
    beans, rinsed and drained
1   can (14 ounces) kidney
    beans, rinsed and drained

Warm the oil in a Dutch oven over medium heat. Add the onion and green pepper. Cook, stirring occasionally, for 5 minutes, or until softened. Add the garlic and jalapeño pepper. Cook for 2 minutes, or until the vegetables are tender.

Warm a small nonstick skillet over medium-high heat. Add the oregano, chili powder, cumin, coriander, and ground red pepper. Stir for 1 to 2 minutes, or until fragrant. Add to the vegetable mixture. Add the tomatoes (with juice), tomato sauce, water, and sugar.

Cook, stirring occasionally, for 5 minutes. Stir in the bulgur, cannellini beans, and kidney beans. Reduce the heat to medium and cook for 15 minutes, or until thickened.

Makes 4 servings

Per serving: 309 calories, 15 g protein, 67 g carbohydrates, 9 g fat, 0 mg cholesterol, 17 g fiber, 156 mg sodium

Very Berry Shortcakes

Berries are among our tastier sources of fiber. If fresh aren't available, frozen will do nicely.

  2 cups unbleached or
     all-purpose flour
  3 tablespoons + ⅓ cup sugar
  2 teaspoons baking powder
  ¼ teaspoon baking soda
  ¼ cup butter or margarine, cut
     into small pieces
  ⅔ cup + 2 tablespoons
     buttermilk
1½ pints assorted berries
  2 tablespoons orange juice
  2 cups fat-free frozen vanilla
     yogurt

Preheat the oven to 400°F. Coat a baking sheet with cooking spray.

In a large bowl, combine the flour, 2 tablespoons of the sugar, and the baking powder and baking soda. Cut in the butter or margarine until the mixture resembles cornmeal. Add ⅔ cup of the buttermilk, stirring with a fork until the dough comes together.

Turn the dough out onto a lightly floured surface. Gently pat or roll to ½" thickness. Using a 3" round cutter or large glass, cut 8 biscuits. (You may have to pat the dough scraps together to cut out all the biscuits.) Transfer to the prepared baking sheet. Brush with the remaining 2 tablespoons of buttermilk. Sprinkle with 1 tablespoon of the remaining sugar.

Bake for 12 to 15 minutes, or until golden. Remove to a rack to cool.

Meanwhile, in a large bowl, combine the berries, orange juice, and the remaining ⅓ cup of sugar. Allow to sit for 10 minutes to draw out the berry juices.

Split the biscuits in half crosswise. Place a biscuit bottom on each of 8 dessert plates. Top with the berry filling and a scoop of yogurt. Cover with the biscuit tops.

Makes 8

Per shortcake: 319 calories, 7 g protein, 59 g carbohydrates, 7 g fat, 2 mg cholesterol, 5 g fiber, 289 mg sodium

‖ Protein

After water, protein is the largest component of the human body, which makes sense considering its versatility. Besides building skin, muscles, bones, and organs, protein assists in functions as diverse as blood clotting, water balance, hormone production, and immunity.

When protein comes from an animal source—beef, pork, chicken, fish, eggs, milk, cheese, or yogurt—it contains the nine essential amino acids to make it a "complete" protein. Animal sources of protein tend to be high in saturated fats and cholesterol, however, which is why nutritionists recommend a diet that combines plant and animal sources of protein. Nuts, seeds, grains, legumes (beans, peas, and lentils), and vegetables all contain protein and can be combined to create the essential amino acids you need.

Most health experts recommend that the average person consume between 12 and 15 percent of their calories from protein. For example, a person eating 2,000 calories daily would consume 60 to 75 grams of protein. Just one 3-ounce serving of lean beef, chicken, or fish (about the size of a deck of cards) would supply about one-third of that minimum amount—21 grams of protein.

Surprising Snacks

Would you be shocked to learn that snacking can help you maintain a healthy diet?

It's true. The reason is that the right kind of snacks can keep you from getting too hungry between meals. If the snacks you choose are nutritious, so much the better.

Here are some delicious and nutritious snack ideas to get you started.

- Baked tortilla chips and salsa are an excellent source of vitamin C and a good source of fiber and vitamin A.
- Cheese and crackers are an excellent source of calcium and a good source of fiber, vitamins A, B_2, B_{12}, and zinc.
- Vegetable chili and crackers are an excellent source of fiber and vitamins A and C as well as a good source of iron.
- Hummus with a pita is an excellent source of fiber and vitamin B_6 and a good source of vitamins B_1 and B_3, folic acid, copper, iron, magnesium, and zinc.
- Shredded wheat cereal with fat-free milk is a good source of fiber; vitamins B_1, B_2, B_3, and D; calcium; copper; iron; magnesium; potassium; and zinc.
- Bell peppers and dip are an excellent source of vitamins A and C and a good source of vitamins B_1 and B_6, calcium, and potassium.

Italian Frittata

A frittata is a simple one-pan egg dish from Italy. This savory version is high in folate, vitamins A and C, fiber, and—thanks to the eggs and cheese—protein.

1   teaspoon olive oil
1   shallot, chopped
1   medium new potato, cooked and cut into ½" cubes
½   cup sliced artichoke hearts
1   roasted red bell pepper, chopped
1   teaspoon chopped fresh thyme
1   egg
5   egg whites
1   tablespoon water
    Salt and ground black pepper
2   tablespoons grated Parmesan cheese
1   tablespoon chopped Italian parsley

Warm the oil in a medium ovenproof nonstick skillet over medium heat. Add the shallot. Cook for 2 minutes, or until tender. Add the potato, artichokes, red pepper, and thyme. Cook for 2 minutes.

In a medium bowl, whisk together the egg, egg whites, and water. Season with the salt and black pepper. Pour over the vegetables and cook while gently moving a spatula across the bottom of the skillet for 3 minutes, or until the base of the frittata is almost set.

Coat a broiler pan with cooking spray. Preheat the broiler.

Place the frittata on the prepared pan. Sprinkle the frittata with the cheese and parsley. Broil 3" from the heat for 1 to 2 minutes, or until the frittata is cooked through and golden.

Makes 2 servings

Per serving: 204 calories, 18 g protein, 19 g carbohydrates, 7 g fat, 111 mg cholesterol, 4 g fiber, 381 mg sodium

To make 4 servings, double the recipe and use 2 separate skillets. Or keep one frittata warm while preparing the second one.

Chunky Turkey Salad

The turkey and nuts in this quick dish will give you a healthy protein fix. The salad takes only about 15 minutes to make.

¼ cup low-fat mayonnaise
½ cup fat-free sour cream
2 teaspoons chopped fresh thyme or 1 teaspoon dried
2 teaspoons lemon juice
½ teaspoon grated lemon peel
1 pound cooked skinless turkey breasts, cut into ½" cubes
2 ribs celery, chopped
1 apple, cut into ½" cubes
⅓ cup dried apricots, sliced
¼ cup toasted coarsely chopped walnuts

In a large bowl, whisk the mayonnaise, sour cream, thyme, lemon juice, and lemon peel until smooth. Add the turkey, celery, apple, and apricots. Toss gently to coat.

Sprinkle with the walnuts.

Makes 4 servings

Per serving: 281 calories, 37 g protein, 21 g carbohydrates, 5 g fat, 95 mg cholesterol, 3 g fiber, 225 mg sodium

Beef Stroganoff

What's a beef dish doing in a natural-healing book? It has every right to be here if you follow the maxim "All things in moderation," including animal proteins.

12 ounces medium no-yolk egg noodles
 1 teaspoon vegetable oil
 ¾ pound beef tenderloin or top round, trimmed of all visible fat and cut crosswise into thin strips
 ¼ teaspoon salt
 1 small onion, quartered and thinly sliced
 ½ pound mushrooms, stems removed and caps sliced
1½ tablespoons unbleached or all-purpose flour
 1 can (14½ ounces) fat-free, reduced-sodium beef broth
 1 teaspoon Worcestershire sauce
 ¼ cup (2 ounces) fat-free sour cream
 2 tablespoons chopped parsley

Cook the noodles according to the package directions. Drain and place in a serving bowl.

Meanwhile, warm the oil in a large nonstick skillet over medium-high heat. Sprinkle the beef with the salt. Place in the skillet. Cook, turning occasionally, for 2 to 3 minutes, or until browned. Remove to a plate.

Coat the skillet with cooking spray. Reduce the heat to medium. Add the onion. Cook, stirring occasionally, for 3 minutes. Add the mushrooms. Cook, stirring occasionally, for 2 to 3 minutes, or until the mushrooms begin to release liquid. Sprinkle with the flour. Cook, stirring constantly, for 1 minute. Add the broth and Worcestershire sauce. Cook, stirring, for 2 to 3 minutes, or until slightly thickened. Remove from the heat. Add the sour cream and parsley. Stir to mix. Return the beef to the skillet. Place over low heat. Cook for 3 minutes, or until heated through.

Serve the stroganoff over the noodles.

Makes 6 servings

Per serving: 430 calories, 26 g protein, 52 g carbohydrates, 12 g fat, 49 mg cholesterol, 4 g fiber, 167 mg sodium

Chicken Paprikash

Nonfat sour cream works wonders in this classic one-pot dish. The sauce is creamy, and the chicken is moist and tender.

1 teaspoon olive oil
2 cups chopped onions
1 teaspoon minced garlic
4 boneless, skinless chicken breast halves (5 ounces each)
Salt and ground black pepper
1 tablespoon paprika
1 cup fat-free, reduced-sodium chicken broth
2 teaspoons tomato paste
½ cup nonfat sour cream
1 tablespoon all-purpose flour
1 tablespoon chopped Italian parsley

Warm the oil in a large nonstick skillet over medium heat. Add the onions and garlic. Cook, stirring often, for 5 minutes, or until softened. Season the chicken with the salt and pepper. Add to the skillet and cook for 2 minutes per side, or until lightly golden. Sprinkle with the paprika and cook for 30 seconds longer. Flip the chicken and cook for 30 seconds longer.

In a small bowl, whisk together the broth and tomato paste until thoroughly combined. Pour into the skillet. Cover and cook for 20 minutes, or until the chicken is no longer pink in the center when tested with a sharp knife. Transfer the chicken to a plate and keep warm.

In the same small bowl, whisk together the sour cream and flour. Reduce the heat to low and whisk the mixture into the skillet. Cook, stirring constantly, for 3 to 4 minutes, or until thickened and bubbling. Season with the salt and pepper.

Serve the chicken topped with the sauce and sprinkled with the parsley.

Makes 4 servings

Per serving: 254 calories, 33 g protein, 18 g carbohydrates, 5 g fat, 78 mg cholesterol, 3 g fiber, 212 mg sodium

Lemon Cheesecake

There's plenty of protein hiding in all those dairy products—and cheesecake is good for the soul.

Crust

1¼ cups graham cracker crumbs
¼ cup pecans, toasted and ground
¼ cup sugar
3 tablespoons butter or margarine, melted
1 egg white

Filling and Topping

2 packages (8 ounces each) nonfat cream cheese
1 package (8 ounces) reduced-fat cream cheese
¼ cup all-purpose flour
2 cups sugar
½ cup lemon juice
2 eggs
2 egg whites
2 cups nonfat sour cream

To make the crust: Preheat the oven to 350°F. Coat a 9" springform pan with cooking spray.

In a large bowl, combine the cracker crumbs, pecans, sugar, and butter or margarine. Lightly beat the egg white in a cup. Add half of the egg white to the bowl; reserve the remainder for another use or discard. Mix well. Press the mixture into the bottom and 1" up the sides of the prepared pan. Bake for 10 minutes, or until lightly browned. Cool on a wire rack.

To make the filling and topping: In a food processor, combine the nonfat cream cheese and reduced-fat cream cheese. Process for 1 to 2 minutes, or until smooth. Add the flour and 1½ cups of the sugar. Process for 3 minutes, or until light and fluffy; stop and scrape the sides of the bowl as necessary. Add the lemon juice and process briefly. Add the eggs and egg whites, one at a time, and process until just incorporated.

Pour the mixture into the prepared pan. Bake for 1 hour. Remove from the oven.

In a small bowl, mix the sour cream and the remaining ½ cup of sugar. Spread over the hot cheesecake. Bake for 10 minutes longer. Place on a rack and let cool to room temperature. Cover and refrigerate for at least 8 hours.

Makes 12 slices

Per slice: 388 calories, 13 g protein, 61 g carbohydrates, 10 g fat, 52 mg cholesterol, 1 g fiber, 416 mg sodium

This cheesecake is equally delicious served with a fresh fruit topping. Omit the sour cream topping. Toss 3 cups berries, sliced peaches, or orange segments with 2 tablespoons melted jam or jelly. Decoratively arrange the fruit on top of the cooled cheesecake.

‖ Fats

Not all fats are created equal. Some, like monounsaturated fats, are actually good for you. "Fat is an extremely important nutrient that provides calories, supplies energy, and assists many vital bodily functions," says Chavanne B. Hanson, R.D., licensed dietitian at the University Hospitals of Cleveland Synergy Program in Ohio.

The key is knowing which fats to eat more of and which to eat less of. Here are the basics.

Eat More . . .

Monounsaturated fats. Monounsaturated fats are the liquid fats found in olive oil, canola oil, and peanut oil. They become partly firm when chilled. They're healthy because they may help lower your total blood cholesterol level.

That's Heavy, Man

Apparently, it isn't all the calories that make those double-cheeseburgers so tempting—it's their size.

How much a food weighs has a lot to do with whether you'll feel satisfied after you eat it, according to nutritionists at Tufts University in Boston. Studies have shown that people will eat about the same weight of food each day, regardless of how many calories from fat grams the food contains. For that reason, dieters are better off choosing foods that contain plenty of fiber and water, which have more bulk than calories.

Nutritionists recommend that you get up to 15 percent of your daily diet in the form of monounsaturated fat, which you can do by swapping solid fats like butter and margarine for oils.

Polyunsaturated fats. Also found in liquid oils, polyunsaturated fats are abundant in corn, safflower, soybean, and sunflower oils. Like the monos, the polys are liquid at room temperature. The polys stay liquid in the fridge, however. These fats tend to lower your blood cholesterol level when they replace saturated fats like butter in your diet. Getting up to 10 percent of your daily diet as polyunsaturated fat is recommended.

Another healthful type of poly fat is called omega-3 fatty acids. These are found mostly in fish. Studies show that omega-3's may help reduce the risk of heart attack by up to 50 percent. So start eating fish such as salmon, Atlantic mackerel, trout, sablefish, and tuna (fresh and canned).

Eat Less . . .

Saturated fats. These fats come mostly from animal sources, such as red meat, butter, and egg yolks. But there are some plant sources, too, like coconut oil and other tropical oils. Eat these fats sparingly because they tend to raise blood cholesterol levels, increasing your risk of heart disease.

Trans fatty acids. These are found in partially hydrogenated oils—the kind used to make processed snack foods like chips, crackers, and cookies. Many margarines and shortenings are also high in trans fats. These fats tend to act like saturated fats because they can raise blood cholesterol levels.

Cholesterol. This fatlike substance is found only in animal-based foods such as meat, poultry, dairy products, and seafood. Although dietary cholesterol is not a saturated fat, it can contribute to increased blood cholesterol levels.

Teriyaki Tuna with Pineapple

Tuna, one of America's most popular fish, also ranks high on the omega-3 scorecard.

¼ cup soy sauce
3 tablespoons dry sherry or fat-free, reduced-sodium chicken broth
1 tablespoon sugar
1 tablespoon grated fresh ginger or 1 teaspoon ground
3 cloves garlic, chopped
4 tuna steaks (5 ounces each)
1 pineapple, halved, cored, peeled, and cut into 8 wedges
1 red bell pepper, quartered lengthwise

In a small bowl, combine the soy sauce, sherry or broth, sugar, ginger, and garlic. Stir to blend. Divide the marinade into 2 medium shallow bowls. Place the steaks in one bowl and the pineapple and pepper in the other. Turn the tuna, pineapple, and pepper to coat both sides. Cover and refrigerate for 15 minutes.

Coat a grill rack or broiler pan with cooking spray. Preheat the grill or broiler.

Arrange the tuna, pineapple, and pepper on the rack or pan. Discard the marinade from the tuna bowl. Grill or broil, basting occasionally with the marinade from the pineapple bowl, for 4 to 5 minutes per side, or until the tuna is just opaque and the pineapple and pepper are heated through and glazed.

Makes 4 servings

Per serving: 261 calories, 35 g protein, 24 g carbohydrates, 2 g fat, 64 mg cholesterol, 3 g fiber, 593 mg sodium

Pasta with Beans and Cajun Salmon

Four ounces of salmon contain 2 grams of omega-3 fatty acids. That's more than half the amount that *Prevention* magazine suggests you aim for each week.

8 ounces penne
1 onion, chopped
2 cloves garlic, minced
6 plum tomatoes, chopped
⅓ cup chopped fresh basil
1 can (15 ounces) cannellini beans, rinsed and drained
1½ cups fat-free, reduced-sodium chicken broth
4 salmon fillets (4 ounces each), skin removed
½ teaspoon Cajun seasoning

Cook the penne according to the package directions. Drain and return to the pot.

Meanwhile, coat a large nonstick skillet with cooking spray. Set over medium heat. Add the onion and garlic. Cook, stirring often, for 5 to 7 minutes, or until soft. Add the tomatoes and basil. Cook, stirring occasionally, for 4 to 5 minutes, or until the tomatoes are soft. Add the beans and broth. Simmer for 3 to 4 minutes, or until slightly reduced. Stir into the penne and cover partially.

Rinse the skillet and wipe dry with paper towels. Set over medium-high heat until hot. Coat both sides of each salmon fillet with cooking spray. Sprinkle with Cajun seasoning. Place the fish in the pan. Cook for 4 to 5 minutes per side, or until the fish flakes easily.

To serve, spoon the penne mixture onto 4 plates. Top each serving with a salmon fillet.

Makes 4 servings

Per serving: 509 calories, 36 g protein, 57 g carbohydrates, 14 g fat, 67 mg cholesterol, 7 g fiber, 382 mg sodium

Most supermarkets carry Cajun seasoning in the spice section.

Seafood Potpie

Shrimp aren't shrimpy when it comes to omega-3 fatty acids. Four ounces of shrimp boast 0.4 gram.

1 large leek, white part only, sliced

4 ounces mushrooms, sliced

2 teaspoons dried tarragon

½ cup dry sherry or nonalcoholic white wine

2½ tablespoons unbleached or all-purpose flour

1½ cups 1% milk

1 bottle (8 ounces) clam juice

½ pound bay scallops

¼ pound small shrimp, peeled and deveined

¾ cup frozen peas

1 jar (2 ounces) pimiento strips, drained

1 package (7½ ounces) reduced-fat refrigerated biscuit dough

Preheat the oven to 400°F. Coat a medium baking dish with cooking spray.

Coat a Dutch oven with cooking spray. Add the leek and mushrooms. Coat with cooking spray. Cook, stirring occasionally, over medium heat for 5 to 7 minutes, or until soft. Add the tarragon and sherry or wine. Increase the heat to medium-high. Cook for 2 to 3 minutes, or until the liquid is almost evaporated. Sprinkle with the flour. Cook, stirring constantly, for 2 minutes to coat the vegetables with the flour. Add the milk and clam juice. Stir, scraping the bottom and sides of the pan, for 4 to 5 minutes, or until thickened. Remove from the heat. Add the scallops, shrimp, peas, and pimientos.

Arrange the biscuit dough over the top in a single layer. Bake for 25 minutes, or until the filling bubbles and the biscuits are golden brown.

Makes 4 servings

Per serving: 319 calories, 24 g protein, 46 g carbohydrates, 4 g fat, 78 mg cholesterol, 3 g fiber, 949 mg sodium

Tuna Salad Pockets

This recipe calls for white, not light, tuna. That's a healthy distinction because white tuna contains more than twice the amount of omega-3 fatty acids as light tuna.

Dressing

½ cup balsamic or cider vinegar
2 teaspoons olive oil
1 teaspoon Dijon mustard
1 teaspoon Italian seasoning
1 clove garlic, chopped

Sandwiches

¾ pound red potatoes, cut into ¼"-thick slices
¼ pound small green beans
1 can (6 ounces) water-packed white tuna, drained and flaked
¼ red onion, thinly sliced
2 hard-cooked egg whites, coarsely chopped
¼ cup coarsely chopped niçoise olives
4 leaves lettuce, chopped
4 pitas

To make the dressing: In a medium bowl, combine the vinegar, oil, mustard, Italian seasoning, and garlic.

To make the sandwiches: Set a vegetable steamer in a medium saucepan filled with 2" of water. Cover and bring to a boil. Steam the potatoes and beans for 6 to 8 minutes, or until tender. Remove to a colander and rinse with cold water. Pat dry.

To the bowl with the dressing, add the potatoes, beans, tuna, onion, egg whites, olives, and lettuce. Toss gently to combine.

Cut each pita in half crosswise. Spoon the tuna mixture into each pocket. Drizzle lightly with any dressing left in the bowl.

Makes 4 servings

Per serving: 353 calories, 20 g protein, 54 g carbohydrates, 6 g fat, 18 mg cholesterol, 5 g fiber, 627 mg sodium

Cornmeal-Crusted Catfish

While not the highest omega-3 fish, catfish tastes great and adds a little variety to your healthy-fats choices.

½ cup buttermilk
1 tablespoon lime juice
⅓ cup cornmeal
⅓ cup unbleached or all-purpose flour
4 scallions, minced
¼ teaspoon salt
¼ teaspoon ground cumin
4 catfish fillets (5 ounces each)

Line a large plate with waxed paper.

In a medium shallow bowl, combine the buttermilk and lime juice. In another shallow bowl, combine the cornmeal, flour, scallions, salt, and cumin. Stir to mix. Dip the fillets into the buttermilk mixture, then into the cornmeal mixture, pressing gently to adhere. Place on the prepared plate. Refrigerate for 15 minutes.

Set a large nonstick skillet over medium-high heat. Coat the tops of the fillets with cooking spray. Place the fillets, coated sides down, in the skillet. Cook for 4 to 5 minutes, or until golden brown on the bottoms. Remove the skillet from the heat. Coat the tops of the fillets with cooking spray. Turn and cook for 4 to 5 minutes longer, or until the fish flakes easily.

Makes 4 servings

Per serving: 339 calories, 31 g protein, 20 g carbohydrates, 14 g fat, 84 mg cholesterol, 0 g fiber, 264 mg sodium

‖ Calcium

Most of us know that calcium helps the body build and maintain bones, but that's just the start of this mineral's contribution to the ongoing bodily enterprise. Calcium is also involved in helping your muscles contract—and that includes the beating of your heart. There's also evidence that calcium intake influences blood pressure.

You probably know that dairy foods such as milk, yogurt, and cheese are all excellent sources of calcium. You may not know that fat-free and reduced-fat dairy products may actually provide you with slightly more calcium than their full-fat counterparts. Other sources of calcium include bok choy, kale, almonds, oranges, and fish with edible bones, such as salmon.

The amount of calcium that your body needs changes at different stages in your life. The Daily Value for most adults is 1,000 milligrams a day. For adults over age 50, it's 1,500 milligrams a day.

With the heightened awareness of daily calcium needs, foods such as breakfast cereals, tofu, soy milk, orange juice, white rice, and cereal bars have been fortified with calcium by food manufacturers. To make sure that calcium is absorbed readily by your body, be sure to also eat foods rich in vitamin D. These include milk, fortified cereals, eggs, and canned salmon with bones.

Osteoporosis: Not for Women Only

Public health warnings about osteoporosis have targeted women, but men are not immune. One in five of the people affected by osteoporosis is a man. One out of every eight men over age 50 will have a bone fracture due to osteoporosis.

Both men and women lose bone density as they age, surprisingly for the same reason: too little estrogen. Certain bone cells actually transform testosterone to estrogen, but the number of those cells diminishes with age. The decline in bone density is not as rapid in men as it is in women, so men get osteoporosis about 10 to 15 years later. But much of the osteoporosis seen in men is not due to simple aging; underlying disorders such as rheumatoid arthritis, liver disease, or cancer can also be responsible.

Osteoporosis prevention is straightforward. Get plenty of exercise, which will keep your bones strong. Also make sure you get plenty of calcium, preferably along with other nutrients that will help your body absorb it. These include vitamin D, magnesium, and vitamin K. A deficiency in vitamin D can lead to soft bones, which in turn can lead to fractures. Magnesium helps transport calcium to the bones; it also helps convert vitamin D to its active form in the body. Vitamin K helps reduce the amount of calcium you lose through urine and is also crucial to the formation of osteocalcin, a protein that helps form the foundation for calcium in the bone.

Berry Berry Smoothie

The yogurt in this smoothie gives you calcium, while the fruits provide you with vitamin C, fiber, and a compound called ellagic acid. All are believed to be effective at warding off heart disease and cancer.

½ cup frozen unsweetened
   raspberries
½ cup frozen unsweetened
   strawberries
¾ cup unsweetened pineapple
   juice
1 cup (8 ounces) fat-free
   vanilla yogurt

In a blender, combine the raspberries, strawberries, pineapple juice, and yogurt. Blend until smooth.

Makes 2 servings

Per serving: 195 calories, 7 g protein, 43 g carbohydrates, 1 g fat, 2 mg cholesterol, 3 g fiber, 79 mg sodium

Double-Crust Pizza

This cheesy pizza tastes as good as it looks. Plus, your bones will thank you for eating it—putting more cheese on the menu is an excellent way to get more calcium.

1 tablespoon cornmeal
1 onion, chopped
2 cloves garlic, chopped
½ pound extra-lean ground round beef
1½ cups pasta sauce
¼ cup chopped fresh parsley and/or oregano or 2 teaspoons dried
2 cups (16 ounces) fat-free ricotta cheese
1 cup (8 ounces) shredded low-fat mozzarella cheese
¼ teaspoon ground nutmeg
2 egg whites, divided
2 tubes (10 ounces each) refrigerated pizza dough
2 tablespoons (½ ounce) grated Parmesan cheese

Preheat the oven to 400°F. Coat a large round pizza pan with cooking spray. Sprinkle with the cornmeal.

Coat a medium nonstick skillet with cooking spray. Set over medium heat. Cook the onion and garlic, stirring often, for 3 minutes, or until almost soft. Add the beef and cook, stirring occasionally, for 3 to 5 minutes, or until no longer pink. Stir in the pasta sauce and parsley and/or oregano.

In a medium bowl, combine the ricotta, ½ cup of the mozzarella, the nutmeg, and one of the egg whites.

Place the dough onto a lightly floured work surface. Divide the dough into 2 balls. Roll 1 ball into a 12" circle. Place on the prepared pan. Spread the ricotta mixture evenly over the dough, leaving a 1" border. Top with the beef mixture and the remaining ½ cup mozzarella. Sprinkle with the Parmesan.

Place the remaining egg white in a small bowl. Beat lightly with a fork.

On a lightly floured work surface, roll the remaining dough ball into a 12" circle. Place over the filling. Fold in the edges of the bottom crust. Pinch the crusts to seal. Brush the top and sides of the pie with the beaten egg white. With a sharp knife, make several small slashes in the top crust.

Bake for 20 to 25 minutes, or until golden brown.

Makes 10 servings

Per serving: 315 calories, 21 g protein, 42 g carbohydrates, 6 g fat, 30 mg cholesterol, 2 g fiber, 492 mg sodium

The New Classic Reuben

One slice of Swiss cheese has a whopping 272 milligrams of calcium. Although the fat and sodium in this sandwich are relatively high, the overall nutritional profile is profoundly better than the original Reuben, which contains around 30 grams of fat and 2,000 milligrams of sodium.

8 slices soft rye bread
6 tablespoons fat-free Thousand Island dressing
¾ pound very thinly sliced cooked turkey breast
1 cup sauerkraut, rinsed and drained
4 slices (4 ounces) low-fat, reduced-sodium Swiss cheese

Place 4 slices of the bread on a work surface. Spread evenly with the dressing. Top with layers of the turkey, sauerkraut, and cheese. Cover with the remaining bread slices. Coat the tops with cooking spray.

Set a large nonstick skillet over medium heat. Place the sandwiches, coated side down, in the skillet. Cover and cook for 3 to 4 minutes, or until the bottoms are golden brown. Coat the tops of the sandwiches with cooking spray. Carefully turn the sandwiches over. Cover and cook for 3 to 4 minutes, or until the bottoms are golden and the cheese is melted. Cut each sandwich in half.

Makes 4

Per sandwich: 417 calories, 40 g protein, 42 g carbohydrates, 9 g fat, 91 mg cholesterol, 5 g fiber, 836 mg sodium

New England Clam Chowder

Milk is still the easiest, best way to get your calcium—and low-fat doesn't mean low in calcium.

2 cans (6½ ounces each) minced clams
2 strips bacon, chopped
1 large onion, chopped
3 ribs celery, chopped
2 cans (14½ ounces each) fat-free, reduced-sodium chicken broth
1 teaspoon dried thyme
1 bay leaf
1 pound potatoes, cut into ½" chunks
1/4 cup unbleached or all-purpose flour
1½–2 cups 2% milk
1½ cups frozen corn kernels
1/4 cup chopped parsley

Drain the clams and reserve the juice. Set aside.

In a Dutch oven, cook the bacon, stirring often, over medium heat for 3 minutes. Add the onion and celery. Cook for 5 minutes, or until the onion is soft. Add the broth, thyme, bay leaf, and reserved clam juice. Bring to a boil and stir well. Add the potatoes. Cook for 20 to 25 minutes, or until the potatoes are tender.

Meanwhile, place the flour in a small bowl. Gradually add 1½ cups of the milk, whisking until smooth. Add to the pot, along with the corn, parsley, and reserved clams. Cook, stirring frequently, for 10 minutes, or until thickened. Add up to ½ cup more of the remaining milk for a thinner chowder, if desired. Remove and discard the bay leaf.

Makes 8 servings

Per serving: 237 calories, 12 g protein, 32 g carbohydrates, 5 g fat, 17 mg cholesterol, 4 g fiber, 359 mg sodium

Banana Ice Cream with Silky Chocolate Sauce

There's no sweeter way to get calcium than by eating ice cream. The natural creaminess of bananas makes it the perfect fruit to whirl into a smooth and sensuous ice cream that's virtually fat-free.

Ice Cream
2 large bananas, ripe, frozen, and sliced
2 tablespoons sugar
1½ cups 1% milk
½ teaspoon ground cinnamon
½ teaspoon vanilla extract

Chocolate Sauce
⅔ cup water
¼ cup sugar
3 tablespoons unsweetened cocoa powder
2 teaspoons cornstarch
2 teaspoons unsalted butter
½ teaspoon vanilla extract

To make the ice cream: In a food processor or blender, combine the bananas, sugar, and ½ cup of the milk. Puree until smooth.

Add the cinnamon, vanilla, and the remaining 1 cup of milk. Puree until smooth. Transfer into an 8" × 8" metal or plastic container. Cover and freeze for 4 hours or overnight.

Remove from the freezer and break up the mixture with a knife. Working with half of the mixture at a time, process briefly in a food processor or blender. The mixture will transform from icy to smooth. Use a rubber spatula to poke the mixture down. Return it to the container, cover, and freeze for at least 30 minutes before serving.

To make the chocolate sauce: In a medium saucepan, combine the water, sugar, cocoa, and cornstarch. Stir with a wire whisk until smooth. Cook over medium heat, stirring frequently with a wooden spoon, for 5 minutes, or until smooth and thickened. Remove from the heat. Stir in the butter and vanilla.

Makes 6 servings

Per ½-cup serving of ice cream with 2 tablespoons sauce: 129 calories, 3 g protein, 27 g carbohydrates, 3 g fat, 6 mg cholesterol, 1 g fiber, 34 mg sodium

Part Six

The Healing Power of **Herbs**

Sure, herbs can be used to treat specific conditions.
But they can also keep you feeling young, fit, and full of vitality.

Chapter 12

The Miracle of Antiaging Herbs

For disease protection and nonstop energy, you can't beat the power of Mother Nature

Running on empty.

Jackson Browne's song of that title was about being on the road with a rock-and-roll band, but if you have kids, a job, or both, chances are you know the feeling too.

Herbs can help. There's a whole class of herbs that can give you energy—enough energy to carry you through your busiest day. Another class of herbs can stop the aging process in its tracks by fighting the biological processes that wear down your body.

In this chapter and the next, we'll give you a full report on both of these classes of herbs. Use them, and you won't feel as if you were running on empty. On the contrary, you will feel younger than you have in years.

The Energy Herbs

Russian scientists coined a word to refer to a class of plants that can boost physical energy, increase mental capacity, and make you feel better in general. Adaptogens, they called them.

Adaptogens are herbs that help your body adapt. Adapt to what? To challenges posed by physical, chemical, and biological stress.

Sound useful? Here's a rundown on some of the best-known adaptogens.

Ginseng

Ginseng is, quite simply, a legendary herb—perhaps the most legendary herb of all. Its root has been used for centuries in China as a sexual stimulant and tonic.

There are several ginseng varieties, but all of the true ginsengs are species of *Panax*. The best known are *Panax ginseng*, the Asian species, and *Panax quinquefolius*, the American variety. Sometimes, ginseng is steam-cured prior to drying to

NATURALFACT

Avoid bargain brands of ginseng. The cheaper the product, the less chance that it's pure ginseng.

produce red ginseng; if the roots are bleached and dried quickly, white ginseng results. Both species and both types of processing yield products that produce similar, but not identical, tonic effects.

A 1996 double-blind study of 501 volunteers found a significant improvement in quality of life when people took 40 milligrams of ginseng extract and multivitamins, compared with people who took only multivitamins. The participants rated themselves on issues such as depression, personal satisfaction, energy level, sex life, and sleep. The ginseng takers showed significant improvements in these areas, but those who took only vitamins showed only slight improvements. Another study of 232 people showed distinct improvements in energy levels. Side effects were minimal.

How to take ginseng: Brew a healthful tea from 1 teaspoon of the finely chopped root steeped for 10 minutes in a covered cup of boiling water. Drink 1 cup one to three times daily.

Or take capsules or tablets containing 100 to 250 milligrams of ginseng extract standard-

Backed by Science

All of the energy herbs have long histories of use in traditional medicine, which for many people is proof enough of their effectiveness. Other people, though, feel more comfortable knowing that there's scientific proof behind any medicine they take.

As far as well-designed studies go, ginseng has the most documentation behind it, followed by Siberian ginseng, cordyceps, and ashwaganda, in that order.

HEALING SPOTLIGHT
Sharon Lawrence

Sharon Lawrence's acting career is going wonderfully, which means it's also stressful. You've seen her as a regular on such TV series as *NYPD Blue* (she spent 6 years playing district attorney Sylvia Costas, wife of detective Andy Sipowicz) and *Ladies Man*. If you were lucky, you caught her during her recent stint on Broadway in the musical *Chicago*.

To keep herself up to the physical demands of her success, Lawrence has a secret weapon. "I'm a strong believer in preventive medicine," she says, "and one of the healthiest things I do in that regard is take herbal supplements."

Lawrence patronizes a Los Angeles boutique where combinations of Chinese herbs are made to order for each customer, depending on his or her particular needs. But she also relies on simpler remedies for specific problems.

"Ginger is terrific for settling your stomach and preventing motion sickness," Lawrence says. "In my twenties, I worked singing and dancing on a cruise ship, and I regularly used raw ginger, grated or sliced and steeped in tea, to prevent me from getting seasick. It really works."

A frequent flier, Lawrence also uses herbs to fight off the cold and flu bugs that seem to swarm through the ventilation systems of planes. "I don't get a lot of colds, and I think it's because I take echinacea," she says. "I take heavy doses of echinacea before I get on a plane and during the flight."

ized to contain 4 to 7 percent of the active ginsenosides. Dosage varies from two to eight capsules daily.

Ginseng is also available as a tincture. Follow the label instructions.

Avoid ginseng soft drinks, candies, chewing gum, and snack foods—unless you can determine from the label that an effective amount is actually present.

Siberian Ginseng (Eleuthero)

Another popular energy-boosting herb is Siberian ginseng, or eleuthero, the root of *Eleutherococcus senticosus*. It belongs to the same plant family, Araliaceae, as the true ginsengs but is not a species of *Panax*. It is, however, much less expensive than true ginseng, so it is widely used.

Most of the clinical investigations of eleuthero have been carried out in Russia. Studies there on thousands of human subjects from the 1960s to the 1980s revealed beneficial tonic effects very similar to those reported for ginseng. Unfortunately, most of these studies were not double-blind and lacked adequate controls, so the results aren't as reliable as more stringent tests would produce.

A more recent, well-designed clinical study was conducted in 1996 on 20 highly trained long-distance runners. After 6 weeks, researchers concluded that the energy-building claims made for eleuthero could not be verified, at least in those well-conditioned athletes. More study is needed to define the exact benefits of this popular herb.

How to take Siberian ginseng: Buy Siberian ginseng products only from the most reliable sources. Because of confusion caused by similar Chinese names, an altogether different herb, Chinese silk vine (*Periploca sepium*), is often substituted in its place. Due to the popularity of Siberian ginseng among athletes, it is also sometimes adulterated with stimulants such as caffeine.

Siberian ginseng is available in a variety of forms ranging from tinctures to powdered extracts. Its active principles are a mixed bag of chemicals called eleutherosides, but research hasn't proved the relationship of specific compounds to specific activities. The dose is 2 to 3 grams of the dried root, or the equivalent.

‖ Cordyceps

Probably the most unusual energizer ever to become popular in the United States is cordyceps. This is a peculiar fungus (*Cordyceps sinensis*) that grows on certain adult caterpillars native to the high mountains of China. The fruiting bodies of the fungus have long been used in that country to enhance endurance and to speed recovery from exhaustion.

Scientists have been able to grow these fungal cells in artificial cultures, and the harvested product

---

NATURALFACT

Some adaptogenic herbs have antioxidant properties as well. These include Asian ginseng (*Panax ginseng*) and schisandra (*Schisandra chinensis*) as well as cat's claw (*Uncaria tomentosa*).

The Energy Herbs at a Glance

Common Name	Also Known As	Scientific Name
AMERICAN GINSENG	Sang, red berry	*Panax quinquefolius*
ASIAN GINSENG	Chinese ginseng, Korean ginseng, rin shen	*Panax ginseng*
SIBERIAN GINSENG	Eleuthero, devil's bush, ciwujia, wu-jia	*Eleutherococcus senticosus*
CORDYCEPS	Caterpillar fungus, vegetable caterpillar	*Cordyceps sinensis*
ASHWAGANDA	Winter cherry, Indian ginseng	*Withania somnifera*

is dried and sold as an adaptogen to enhance stamina, reduce symptoms of fatigue, and energize body systems. These effects are supported by a number of pharmacological and clinical studies carried out in China, but they have not been studied in the West.

How to take cordyceps: The recommended dose is 3 to 9 grams per day. Side effects are not common but include skin rashes, nausea, and diarrhea.

Because cordyceps increases male hormone levels, it should probably not be used by men with prostatitis; no adverse hormonal effects have been reported in women.

"Cordyceps relieves mental exhaustion and aids recuperation from illnesses."

—Dr. Douglas Schar, medicinal herbalist

somnifera—is sometimes referred to as Indian ginseng. The roots particularly have long been used in Ayurvedic medicine for a variety of conditions ranging from debility to senility and for sexual stimulation.

Although it has attained a considerable reputation as a useful tonic, scientific evidence supporting its activity is scant. Studies in small animals have demonstrated anti-inflammatory and antioxidant effects. A 1980 clinical trial found some benefits in middle-age men, including increases in hemoglobin and red blood cells, both of which transport oxygen throughout the body.

How to take ashwaganda: A dose of 2 to 3 grams of the powdered root is commonly taken three times daily in India. Toxicity is mostly limited to stomach upset, but keep in mind that the plant may have some sedative properties as well.

‖ Ashwaganda

Because of its adaptogenic properties, ashwaganda—the roots, shoots, and leaves of *Withania*

Chapter 13

Fighting the Good Fight for Your Health

Antioxidant herbs protect you from free radical attacks and aging

What would you call an herb that could safely help slow aging, promote heart health, and reduce the risk of a whole host of diseases—not least among them cancer? A miracle? Well, maybe. But science calls it an antioxidant.

When most people think of antioxidants, they think of pills: a few hundred milligrams of vitamin C in the morning, a vitamin E supplement to stave off heart disease.

But vitamin supplements are far from the only sources of antioxidant protection. Plenty of herbs offer it, too. Some herbs, in fact, are as much as 50 times more powerful than the most popular antioxidant vitamins.

Want to know which herbs provide nature's best antioxidant protection? Read on.

Trapping Radicals

The term *free radical* sounds like it describes an escaped terrorist. In a sense, it does. Free radicals are highly reactive oxygen molecules that are formed as by-products of normal metabolic reactions. They act upon the cells and tissues of your body to produce significant damage—terrorizing them, if you will.

Antioxidants come to our rescue by neutralizing these free radical molecules. If they aren't neutralized, free radicals create all sorts of trouble, reacting with proteins, fats, and nucleic acids to cause changes that can lead to heart disease, arthritis, cancer, and various degenerative conditions. Almost all of these conditions are associated with the aging process, so the direct effects of antioxidants can actually reduce some of the effects of growing old.

Among the most effective herbal antioxidants are a series of compounds known collectively as polyphenolic derivatives. Individually, they have a bewildering number of names that are even more confusing, so herbalists lump them together under the nickname OPCs.

OPCs are found in a number of species of higher plants, ranging from foods such as blueberries to grape seeds, pine bark, and green tea. Their primary antioxidant activity is preventing the oxidation of low-density lipoprotein (LDL), or "bad," cholesterol in the blood. That makes the LDL less sticky and less likely to build up on artery walls. When your arteries are clear, you're far less likely to have a heart attack. OPCs also help strengthen tiny blood vessels, thus improving circulation.

Grape Seed Extract

One of the most effective of the OPC antioxidants—the one that is some 50 times as powerful as vitamin E and 20 times more powerful than vitamin C—is derived from grape seed (*Vitis vinifera*). Grape seed used to be considered a worthless by-product of wine production, but after careful study in France and Italy (two countries where grapes abound), we now know that's not the case.

Grape seed extract has proven to be valuable in the treatment of inadequate bloodflow in the veins, helping to relieve the pain, nighttime cramping, and edema (swelling) associated with that disorder. The extract has also been found to be of potential value in treating certain eye problems, including ocular stress and macular degeneration (the leading cause of irreversible vision loss in people over age 50). It even shows value in reducing the effects of glare from bright lights.

Another important feature of grape seed extract is its ability to act synergistically with vitamin C. The term *synergistic* simply means that the

An Added Bonus

In addition to protecting your heart, the antioxidant power of grape seed extract can help you look better in a swimsuit this summer. Its ability to strengthen the walls of tiny blood vessels helps reduce the tendency toward varicose veins.

combination of the two antioxidants is more effective than either of them alone. This combination facilitates wound healing and even tends to promote the elimination of excess cholesterol.

How to take grape seed extract: OPCs occur in the skins of the fruit as well as in grape seeds and are believed to be partly responsible for the so-called French Paradox. Even though the French diet includes plenty of fatty foods that are high in cholesterol, statistics indicate that the French people who eat that diet don't suffer the consequences that you would expect in terms of heart disease.

The explanation for this seems to lie in the fact that they also consume lots of red wine, fruits, and vegetables. Scientists agree that the OPCs in red wine exert a protective effect against the cardiovascular damage caused by a high-cholesterol diet.

If you want to avoid alcohol, drink nonalcoholic red grape juice. It offers the same antioxidant protection as red wine. In fact, you don't have to drink your herbal antioxidants at all. You can get the same healthy benefits simply by taking grape seed extract capsules. These are readily available throughout the United States and have become a popular dietary supplement.

To help prevent the various conditions we've described, the recommended maintenance dosage is 50 to 100 milligrams per day of a 100:1

"There are more old wine drinkers than old doctors."

—Sign often seen in European bistros

concentrated grape seed extract. Such extracts should contain 80 to 85 percent OPCs. Actual treatment of the various conditions (a therapeutic dose) involves the consumption of somewhat larger quantities, up to 300 milligrams daily.

The safety of consuming grape seed extract has never been questioned.

‖ Rosemary

Another of the most effective herbal antioxidants is hiding in your kitchen spice rack. Rosemary's spiky, evergreen-like leaves contain plant pigments called bioflavonoids that have antioxidant properties. In fact, this tasty herb's antioxidant power was used for centuries to preserve food. One bioflavonoid in rosemary, diosmin, is reported to help strengthen capillaries, which can ease problems such as varicose veins and hemorrhoids.

Can rosemary help you stay young? In 1995, Japanese researchers found that two compounds in the herb, carnosol and carnosic acid, may help to protect body tissues and cells against the oxidative stresses that have been linked to diabetes, aging, and coronary arteriosclerosis. Germany's Commission E, an expert committee on herbal remedies that evaluates the safety and efficacy of herbs for medical use, has given the nod to using rosemary for circulation problems, such as low blood pressure, and for painful joints or muscles.

The Herbal Difference

With all the antioxidant supplements available these days, why resort to herbs?

We put that question to *Prevention* magazine's herb columnist, Varro E. Tyler, Ph.D., Sc.D., dean emeritus of the Purdue University School of Pharmacy and Pharmacal Sciences in West Lafayette, Indiana. Here's his answer.

"The antioxidant properties of herbs are just one of their many health benefits. They contain a number of chemicals that do many things. The antioxidant ginkgo, for instance, also improves circulation.

"Most single chemical products do only one thing. They also usually act through a single mechanism, such as exerting a pronounced action on one particular receptor site in the body. The end result is a strong action—along with the strong possibility of a reaction. The multiple compounds in herbs act weakly on many different receptor sites. Since no single receptor site is strongly affected, side effects are minimal."

How to take rosemary: Rosemary (*Rosmarinus officinalis*) is often taken as a tea made from 1 teaspoon of the dried leaves per cup of water. To make tea using fresh leaves, double or triple the amount. You can also use rosemary to flavor lamb, chicken, or roasted vegetables—it's tasty as well as healthy.

Other Antioxidant Herbs

There are a number of herbs that have antioxidant properties, although that is not their major health benefit. These include ginkgo (*Ginkgo biloba*), which is recommended for cognitive deficiencies; garlic (*Allium sativum*) for circulatory benefits; and turmeric (*Curcuma domestica*) for its digestive properties. Because these herbal products exist in so many forms (capsules, tablets, tinctures, and so on) and concentrations, follow the dosage instructions on the labels and look for standardized products.

Sage (*Salvia officinalis*) is another herbal antioxidant that has multiple talents. Commission E approves its internal use for indigestion and excessive perspiration, while many traditional herbalists recommend sage tea as a remedy for menopausal night sweats. Commission E also approves sage as a gargle for throat irritations. It may be drunk as a tea, using 1 teaspoon of the dried leaves per cup of water. Some people report irritation and dryness of the mouth after consuming sage tea, so be cautious about using it too frequently.

Chapter 14
Try the Tonic Approach to Healthy Living

For centuries, herbal tonics have helped prevent illness and promote vitality

Most of us think of a tonic as a sparkling drink that's mixed with gin on a sunny summer afternoon.

Herbalists see it differently.

To them, a tonic is an herbal preparation that promotes good health and well-being in general. It's also a preparation that you can take to help prevent an illness you hope to avoid rather than to cure one you already have.

Tonics can be taken on an on-going basis, for weeks, months, even years at a time. Some keep killer diseases such as cancer or heart disease at bay. Others reduce the discomfort of conditions that are more annoying than life-threatening, such as hemorrhoids or colds.

The end result is good health and vitality.

‖ Meet Dr. Schar

In order to get the lowdown on herbal tonics, we consulted one of Europe's leading medicinal herbalists, Dr. Douglas Schar. Based in London, Dr. Schar specializes in disease-preventing herbal medicines. He has a Diploma in Phytotherapy, which is an herbal medical degree, and is a member of the College of Practitioners of Phytotherapy. He is also editor of the *British Journal of Phytotherapy*, Europe's oldest journal of herbal medicine.

Mail-Order Herbs

Tonic herbs are widely available at health food stores and also by mail order. Here are two mail-order firms.

Blessed Herbs
109 Barre Plains Road
Oakham, MA 01068
800-489-4372
www.blessedherbs.com

Mountain Rose Herbs
20818 High Street
North San Juan, CA 95960
800-879-3337
http://botanical.com/mtrose

A mail-order source for maitake is:

Maitake Products
222 Bergen Turnpike
Ridgefield Park, NJ 07660
800-747-7418
www.maitake.com

According to Dr. Schar, a century ago taking tonics was as common as popping aspirin is today. But then tonic use died out. Why?

"Because the more cures medical science developed, the more people turned away from using tonic plants to prevent disease," Dr. Schar says. "Why bother growing and brewing echinacea to keep the kids free of sore throats when you could run to the doctor and get an antibiotic? Tonics were abandoned for less time-consuming options."

Today, Dr. Schar believes, tonics are coming back into vogue. Most of us have heard about the energy you can get from taking ginseng, he points out, or the memory boost offered by *Ginkgo biloba*. But those are only two of the tonic herbs that nature's garden has provided.

We asked Dr. Schar to share some of his favorite tonic herbs, specifically those that target the most common health problems. You can find these herbs at local health food stores or through mail-order sources (see "Mail-Order Herbs").

‖ The Woman's Tonic

Black Cohosh (Actea Racemosa)

What it's good for: It alleviates premenstrual symptoms, irregular periods, and menopausal symptoms.

"This American native plant was beloved by Native Americans," Dr. Schar says. "They used it to treat infertility, irregular menstruation, and menopausal symptoms."

Why it works: A double-blind study of 80 patients compared two remedies for meno-

A Word of Caution

If you have a serious condition, such as heart disease, cancer, or asthma, or if you suffer from allergies, see your doctor before using herbal remedies. Never stop taking your prescribed medication or substitute herbs for prescription meds unless your doctor says it's okay.

pausal symptoms—black cohosh and conjugated estrogens—over a 12-week period. Some patients received a placebo (sugar pill) as a control. Black cohosh was found to be the superior treatment for easing hot flashes, headache, joint pain, heart palpitations, sleep disturbances, and depression, Dr. Schar says.

In another trial, black cohosh beat a placebo for relieving hot flashes and vaginal dryness. Germany's Commission E, an expert committee on herbal remedies that evaluates the safety and efficacy of herbs for medical use, considers black cohosh effective for treating PMS and painful periods as well as nervous conditions associated with menopause.

Who should consider it: Dr. Schar recommends this herb for women of all ages, in-

cluding those who have painful periods and those troubled by menopausal symptoms such as hot flashes.

"Women who suffer terrible emotional ups and downs in connection with menstruation tell me that black cohosh is a lifesaver," he says. "I also use it successfully for women who experience PMS-related problems such as depression, nervousness, and irritability."

At menopause, black cohosh can ease many of the symptoms without the side effects that some women experience with hormone replacement therapy (HRT). And, unlike HRT, black cohosh is not associated with increased risk of breast or endometrial cancers.

How to use it: To make a tea, cover 1 tablespoon of dried root with boiling water. Steep, covered, for about 10 minutes. If you prefer capsules, take 40 milligrams a day. The dosage for a tincture is 1 teaspoon a day.

‖ The Heart Tonic

Hawthorn (*Crataegus Oxycantha*)

What it's good for: It lowers blood pressure, prevents atherosclerosis (hardening of the arteries), and helps other circulatory problems, such as varicose veins.

Hawthorn can help you beat the odds against heart disease, America's number one killer, Dr. Schar says. In Europe, hawthorn is considered a mainstream medicine for strengthening the heart and blood vessels.

Why it works: "Hawthorn can reduce blood pressure, a known risk factor for heart disease,"

Dr. Schar says. "It contains the antioxidant hyperin, which mops up free radicals, reactive agents that can damage the blood vessels and lead to atherosclerosis."

In addition, hawthorn contains rutin, which reduces plaque formation. As plaque deposits develop, they eventually block bloodflow, which can lead to a heart attack or stroke.

Who should consider it: "If there's heart disease in your family, you may want to consider taking hawthorn now and using it every day," Dr. Schar says. "It may strengthen your cardiac system and make it more disease-resistant."

In his practice, Dr. Schar has prescribed hawthorn and seen blood pressure lowered, angina eased, shortness of breath and ankle swelling improved, and an overall improvement in heart health and bloodflow. "Of course," he adds, "always talk to your doctor before taking an herb for a serious condition."

Varicose veins, hemorrhoids, and leg ulcers may also be improved with regular hawthorn use.

Caution: If you have a cardiovascular condition, do not take hawthorn regularly for more than a few weeks without medical supervision. You may require lower doses of other medications, such as high blood pressure drugs. If you have low blood pressure caused by heart valve problems, do not use without medical supervision.

How to use it: To make a tea, boil 1 tablespoon of dried berries in 1 cup of water for 10 minutes. Drink 1 cup a day. If you prefer tablets, take 300 milligrams daily. The dosage for a tincture is 1 tablespoon daily.

NATURALFACT

Some herbs— ginseng, garlic, and ginkgo are examples— need to be taken for a month or more before their beneficial effects kick in.

The Respiratory Tonic

Licorice (*Glycyrrhiza Glabra*)

What it's good for: Licorice fights bacteria and viruses, and lessens symptoms of asthma and allergies.

Whether the problem was asthma, chronic sinus infections, chronic bronchitis, allergies, or a tendency to develop coughs and colds, licorice was the first choice of the ancient herbalist, Dr. Schar says, and it remains so for many herbalists today.

Why it works: Licorice contains a wild cocktail of compounds that make the respiratory tract function better. Among them, glycyrrhetic acid, glycyrrhizic acid, and glycyrrhizin have been proven to reduce inflammation, fight viruses and bacteria, and counteract the symptoms of allergies and asthma. (It's worth noting that deaths caused by asthma have risen 117 percent in the last 20 years.) Licorice stimulates the part of the immune system responsible for attacking viruses.

Who should consider it: "In my experience, licorice can lower the frequency of colds, lessen asthma's severity, and reduce allergic reactions," Dr. Schar says. "If you have allergies, I suggest using licorice a month in advance of your personal hay fever season."

How to use it: To make a tea, simmer a heaping tablespoon (about 4 grams) of root, sliced or powdered, in boiling water for 10 minutes. Strain and drink hot daily. To save time,

The King of Immunity

For many herb consumers, maitake is a newcomer when it comes to building immunity. The king of immunity herbs—and the best-selling botanical remedy in the United States—remains echinacea.

"Echinacea has been extensively studied, and there's some pretty good evidence that it does indeed trigger an immune response that can blast away the viruses and bacteria that cause cold and flu symptoms," says *Prevention* magazine's herb columnist, Varro E. Tyler, Ph.D., Sc.D., dean emeritus of the Purdue University School of Pharmacy and Pharmacal Sciences in West Lafayette, Indiana.

Dr. Tyler cites one European study that showed that an extract of echinacea was significantly more effective at shortening the duration of an upper-respiratory illness than was a sugar pill. "On average," he says, "the people who used echinacea got better 4 days sooner than the people who were given placebos."

make 3 cups at once and later reheat 2 in the microwave. The dosage for a tincture is 1 tablespoon daily.

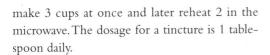

The Immunity Tonic

Maitake *(Grifola Frondosa)*

What it's good for: It stimulates the immune system to fight bacteria, viruses, and cancer and prevents stress-induced flare-ups of hepatitis and herpes.

Maitake is a mushroom-producing fungus found in North America, Europe, and Asia. Japan is the world's leading producer.

The health benefits of maitake were substantiated in cancer research in the early 1980s, when scientists learned of its powerful ability to stimulate the immune systems of laboratory animals.

Why it works: Research in both animals and humans suggests that maitake stimulates the white blood cells responsible for killing bacteria, viruses, fungi, and cancer cells. Maitake seems to fortify immune system helpers known as interferon and interleukin, and it contains substances that directly inhibit bacteria and viruses.

In a study supervised by Dr. Schar, 30 men with HIV, the virus that causes AIDS, experienced increases in T-cell counts (an important disease-fighting cell) after using maitake for periods of 8 months or more. They also demonstrated decreases in viral activity and a reduction of the symptoms associated with the infection, such as night sweats, weight loss, and diarrhea. Many of the participants gained weight and returned to work.

Who should consider it: If you suffer from chronic tonsillitis, sinusitis, urinary tract infections, or any recurring bacterial or viral infections, maitake may help keep these infections from recurring, Dr. Schar says.

People anticipating a stressful period in their lives may want to take maitake ahead of time, he adds. It may prevent problems such as colds and other illnesses that can strike when immune defenses are weakened. People with viral infections such as hepatitis, herpes, and warts often have recurrences when they're under stress and their immune function is depressed. Dr. Schar recommends maitake to help reduce the frequency of their symptoms.

How to use it: As a preventive, Dr. Schar recommends 2 grams of maitake per day, 4 to 6 grams a day when you're sick.

The Energy Tonic

Oats (Avena Sativa)

What they're good for: Oats restore energy, reduce fatigue, improve thinking ability, speed recovery from chronic illness or surgery, and boost sex drive.

For the modern man or woman who's feeling constantly overwhelmed, Dr. Schar recommends oats as the stamina tonic of choice.

Why they work: "Here's a case where science says very little, but centuries of herbal experience speak volumes," Dr. Schar says. "How oats work remains a mystery."

There are clues, however. Ginseng, for example, is a well-known endurance tonic, and herbalists know that its active ingredients are derived from a group of compounds called ginsenosides. According to Dr. Schar, oats contain avenacosides, which are chemically similar enough to ginsenosides to suggest that they may be a fatigue-fighting component. Indeed, Dr. Schar says, one avenacoside (avenin) has been shown to work as a neuromuscular stimulant that theoretically could enhance endurance.

Who should use them: "I've found that oats seem to give busy people enough mental and physical energy to get them through their day," Dr. Schar says. "Afternoon fatigue tends to lessen and clarity of thought tends to increase when people eat their oats."

Oats are especially helpful for people recovering from surgery, serious disease, or viral infection, Dr. Schar believes, as well as for those suffering from the fatigue associated with chronic disease. Finally, oats may be an excellent sex tonic, especially for people whose hectic lives leave their libidos limp. Oats give both men and women a boost in sexual desire and satisfaction.

How to use them: Eat 1 cup of dry oats daily, made into 2 cups of oatmeal or even cookies. Or, use oat tincture made from the whole flowering plant (sometimes called milky oats). Take 1 teaspoon of the tincture in the morning and at night.

The Skin Tonic

Oregon Grape (Mahonia Aquifolium)

What it's good for: It improves skin symptoms and the underlying diseases that cause them.

The chronic skin diseases psoriasis, eczema, and acne aren't life threatening, but they can certainly impair the quality of your life. Of course, there are medical treatments for skin problems—steroid creams quell eczema and antibiotics quiet acne. But when the medication stops, the problem often recurs.

Herbalists prefer to address the problem that lies *beneath* the skin condition, Dr. Schar says, not merely the symptom. And that problem is usually more than cosmetic. Often, it's a sign of weakened immunity. Oregon grape targets the root of the problem.

Why it works: "This medicinal root is made active by two alkaloids, berbamine and berberine," Dr. Schar says. "Berbamine is an antihistamine with antibacterial action. It may stimulate the immune system and liver function." In addition, berberine has been shown to be antiinflammatory, antifungal, anti-ulcer—it's even effective against dandruff.

Who should consider it: Many chronic skin diseases are autoimmune in origin, according to Dr. Schar, meaning that the immune system attacks the body. That's why several different problems often arise at once.

"When I consult patients with eczema and psoriasis," Dr. Schar says, "I often find that they're also troubled by chronic respiratory disorders, digestive disturbances, or joint problems. I believe that in these cases, Oregon grape is an ideal tonic. It can improve the skin problem as well as the associated respiratory, digestive, or joint problems."

Women prone to gallstones often have poor skin, Dr. Schar adds. Oregon grape can reduce both their tendency to gallstones and its associated skin conditions. It may also improve skin problems associated with weak digestion, difficulty digesting fatty foods, and constipation as

well as improve the digestive problems themselves.

Dr. Schar has seen chronic skin conditions simply disappear when Oregon grape was used for prolonged periods of time. It may take a year or more for the condition to clear, he says, though improvement may occur after 3 to 6 months.

How to use it: To make a tea, add 1 tablespoon of dried root to 1 cup of boiling water. Boil for 10 minutes, strain, and drink in the morning. To improve the flavor, add a handful of chamomile, which is also excellent for the skin and makes this skin tonic even more potent. The dosage for a tincture is 1 tablespoon daily.

The Man's Tonic

Saw Palmetto (Serenoa Repens)

What it's good for: Saw palmetto prevents changes in the prostate that can lead to impotence and urinary problems.

"Male 'menopause' is subtler, slower, and far less noticeable than its feminine counterpart," Dr. Schar says. "As testosterone levels drop, muscle tone lessens and sexual drive wanes. The physical changes associated with reduced hormone levels may include benign prostatic hyperplasia"—swelling of the prostate—"which results in frequent bathroom visits and difficulty emptying the bladder completely. Saw palmetto can slow the development of these symptoms."

Why it works: Your body manufactures testosterone and the enzymes that break it down at the same time, Dr. Schar says. Compounds found in saw palmetto destroy those enzymes. The net result is that the testosterone produced by your body stays in circulation longer.

In clinical trials, saw palmetto improved the symptoms of reduced testosterone levels, such as prostate swelling. Saw palmetto also supports joints and muscles, Dr. Schar says, which may help active men stay active well into their golden years.

Who should consider it: "In my experience, when men start using saw palmetto in their forties, their prostates don't swell and their libidos don't drop," Dr. Schar says. "I encourage older men with prostate problems to use the herb to correct existing problems and stave off the possibility of surgery."

How to use it: Saw palmetto works best in tablet or capsule form, Dr. Schar believes. He suggests taking six 250-milligram tablets of saw palmetto daily. Look for products standardized to contain 85 to 95 percent fatty acids and sterols.

Chapter 15

What Are These Herbs Doing to Me?

Here's what you need to know about herb side effects and herb-drug interactions

Are you worried? You're not alone. Millions of Americans are using herbal remedies today, but they're worried about how those remedies might interact with the prescription drugs they're also taking. They worry, too, about the impact that herbal remedies might have on other health concerns, such as fertility.

Is it safe to take ginseng if I'm already on medication for a heart condition? Will St. John's wort keep me from getting pregnant? Can I drink coffee if I'm taking ephedra? Herbal experts hear these sorts of questions every day. Some are based on legitimate concerns; some are fueled by myth.

In hopes of sorting out which is which, we asked *Prevention* magazine's herb columnist, Varro E. Tyler, Ph.D., for a status report.

The Birth of a Myth

Dr. Tyler started out by explaining how one of the more prominent herbal myths got started and where the truth actually lies.

"Back in 1996," he recalls, "there was a report that Siberian ginseng increased blood levels of digoxin, a cardiac glycoside prescribed for heart disease. This caused quite a stir. Many doctors advised their patients not to take the herb if they were also taking the drug.

"But the researcher who conducted the study never analyzed the herb to make sure it was properly identified. Because of a similarity in their Chinese names, Siberian ginseng (*Eleutherococcus senticosus*), which does not contain any cardiac glycosides, is often mistaken for Chinese silk vine (*Periploca sepium*), which does. So this reported interaction was probably due to a misidentified herb. Yet the cautionary statement about toxic effects of digoxin being increased by Siberian ginseng continues to appear in many stories about herb/drug interactions."

The bottom line? Purchase herbs from well-established manufacturers to avoid misidentified products, Dr. Tyler advises. He also suggests that you avoid bargain herbs. "They're usually not a bargain when it comes to quality."

The Sterility Scare

Another herb myth that Dr. Tyler debunked involved the rumors that St. John's wort might hurt your chances of getting pregnant.

"A recent test-tube study in California showed that when hamster eggs were incubated with high concentrations of St. John's wort (*Hypericum perforatum*), sperm failed to penetrate them," Dr. Tyler says. "Even though the conditions of the experiment couldn't remotely occur in living humans, the press stories all emphasized

An Herbal Watch List

Here's an overview of the most important herb guidelines to observe.

1. Don't take comfrey, coltsfoot, sassafras, germander, or chaparral internally.

2. Don't combine ephedra with caffeine or theophylline. Don't use ephedra alone for more than 7 days.

3. Feverfew, garlic, ginger, and ginkgo do thin the blood, but the clinical relevance is not clear. Stop taking any blood thinners 2 weeks before and after surgery.

4. If you are taking prescription medications, check with your doctor before taking St. John's wort.

5. Avoid combining herbs with drugs that have the same action, especially sedatives, antidepressants, and antianxiety agents.

the antifertility effects of the herb. St. John's wort has been used by humans for thousands of years. If it had any effect on fertility in real life, I'm quite certain we'd have made the connection long ago."

The moral of this story is simple, Dr. Tyler says. Don't assume that test-tube studies hold true for humans.

The Starting Point

Why do herb myths get started?

A big part of the problem, Dr. Tyler believes, is that people don't understand the fundamental differences between herbs and prescription drugs and the impact each has within the human body. "In the United States, most herbs are legally classified as foods," he says. "But from the scientific point of view, they are simply diluted drugs." That's because the active principles in herbs are contained in a complex mixture of inert ingredients such as cellulose, lignin, chlorophyll, starch, and similar materials. Drugs, by contrast, are potent, undiluted chemicals, produced specifically to have a single, specific biological effect.

Because the active ingredients of herbs are so diluted, the effects of herbal medications are usually mild—and so are their side effects. So if an herb causes an allergic response, it is more likely to be a runny nose and watery eyes, not the life-threatening situation that can occur when someone is allergic to a drug such as penicillin.

NATURALFACT

Piperine, a pleasant-tasting alkaloid found in pepper, enhances the availability of drugs and nutrients by increasing their absorption in the gut and slowing the rate at which they are metabolized and neutralized.

Some Scary Numbers

The number of fatal adverse reactions to prescription drugs administered in U.S. hospitals in 1994 was estimated to be 106,000, Dr. Tyler says. A study published in the April 15, 1998, issue of the *Journal of the American Medical Association* estimated that adverse drug reactions ranked as the fifth leading cause of death in the United States in 1994.

How does that statistic compare to herb reactions? Although the U.S. Food and Drug Administration doesn't keep close track of adverse herb reactions, we do have some reliable figures from Canada. Since 1990, Dr. Tyler says, there have been a total of 90 reported adverse effects and one death attributed to herbs in Canada. Even if you multiply these figures by 10 to account for the population difference between the two countries, the number of problems with herbal remedies is just a tiny fraction of the adverse reactions experienced with prescription drugs.

If the incidence of adverse herb reactions is so low, why are problems reported so frequently? The answer is simple, Dr. Tyler believes. Many of the reported adverse effects are based on a single or, at most, a very small number of case reports that get widespread notoriety due to sensationalized reporting. Sometimes the problems aren't even caused by the herb, and even when they are, they're not particularly serious because the mild effects of herbs seldom result in serious toxicity. Remember that many herbal side effects or interactions reported in the literature are not necessarily accurate, because the identity of the herb used was not definitely established.

An Action Plan

So what do you need to know to use herbal medications safely and effectively? Here are Dr. Tyler's suggestions.

Avoid these dangerous herbs. Some herbs are just naturally toxic and shouldn't be used internally at all. These include comfrey (*Symphytum officinale*), coltsfoot (*Tussilago farfara*), sassafras (*Sassafras albidum*), germander (*Teucrium chamaedrys*), and chaparral (*Larrea tridentata*).

Avoid this dangerous combination. Ephedra (*Ephedra sinica*) with theophylline or with caffeine combine to produce an intense stimulation of the central nervous system. The result is increased heart rate, anxiety, and high blood pressure. Avoid this combination, and limit the use of ephedra itself to a maximum of 7 days.

Avoid these herbs if you're taking blood-thinning medications. Feverfew (*Tanacetum parthenium*), garlic (*Allium sativum*), ginger (*Zingiber officinale*), and ginkgo (*Ginkgo biloba*) all have a tendency to prevent platelet aggregation and act as blood thinners, thus prolonging clotting time. The clinical significance of this activity is still unknown. If you are taking other blood-thinning drugs such as warfarin (Coumadin) or even aspirin, consult your

"In general—and this is a very important rule—don't take herbs and drugs that have similar effects."

—Herb expert Varro E. Tyler, Ph.D., Sc.D.

doctor. Also, be sure to stop taking both the herb and the drug for 2 weeks before and after any surgical procedure.

Avoid stimulant herbal laxatives. Stimulant laxatives such as senna (*Cassia senna*) or cascara sagrada (*Rhamnus purshianus*) may cause potassium depletion. Therefore, if you use them, make sure you're getting the recommended Daily Value of potassium (3,500 milligrams) by taking a multivitamin or by eating foods rich in potassium, such as bananas. Otherwise, using stimulant laxatives can cause heart problems. Try not to consume them for more than 3 to 4 consecutive days.

Don't double-team your herbs and prescriptions. "In general—and this is a very important rule—don't take herbs and drugs that have similar effects," Dr. Tyler says. "Don't take St. John's wort with prescription antidepressant drugs such as fluoxetine (Prozac) or paroxetine (Paxil). Don't use kava kava (*Piper methysticum*) with other anxiolytics such as diazepam (Valium) or alprazolam (Xanax). Don't take valerian (*Valeriana officinalis*) with other sedatives such as pentobarbital (Nembutal) or any of the benzodiazepines. Don't take saw palmetto (*Serenoa repens*) with finasteride (Propecia)."

This caution applies to over-the-counter drugs as well as prescription drugs, Dr. Tyler adds. If a drug's effect—or side effect—is the same as an herb's, don't mix them.

THE PREVENTION LIST

Dr. Duke's Picks

James A. Duke, Ph.D., is not only one of America's great herb experts; he's also a very cool guy, a cross between Willie Nelson, Carl Sagan, and Santa Claus.

For nearly 3 decades, Dr. Duke worked as a botanical consultant and ethnobotanist for the USDA, searching the jungles of Central and South America and other remote areas for medicinal plant species. Upon his retirement from that job, he wrote *The Green Pharmacy*, a wonderful combination of scientific knowledge and folk wisdom that has become *the* standard herbal reference book for thousands of people.

At 71, Dr. Duke still plays a mean bluegrass bass and classic guitar and still has a twinkle in his eye. In 1999, he came out with a new book, *Dr. Duke's Essential Herbs*, in which he picks the dozen herbs—a baker's dozen, actually—that he takes most frequently. You'll have to read the book to get the full breadth of his insight on these herbs, but we can give you a sample taste. Here are brief summaries of five of Dr. Duke's absolutely essential herbs.

1. **Garlic *(Allium sativum)*.** This herb is effective for treating high blood pressure, high cholesterol, bacteria, and viruses, plus a few more exotic health problems. "Based on personal experience, I can attest that these pungent cloves do indeed ward off vampire bats."

2. **Ginkgo *(Ginkgo biloba)*.** "The concentrated extract from this tree's leaves improves bloodflow from your brain to your feet, plus strategic points in between."

3. **Celery and celery seed *(Apium graveolens)*.** Dr. Duke recommends this for joint pain, including gout, which he calls "my one big health problem."

"As long as I take my celery seed extract, I no longer need the anti-gout medications that I depended on for most of 2 decades," he says.

4. **Bilberry *(Vaccinium myrtillus)*.** He recommends this for a host of vision disorders, from macular degeneration to glaucoma. "Whatever reason you have for sore eyes, this blueberry relative is quite a sight."

5. **Kava kava *(Piper methysticum)*.** "What coffee is to waking up, kava is to calming down. It's the ideal antidote to an always-on-the-go, stress-filled lifestyle."

Part Seven

Soul Survival

Modern life threatens to crush your spirit in a thousand ways. Don't let it.

Chapter 16

Are You Struggling to Keep Your Balance?

Practice the fine art of going placidly through the noise and the haste

Remember when you were a kid and you used to spin yourself around to make yourself dizzy?

It was fun for a while, but not as a daily habit. Yet that's pretty much what life is like for too many grown-ups today. The competing demands in our lives—family, job, friends, errands, paperwork, and all the rest—pull us in a hundred different directions.

It's easy to lose your balance, and before you know it, you're crashing into things.

The good news is that you don't have to play that game anymore. Keeping in balance is a skill that can be learned.

There are people who have made a personal quest out of living simpler, calmer lives. We asked some of them how to go about it.

The Balancing Act

You may notice an underlying theme running through the simplicity suggestions below. It's time. Quiet time. Fun time. Recharging time. Personal time.

Time has become the ultimate luxury today—and yet it's not a luxury at all. The truth is that if you don't take time for yourself, you risk burnout, which means you'll be less available to do all the things you'd like to do, for yourself and for everyone around you. Given the health risks of stress, if you push yourself hard enough, you might not be available at all.

Time is not only a question of efficiency, though. It's also a question of joy. A philosopher once said that the unexamined life isn't worth living, to which we would add that the over-stuffed, overwhelmed, overstressed life isn't worth living, either.

Here are eight specific steps you can take to restore some sanity to your schedule.

1. Learn to say no. The temptation to take on too much can be hard to resist, but learning to resist it is absolutely crucial. How do you do it? Look at your to-do list and start paring.

For example, think about your commit-ments to the PTA or to your church. Are you on a committee because you really care about it or because someone asked you to join and you didn't know how to say no? If it's the latter, then maybe it's time to bow out. Your goal should be to serve in a way that complements your talents as well as nourishes your soul.

2. Take time to play. When you spend much of your time running from one activity to another, you keep your brain on analytical mode,

Why Am I So Tired All the Time?

Stress has a first cousin: fatigue. By some estimates, fatigue is the reason for one-quarter of all doctor visits. But often, people don't connect their exhaustion to the fact that they're under too much emotional or psychological stress.

constantly solving immediate problems. To relax, you need to balance analytical thinking with playful thinking. You can put yourself in a frame of mind for playful thinking by, well, playing—really playing—with young children.

Make pictures with finger paints, mold clay, blow bubbles. Activities like these not only give you quality time with your children, nieces or nephews, or grandchildren but they also take you to a restful part of your brain where you're more open to creative ideas. Other options if there aren't any young kids around are going on a na-ture hike, stargazing or bird-watching, or singing songs.

You can even incorporate such forms of play into your job. Take a short doodling break during your workday. Go for a quick walk outside and listen to the birds. Close your office door and read a passage from a Dr. Seuss book—out loud. Tell a joke to one of your coworkers.

3. Beat a retreat. A great way to carve out some time just for you is to go on a re-treat. Going to a health spa for a day or two of physical rest and recuperation is one route; going to a retreat house for some spiritual rejuvenation is another. There are hundreds of retreat houses and retreat centers around the country dedicated to just this purpose. Usually, they're located in some peaceful place, with rooms set aside for quiet meditation and prayer and grounds for peaceful walking. Many of them are connected to church denominations, but you usually don't have to be a member of that denomination to spend time there.

Go for a weekend, if you can, or for a day or even a few hours. Don't take your cell phone or anything that resembles work. The idea is to unplug completely—that's why they call it a retreat.

4. Join a group. Small discussion groups provide a shorter-term but more regular opportunity for renewal. The point here is not to add one more draining commitment to your schedule. Rather, the goal is to find a place where there is nourishment and support for *you*. The rule of thumb is simple: If you look forward to going to a small discussion group as an island of refreshing tranquillity in your week and if you leave the group feeling invigorated, that's what you're after.

Find out if your church sponsors a Bible study program or a prayer group, or look in the paper to see if any appropriate self-help groups are available in your community. The range of needs that these groups serve is surprisingly wide-ranging.

5. Ask for help. If you feel overwhelmed, ask for help, says Katherine Brown-

"Taking time for yourself is like taking care of the temple. It's the difference between having a home that's in total disarray and chaos and a home that's in order with fresh air and plenty of light."

—Katherine Brown-Saltzman, R.N.

Saltzman, R.N., clinical nurse specialist at UCLA Medical Center, who helped found the Circle of Care retreat program, which helps nurses and other health-care workers cope with stress. Ask your spouse to share the housework or entertain the kids for the evening. Ask friends to lend you a hand for a few hours. If you belong to a church community, put out the word that you could use a hand.

6. Get your day of rest. Sunday is not necessarily a day off for everybody. In fact, many people are busier cooking and taking care of chores and activities on Sunday than they are during the week. If that's the case with you, make sure to take another day as your personal Sabbath. For most people, it's not the specific day that's important but the idea of setting aside some time for reflection and recuperation. Sleep late. Go for a walk and contemplate the beauty of nature. Lounge around with a good book. Think about truth and beauty and justice and all those other worthwhile subjects for which you usually don't have time.

7. Honor thy vacation. Take the time to which you're entitled. And, if you can, take more than a week at a time. Brown-Saltzman tries to vacation for an entire month. She knows that if she takes just 1 week, she barely gets thoughts of work out of her mind before she has to go back again. Two weeks gives her just enough time to feel rested. But in 4 weeks, she can get into a restful state *and* enjoy quality time with her family. In fact, during that month off, she usually spends some time alone first, before vacationing with her family.

8. Light a candle. Spend some time sitting in front of a lighted candle at the end of every work week, suggests Brown-Saltzman. For centuries, candle lighting has served as a symbolic link with God. It can give you a feeling of peace and help you meditate or pray. Most important, this simple act can help you make the transition from work to rest.

NATURALFACT

A recent study found that women with the most problems at home were four times as likely to have heart attacks as women with the fewest problems at home. High work stress doubled the risk.

A lot of people are stressed out because they're unhappy. If you hate your job, your resilience is compromised. You're more likely to be irritable; you're more likely to be tired. Being in love with your work, on the other hand, *gives* you energy. You feel exhilarated, invigorated, inspired.

Christopher Neck can testify to that. Christopher started his career as an accountant, and he hated every minute of it. It wasn't that accounting was a bad profession. It was just a bad profession for him. He simply found no meaning in crunching numbers all day long.

Eventually, Christopher went back to school for a master's degree in business administration and then

Find Your Calling

Is it naive to think that you might be able to do what you want to for a living? Maybe; maybe not. Certainly, it's worth considering.

his doctorate in management. But one day during his Ph.D. program, while filling in for a professor who was out sick, he discovered his true career: teaching. He felt exhilarated after every class.

Today, Christopher has a Ph.D., and he's an

Lighten Up

Stress hormones can increase the risk of heart attacks, and mirthful laughter can block those hormones. Does it follow then that laughter can reduce the risk of heart attacks?

To find out, a team of researchers from Loma Linda University in California studied 24 patients after heart attacks. The patients all got standard medical care and rehabilitation, but half of them watched a self-chosen humorous video for 30 minutes each day. After 1 year, the humor group had lower blood pressures, lower levels of stress hormones, and fewer arrhythmias than the controls. They required less cardiac medication, and fewer of them had recurrent heart attacks.

A Prayer for Balance

"Lord, I'm doing my best to balance home and work. Sometimes, I feel that there's not enough of me to go around in meeting all the demands. Both my energy and my clock run out before I can get it all done. And when I get really frazzled, the people I love most bear the brunt of my frustration. Help me, Lord, to draw from your strength and peace in ordering my priorities. Help me to use my tongue wisely and always with kindness. Equip me to be the best I can be, both at home and on the job, and bring people into my life who can help me with what I need to do. Thank you for your provision, Lord. Amen."

—Quin Sherrer and Ruthanne Garlock

associate professor of management at Virginia Tech in Blacksburg. He has written two books (*Medicine for the Mind* and *Mastering Self-Leadership*), but it's still teaching that most excites him. "I get a high many times a week that some people never get in their entire lives," says Christopher, who is now also known as Dr. Neck.

He believes that he gets that high because he is following his inner purpose. Preachers and other religious types refer to it as a calling. Others might call it destiny. Whatever your name for it, it's the thing that you do that makes you feel like life is truly worth living.

Finding and following your inner purpose can bring a new clarity to your life. Suddenly, you know which tasks to take on and which to turn down. You commit yourself only to jobs, hobbies, and other pursuits that exhilarate you. You feel at one with yourself, your career, your family, and your acts of charity. In short, your life is filled with a meaningful balance.

So, how do you find your inner purpose? Here are four suggestions that can help lead you toward it.

1. Listen for the "wow." Remember the times in your past when you felt exhilarated by what you were doing? Those are "wow" moments.

The first such moment that Dr. Neck can remember dates back to ninth grade. His speech-class teacher gave him a slip of paper with the word *bowling* written on it and told him to talk about that word for 5 minutes. "At first, I thought, 'Five minutes! That's an eternity!'" he recalls. "I had only bowled once before. But then, as I started talking, the time just flew. When I was done, all I could think was 'Wow!'"

Try to remember your own "wow" moments. What common link runs through them? For Dr. Neck, the link turned out to be talking in front of large groups of people. For you, it might be singing or writing or riding a horse. Once you pinpoint this link, you're well on your way to discovering your true calling.

2. Take risks. If meditating on your majestic moments makes you feel strongly that you are on the wrong career path, gather the courage to forge a new career.

This doesn't mean you have to quit your

current job tomorrow. Instead, take some time to investigate your new direction to get a reasonably good idea of what you're getting into. Tip your toe into a field that attracts you by taking on part-time, freelance, or volunteer jobs. "Do a trial run and see what happens," suggests Dr. Neck. Also, seek out others who have taken similar risks. Get their advice on what to expect.

3. Look for meaning. If switching careers is impossible for you at this point, there are usually ways to make your current job more meaningful. "Not everyone loves their entire job, but within their job they find some way to make a difference," says Dr. Neck. "It's not the company mission that needs to be important. It's *your* mission that's important." For example, you might find satisfaction in bringing in flowers to a coworker or in starting a company recycling program or in setting up a holiday fund-raiser for underprivileged children.

4. Remind yourself. Whenever you feel overloaded, take a new look at your inner purpose. Have you agreed to tasks that deviate from it? Or has your inner purpose simply changed? That can happen as you age.

If you feel confused about what to do, try praying or meditating for direction. It can also help to talk the problem over with trusted advisors, be they friends, relatives, a career counselor, or a spiritual mentor.

HEALING SPOTLIGHT
Barbara Walters

You think *you* have stress? Barbara Walters stars on two national TV shows: *The View*, which she also produces, and *20/20*. Meanwhile, she continues her more or less nonstop pursuit of the big "catch"—an interview with whichever notable or notorious figure happens to be preoccupying the American imagination at any given moment.

How does Walters handle it? More by taking a philosophic approach to life than by following a rigorous exercise or diet plan, she says.

"It's really a matter of common sense," she says. "I tell myself that this too shall pass. No matter what I'm doing, it's probably not going to matter 2 months from now. If I allowed myself to get stressed over every story, I could go crazy. When something is done and I've edited it, I put it aside and don't go back at it again and again, making changes until I drive myself nuts."

Walters's other favorite antistress weapon is her extensive support network. "I have very close friends and a life outside my work, which I think is very important," she says. "You don't want to be so caught up in your career that your whole life is endless stress. You must have family and friends to maintain a vital life."

Chapter 17

Conquer the Clutter That Binds You

Here's how to set yourself free from mountains of suffocating stuff

It's a fundamental law of the universe: Stuff accumulates. It lurks on desktops, in drawers, in closets, in your garage. It consists of magazines, old clothes, toys, newspapers, bills, reports, lawn-care paraphernalia, notices from your child's school, more old clothes, more toys, homework, photographs, receipts, more bills, telephone messages, shopping lists, and much more.

The piles grow higher at night as you sleep. Eventually, they will bury you alive.

Setting yourself free from the suffocating weight of stuff can be a healing exercise. Feeling encumbered is another version of feeling stressed. Clear away some of the obstacles in your life, and you open up psychic pathways. Once more you can breathe.

Attack of the Piles

Piles are a burden on your consciousness because they embody complexity. The higher the stack and the more diverse the elements composing it, the more complexity the pile represents. Don't be surprised if some researcher finds a link between the incidence of heart disease and the number of piles one accumulates.

Piles also represent unfinished business, a lack of completion of one's affairs. Each pile that you encounter registers in your brain, if only for a nanosecond at a time, as more stuff that you haven't handled.

For all these reasons, reducing or eliminating your pile of piles can significantly reduce the stress in your life. Launch your attack with these steps.

Create a master pile. Round up a pen, some file folders, paper clips, rubber bands, and a stapler. Collect your piles of piles and haul them over to a work area like your kitchen table or a desk. Use a wheelbarrow, if necessary. Stack up all of them in front of you in a temporary master pile.

Divide and conquer. Check your watch, and allow yourself 30 minutes or less to dismantle and reallocate this (no doubt humongous) single pile into four smaller stacks: one for stuff that's important, one for stuff that's urgent, one for stuff that's interesting, and one that's destined for the recycling bin (where most items will go). Don't waste a lot of time worrying about which stack to place each item in. Allocate to the best of your ability.

If an item is urgent *and* important, place it near the top of the important pile. If it's simply urgent, place it in the urgent pile. If you are unsure about any particular item, place it at the bottom of the original large stack. Do this no

The Replacement Principle

One of the easiest ways to control the spaces in your life is to use the replacement principle. Here's how it works.

Say you have a collection of 24 videos that you've accumulated over the years. Some are copies of your favorite movies; others are presidential speeches or football games. When you're about to videotape some new program, record over one of the existing 24 tapes.

You can do it. There is at least 1 video, if not 5 or 10, out of those 24 that you can live without, particularly if it's something that you haven't looked at since you taped it 6 years ago. Keeping your collection at 24 videos (or whatever you deem to be a reasonable number) wins back one more space in your life that was previously dominated by the clutter monster.

The replacement principle can be applied to any number of things, especially those small, unimportant, inexpensive items that tend to accumulate quickly. Examples include batteries, office supplies, and cosmetics.

more than once for each item. Next time you go through the original stack, make a decision.

Dispose and rank. In 30 minutes or less, the master pile should be history, and you'll be left with four semineat little piles. Dispose of the recycle pile. Then, rank the items in the remaining piles, with the most important at the top. Downgrade or toss anything you can.

Finally, you'll be left with three small, precisely arranged piles of important, urgent, and interesting stuff. You probably feel better already.

"Achieving simplicity in your life starts with the simple notion that you are in control."

—Jeff Davidson, author of
The Joy of Simple Living

possible volume and gotten them into slim, trim shape, keep related items together. Use a stapler, paper clips, rubber bands, or other organization tools. In general, the more related items you can fasten together, the easier it will be for you to find any particular item that you need.

Do the math. Make an assessment. Starting with the important pile, estimate how long it will take to complete each item. Add all of your estimates together and multiply that number by 1.5. That will account for the fact that most of us habitually underestimate how long tasks will take. Do the same with the other piles.

Start Trimming

As you study and rearrange the three piles of tasks that you have created, remember that you can always get meaner, leaner, and more focused. What else can you chuck? What items can be combined, ignored, delegated, or used for kindling?

The more items you can downgrade to interesting, the further ahead you'll be, simply because you can deal with these items whenever you feel like it.

Once the piles that haunted your household have been reduced to a few carefully sorted stacks, you're ready to attack the tasks that survived the weeding-out process. Here's some advice to help you accomplish that.

Combine, fasten, compile. When you've pared down your piles to the lowest

As the estimated time of completion climbs to alarming heights, you will see how problematic the pile-building habit is. Don't let that intimidate you from proceeding to the attack, however.

Go to work. Tackle items one by one. After you've identified the most important project or task (the one at the top of the important stack), work on it to its completion. If you can't complete it—perhaps it requires help from others—proceed with it as far as you can go. Then place it back in the stack, either on top or wherever you determine it now belongs.

Next, begin on the next-most-important item and proceed as far as you can go.

Mix it up. When you need a break from working on the important tasks, flip to the urgent stack for a change of pace. Review the interesting pile only intermittently, perhaps every couple of days or weeks. It's okay if the interesting pile grows exceedingly thick. Eventually, you'll reclassify or chuck its contents.

Lower the volume. A small stack of material is easier to manage than a monstrous pile. Always strive to keep only the absolute minimum amount of information on any given matter. Strive to reduce the size, weight, and volume of each pile by systematically reducing the size, weight, and volume of each item within each pile.

Rather than keeping a five-page report, for example, retain only the single page that you actually need. Rather than retaining an entire page, clip the paragraph, address and phone number, or key item of information that you actually need, and chuck the rest of the page. Tape the small clipping you've retained to a sheet that contains other relevant tidbits.

Collect when necessary. On rare occasions, let piles accumulate. Do so when the items in a pile are actually related to one another in some significant way. For example, perhaps every-thing in a stack is related to your child's education, or the pile is temporary and you fully intend to organize it within an identified time frame.

Even in these circumstances, be ruthless. Almost any pile can be pared down. Go on a search-and-destroy mission. Look for duplicate information and chuck the excess. Reexamine everything with this question in mind: What am I continuing to retain that adds unnecessary complexity?

Perhaps you are already familiar with the issue an item represents and you don't need to retain printed information relating to it. From that viewpoint, you may be able to chuck a third or more of the documents remaining in your already-stripped-down pile.

Use keywords. If you are keeping items in your pile that merely serve as reminders to you, maybe a list of keywords would work better instead. Such simple words and phrases written on a single slip of paper can substitute for pages and pages of items. The keywords used to devise the writing of this chapter, for

Only the Best

Whether you're into souvenir plates or beer steins, collectibles can all too easily take over life, if you let them. Free yourself by choosing an all-star team.

Let's say you're a coin collector whose collection has gotten unduly large. What if you were to focus on the most rare, most valuable, most beautiful, or most pleasing items in your collection—the best of the best? Your goal is to keep the truly worthwhile items. The rest can be sold, traded, given away, or stored.

The next step is to sort through the items you choose to display. Box up the excess and live without it in your visual field for several months. You'll breathe easier, having reclaimed the open spaces in your home. After several months, revisit your boxed-up knickknacks and critically examine each item. If you can't bear to part with it, return it to the land of the living, or keep it stored. Otherwise, sell it, trade it, or give it away.

HEALING SPOTLIGHT
Tracey Ullman

Count comedic actress Tracey Ullman among those who long for less stuff and more simplicity. "I'd like my life to be quieter," she told *Ladies' Home Journal*. "My husband has this TV with this satellite thing moving on the roof. The whole house is buzzing, and I wish we could just light a candle and sit around and talk."

example, included "piles," "trimming," and "holding bins."

Arrange for access. If you've slimmed down several piles, try arranging them in a cascading or stair-step manner down one side of your desk or table. Each would have the top inch visible before being covered by the next. This kind of arrangement allows you to draw upon any one of the piles while keeping the others in order.

An even better solution in many cases is to get the piles out of sight. You don't have to spread your piles out on your desktop to know where they are. Use file cabinets, desk drawers, and so forth to store things where they're easily retrievable. Use a visible arrangement of your piles on a desktop only when you intend to deal with the piles sooner rather than later.

Taming Big Stuff

You don't have to be rich to find yourself with more possessions than you know what to do with. In any household today, particularly one with kids, you're likely to have more stuff in more rooms than you could have witnessed at any other time in history.

Is it possible to tame this tidal wave of stuff? Yes, but it takes some concentrated effort.

A fundamental step in the right direction is to start using holding bins. In its simplest form, a holding bin can be a file that is simply labeled "Review these items on January 1." Or a holding bin can be a shoe box, a plastic bag, a packing box, or a shipping crate. Whether large or small, thin or voluminous, holding bins afford you the opportunity to park items for later review.

Here are some tips that can help you get the most out of this superb tool for stuff management.

Let a folder hold it. Anytime you receive printed information that you suspect may be worth retaining but cannot determine where it ought to go, the answer is clear: Put it in a holding bin. In this case, the holding bin could actually be a file folder with a creative label such as "Monthly review," "Not pressing," or "Read on retirement." There is a tremendous measure of freedom to be gained by stashing away the tons of stuff you would otherwise not know what to do with but sense that you cannot chuck.

Box it up. Clothing may be second only to paper as the most suffocating possession in the average person's life, and holding bins can be especially important in keeping old clothing in some semblance of order. If you haven't worn something in at least a year or two, put it in a box to free up your dresser drawers and closets. Close the box and label it as you see fit. You might write "Out of fashion?" "Open after I've dropped 10 pounds," or "Examine contents after June 1." The mere act of freeing up the space in your dresser drawers and closets yields a feeling of simplicity and enables you to more easily find and wear current clothing.

Disperse, discard, decide. When you do get around to reviewing the contents of the clothes you've boxed, you have several options. You can return them to your wardrobe, and this time actually wear them; continue to keep them boxed, which guarantees that you'll have to go through this process again (ugh); rip them to shreds and use them as rags; or give them away (usually the best choice).

Rate by season. There's no need to have all of your clothes crammed into your closets all year long. If spring is coming, pack away all of your winter clothes. With the first frost, it's a safe bet that you can stow all of your summer clothes.

This is also true of garden utensils, athletic equipment, toys, and anything else that you only use during particular seasons. The hour or so that it takes to put your possessions into seasonal storage is more than offset by the freed-up space and the sense of simplicity you gain thereafter.

‖ Creating Clearings in Your Life

Magical and mystical things begin to occur as you begin to clear out the vast accumulations of stuff that have been cluttering your home, car, and office. You gain a feeling of space, ease, and control. This is the blessing of simplicity.

What do you do with the space you've created? What you *don't* do is fill it up again with more things that will clutter and complicate your life all over again. Remember: "Stuff accumulates" is a fundamental law of the universe. Thus, all the spaces you've so laboriously created in your life will automatically and inevitably fill up again unless you exercise discipline.

Here are some steps you can take to preserve that precious resource of simplicity.

Leave some blanks. Where is it written that every square yard of floor space has to be covered or that every wall has to have something in front of it? One obvious place to keep clear is in front of windows. Others are near doorways and entrances. You can get used to having less in each room, just as you were once used to having your rooms filled.

Stop clutter at the border. Keep your holdings simple by evaluating and reevaluating every new item that crosses your threshold. Whether it's paper and documents, knickknacks, kitchen utensils, clothing, or larger items like furniture, be vigilant about what you acquire. By keeping watch over what enters your personal kingdom, you avoid having to initiate these possession-purging exercises.

Talk to yourself. Each time you encounter a new item, ask yourself questions like: What impact will this have on my life? Will this make a difference in my life? Do I need to have this at all? Is this easily retrievable if I decide I need it in the future? Are there any consequences of not retaining it? Will this make things simpler for me?

With vigilance, you can keep clutter from re-invading your home. Eventually, peaceful simplicity will become a way of life.

Don't worry. You'll get used to it.

Chapter 18

Are You a Dragon Lady or a Nice Girl?

Women get angry, but they have their own ways of expressing it

I n the drama of human emotions, anger occupies a leading role. That's normal. Unfortunately, it can also be extremely unhealthy. If it's not handled correctly, anger can act as a poison to your system, vastly increasing your chances of a heart attack (both immediately and in the long run) and weakening your immune system. Anger can also set you up for all sorts of unhealthy behaviors, from reckless driving to overeating.

Social convention has made anger a difficult and confusing issue for women. Many women feel guilty about being angry and confused about their anger's true source. Most of all, women struggle with how to express anger appropriately.

If anger is a problem for you, stay cool. We can help.

The Misunderstood Emotion

Anger is a murky emotion that pretends to be things it isn't. Perhaps that's why there are so many myths surrounding it. For example:

Myth: When you're angry, you should let it all out by pounding a pillow or honestly unloading on the source of your upset.

Fact: Research shows that venting angry feelings in an aggressive way can actually increase anger.

Myth: Men get angry more than women do—and *ladies* don't get angry at all.

Fact: "That's part of the old sugar-and-spice stereotype of women," says Carol Tavris, Ph.D., a social psychologist in Los Angeles and author of *Anger: The Misunderstood Emotion.* In fact, research shows that women's anger is as frequent and as intense as men's.

Women do tend to express anger differently than men do. For instance, men are more likely to get angry in public and to express anger aggressively.

But just because they're quieter with their anger doesn't mean women don't realize they're upset. "Women do know when they're angry. They told us about it," says Sandra Thomas, Ph.D., principal investigator of the Women's Anger Study, the first large-scale, comprehensive study of everyday anger in women's lives.

It's also a myth to say that anger, in and of itself, is unhealthy. What's unhealthy is hostile, aggressive behavior and suppressed anger. Normal, everyday anger can actually be an extremely helpful signal, pointing the way toward constructive problem solving in your relationships and, ultimately, mutual respect.

Holy Anger

If anger is a sin, then God is a sinner. So says the Reverend Gary J. Oliver, Ph.D., executive director of the Center for Marriage and Family Studies at John Brown University in Siloam Springs, Arkansas.

He points out that of the 455 references to anger in the Old Testament, 375 of them refer to the anger of God.

Anatomy of Anger

To chip away at the anger myths, we need to understand what anger actually is and what it is not.

Anger is a strong feeling of emotional distress in response to a threat, insult, or injustice, according to Dr. Tavris. Anger, she says, is an emphatic message: Pay attention to me. I don't like what you are doing. Restore my pride. You're in my way. Danger. Give me justice.

By contrast, anger is not hostility, which can be more accurately described as the enduring belief that the world is out to do you wrong. Hostility is more pervasive and lasts longer than anger. Nor is anger frustration, which is the frequent response to everyday annoyances, from traffic jams to busy signals. "Unlike anger, frustration doesn't threaten our integrity or values," says Dr. Thomas.

Anger is also not aggression. The former is a feeling, says Dr. Tavris, while the latter is the expression of that feeling.

There's no shortage of reasons to get hopping, boiling mad. A spouse who doesn't treat you right. Kids who refuse to do what you ask them to do. Lazy coworkers. An unscrupulous boss. Relatives of every shape, size, and variety.

As maddening as all those things can be, the true source of our anger is usually something deeper, Dr. Thomas says. Surface irritations can push your buttons, but they are not the buttons themselves.

Here is a list of core issues that are most likely to stimulate anger.

Powerlessness. Feeling unable to get someone or something to change, or to make yourself heard, triggers anger more frequently than anything else, Dr. Thomas says.

Injustice. Being treated unfairly or disrespectfully also ranks high on the list of anger's greatest hits. "The women in our study talked about people lying to or betraying them," says Dr. Thomas. "They were also angry on behalf of others who were treated unjustly. For example, they might be furious at a teacher who seems to have it in for their child."

Irresponsibility. People often get angry when we feel others don't pull their weight at home or at work. This can range from the spouse who blithely leaves his underwear on the bathroom floor to the coworker who takes 3-hour

"When I get mad at (my partner), I just clam up. Sometimes I'm so angry that I enjoy watching him squirm as he tries to figure out what's wrong."

—Christine, a respondent in the Women's Anger Study

lunch breaks, leaving more for us to do.

Stress. Anger is a major by-product of stress. Quite simply, the more stressed we get, the more we tend to explode or lash out.

Two Angry Women

Life gives women just as many reasons to get angry as it does men, but somehow women aren't as likely to express their anger. Why is that?

Because society doesn't approve of it, according to Harriet Lerner, Ph.D., clinical psychologist and psychotherapist at the Menninger Clinic in Topeka, Kansas, and author of *The Dance of Anger*. That leaves women with two basic options, one socially acceptable, one not. Call them the Nice Girl and the Dragon Lady.

Rather than express her anger, the Nice Girl gives in, goes along, and accommodates. She avoids conflict at all costs. "Nice Girls never say, 'This is what I believe. This is how I see it,'" Dr. Lerner says.

Why do Nice Girls find anger so threatening? Speaking up, in anger or otherwise, might be disruptive, which conflicts with the social roles that Nice Girls have traditionally occupied, among them cook, cleaner, comforter, and keeper of harmony.

Another reason why Nice Girls hold their

anger is that they've repressed it for so long that they fear that letting it out might unleash a terrible destructive force. "I've heard women say, 'If I were ever to get really angry, we'd all burst into flame,'" says Deborah Cox, Ph.D., anger researcher at Southwest Missouri State University in Springfield.

Unfortunately, anger that isn't expressed consciously and directly has a way of coming out anyway—unconsciously and indirectly. Worse, it

When Anger Turns Violent

Is male anger more dangerous than female anger?

Supposedly, that's true. Women's nurturing instincts, we are told, make them all but incapable of extreme violence.

Not so, says Patricia L. Kirby, Ph.D., a former psychological profiler in the FBI's Behavioral Sciences Unit who is now assistant professor of sociology and criminology at the College of Notre Dame of Maryland in Baltimore. "It's true that men are more than twice as likely to commit acts of extreme violence than women are," she says. "But I've found that the women who work with men in armed robberies or team killings are every bit as violent."

Dr. Kirby has found that the personal backgrounds of extremely violent men and women are "virtually identical." For example, male and female serial killers tend to be similar in intelligence, personal achievement, and criminal motivation. Both also tend to have been physically, emotionally, or sexually abused as children.

Male and female serial killers do show some differences. "There's no doubt that serial killers are angry," Dr. Kirby says. "Often, murder is a manifestation of extreme anger. What's interesting is that many extremely violent women—like many normal women—turned their anger on themselves before they turned it on others. Many have attempted suicide, which is the extreme of turning anger inward. Violent men have not."

The bottom line is that women do not appear, in Dr. Kirby's view, to be any more or less genetically predisposed toward violence than men. What's more likely, she feels, is that violent people of either sex have something faulty in their genetic wiring.

can emerge in harmful ways, often hurting the women themselves. Drugs, alcohol, cigarettes, and food can all be used to temporarily mask the emotional arousal that anger causes, Dr. Thomas says.

But even Nice Girls eventually explode, says Christine Padesky, Ph.D., founder and director of the Center for Cognitive Therapy in Newport Beach, California, and coauthor of *Mind over Mood.* "It's common for a woman to be overaccommodating and hold in a simmering resentment," she says. "Eventually, given enough resentment or stress or fatigue, she'll explode, usually over something fairly minor. And because her anger is so extreme relative to the situation, it fuels her guilt about getting angry and her reluctance to be angry. She thinks, 'Look what anger does. It turns me into a monster.'"

"I scream, rant, rave, throw things, and drive my car too fast! When I get mad, I say nasty things to my husband and my sister-in-law, and I all too often yell at my kids when I'm not even angry at them."

—Marcia, a respondent in the Women's Anger Study

complain to their partners, their kids, their colleagues, not to mention salesclerks and waiters. An annoyance is enough to start a tirade; significant problems can generate a nuclear firestorm.

Ironically, in the end, the Dragon Lady's tirade produces exactly the same result as the Nice Girl's silence, Dr. Lerner says. The anger remains unheard because people who find themselves in the path of an angry outburst tend to turn away, not listen; the issues that provoked it go unresolved.

Dragon Ladies may also use anger to cover up other, more threatening feelings, such as sadness or fear. Such emotions evoke feelings of vulnerability, while anger evokes a sense of power. Thus, anger becomes a crutch, used to keep uncomfortable feelings at bay. But there are consequences attached to its use. Relationships can be damaged, jobs or promotions can be lost, and guilt, depression, and self-loathing can sink in.

Enter the Dragon Lady

While Nice Girls reveal their anger only rarely, after it has built up over a significant period of time, Dragon Ladies explode as a matter of course. They threaten, shout, swear, bitch, and

In the next chapter, we'll take a look at how you (whether you're a Dragon Lady or a Nice Girl) can begin to confront your own anger—not so you can tame it but so you can work with it and make it work *for* you.

Chapter 19

Take Your Anger Where It Belongs

Once you understand your anger, you can make it work for you

Angry people are often unaware of how angry they really are, just as they're often unaware of who is really making them angry. They'd also be surprised, in many cases, about whom their anger is hurting.

Because Nice Girls and Dragon Ladies express their anger in different ways, it affects their relationships differently. Nice Girls tend to withdraw and retaliate with passive-aggressive behaviors, which include everything from withholding sex to dragging their feet on projects at work.

Dragon Ladies tend to focus all their energy on a target who may or may not be the genuine cause of their anger. This is where innocent bystanders can be caught in the line of fire.

Taking Charge of Anger

Getting a handle on your anger is extremely important, both for your own sake and for the sake of those around you.

How do you do that? You must become conscious of it, understand it, and learn to manage it appropriately.

Dissecting your anger in such a direct and comprehensive manner may sound a little intimidating, especially for Nice Girls, who tend to believe that their anger is so dangerous that it must remain hidden at all costs.

Have no fear, says Deborah Cox, Ph.D., anger researcher at Southwest Missouri State University in Springfield. When women allow themselves to fully and honestly feel their anger, *good* things happen. "All that buried anger becomes a catalyst for positive change and growth," she says.

The first step in changing your behavior is to identify the true source of your angry feelings, says Sandra Thomas, Ph.D., principal investigator of the Women's Anger Study, the first large-scale, comprehensive study of everyday anger in women's lives. Toward that end, she recommends keeping an anger journal, which is a detailed log of incidents that incite your wrath. "By recording your anger incidents as they occur," Dr. Thomas says, "you will be able to identify the repetitive themes and patterns in your anger behavior."

To start an anger journal, simply buy an inexpensive notebook that is small enough to carry with you. Commit yourself to write in your journal every day for at least a month. The best time to make an entry is when the incident that provoked your anger is still fresh in your mind

but *after* you've calmed down enough to think about it logically. The longer you keep your journal, the more adept you'll become at recognizing your anger "style" and the situations that fuel your anger, Dr. Thomas says. (See "Evidence of Anger" for more suggestions on keeping an anger journal.)

Once you've identified what provokes your anger, you can then proceed to the nitty-gritty: incorporating into your life practical strategies to help you use your anger productively. Not surprisingly, different strategies are recommended for Nice Girls and Dragon Ladies.

An Assertive Approach

Nice Girls who wish to express their anger in a positive way need to learn to communicate two things, says Christine Padesky, Ph.D., founder and director of the Center for Cognitive Therapy in Newport Beach, California, and coauthor of *Mind over Mood*: (1) what they're angry about and (2) what they want to change in order to not be angry.

In other words, they need to become more assertive.

Here are nine steps that together add up to a crash course in assertiveness.

1. Listen to your body. Nice Girls may not even be aware that they're angry, says Dr. Padesky. But your body has ways of telling you, if you listen. "Perhaps you become quieter or your muscles get tense or you get a headache or stomachache," she says. "While you may not have linked these physical reactions to anger, they may be a signal that something about a situation is disturbing you."

Evidence of Anger

Keeping an anger journal is an excellent way to uncover the true sources of your anger, which is a first step in breaking free of it.

Here's a step-by-step strategy for keeping track of what bugs you, provided by Sandra Thomas, Ph.D., principal investigator of the Women's Anger Study.

1. Describe who or what provoked your anger. Be sure to include whether the perpetrator was male or female and whether they're above or below you in status.

2. Describe your first reaction. Was it "There he goes again!" or "Her condescending attitude drives me nuts!" or even "What a bitch!"

3. Describe the tactics you used to handle your anger. Did you smile and accommodate, or yell, kick the dog, or throw a potted plant? Did you pout and sulk, or employ a lot of eye rolling or sarcastic remarks? Did you talk about your anger with your partner or a close friend, or keep it to yourself?

4. Think about the physical sensations or reactions that accompanied your anger. Did you cry? Get a stomachache or headache? Breathe more rapidly, get a lump in your throat, experience shakiness? Reach for a cigarette, a doughnut, or a glass of wine?

5. Record how long you stayed angry. Fifteen minutes? Three hours? All day? Longer?

6. Describe how you felt when the incident was over. Did you feel guilty, wiped out, depressed? Or proud of yourself?

7. Finally, analyze your anger. What was it that really set you off? What was most threatening or hurtful about the incident?

2. Listen to your thoughts. Consciously identify thoughts that could be making you hold in your anger. This self-talk often goes something like this: "If I get angry at this person, it will hurt or upset them" or "Maybe I'm overreacting. I'll just let it go."

"Women feel extra responsible for making relationships go smoothly," says Dr. Padesky. "Or you may be used to seeing other people's feelings as more valid than your own." In either case, the point is to learn to identify and express how *you* feel.

3. Learn another language. Learn "I-language," that is. Using "I-messages" when you're angry can help you focus your anger and state your feelings in a clear, straightforward way, says Dr. Padesky. To give an I-message, use this simple fill-in-the-blanks template.

- "When you do . . ." (describe the behavior) .
- "It makes me feel . . ." (describe how the behavior affects you)
- "I want . . ."

For example, you might say to your mother-in-law, "When you criticize my cooking, it makes me feel hurt and unappreciated. I want you to stop."

Or link how you feel with a specific behavior in the other person. For example, you might say, "I felt hurt when you said the casserole was too salty" rather than "You were rude."

4. Be persistent. Say your mother-in-law fails to respond to your I-message. Give it again, over and over, if need be. Repeat yourself until the other person runs out of steam—or excuses.

In the Women's Anger Study, stress was found to be the most frequent and powerful predictor of female wrath.

5. Use body language. "Our posture makes a tremendous difference in how we feel," says Dr. Padesky. So when you confront the target of your anger, look them directly in the eye, keep your body open and relaxed (no shuffling of feet or twisting of hair), and speak in a strong, clear voice.

To sample the power of body language, try this exercise, suggests Dr. Padesky. First, slump in a chair, look at the ground, and say softly, "No, I don't want that." Then, sit straight and tall and say in a clear, strong voice, "No, I don't want that" while looking directly at a lamp or some other object.

Feel the difference?

6. Start small. Before you take on your spouse or boss, practice assertive behavior in low-risk relationships.

"If you have anger issues with your partner, he may not be the person you want to confront first, particularly if you tend to get into tumultuous arguments," says Dr. Padesky. Instead, start with low-risk encounters and relationships: store clerks, bank tellers, bag boys at the grocery store. This is not a license to abuse service people, only an encouragement to practice telling them, clearly and straightforwardly, what you think and what you need.

When assertive behavior becomes more natural and you're feeling more confident, you can graduate to a more high-stakes relationship.

7. Enlist support. Before you start asserting yourself all over the place, let family and friends know that your behavior is going to change. "You might call your family together and say, 'I have a hard time saying no and expressing my anger, but I'm going to change that. So when I get angry or say no, please don't take it personally. I'm changing my behavior for me,'" says Dr. Padesky. "This message can help make people your allies."

8. Practice, practice, practice. In the car or shower, or in front of a mirror, stage a mental dress rehearsal of exactly how you'll confront an anger-provoking person or situation. "If I know I'm likely to get angry or be too much of a doormat in a certain situation, I rehearse different approaches and responses," says Dr. Padesky.

You might also come up with two or three lines that will buy you time in an anger-provoking situation. Useful stock lines include "Let me think about this for a few minutes and get back to you" or the time-honored, "Excuse me; I need to visit the ladies' room." Use the time you buy with such lines to figure out how you want to respond.

9. Stick to your guns. If you've been picking your mate's underwear off the bathroom floor for the past 15 years, his jaw may drop when you tell him that it makes you angry and that, from now on, you want him to put them in the hamper. "People will try to make you go back to the meek little mouse that you were," says Dr. Thomas. "They may say things like 'What's gotten into you?' or 'You're being a real bitch about this!'"

That's not exactly the understanding response you might have hoped to get. Nonetheless, don't back down, says Dr. Thomas. Tell whomever it is you're dealing with that your request is not unreasonable. Then, keep repeating your request for a change in their behavior for as long as it takes him or her to get it.

Taming Dragons

You Dragon Ladies, as we've explained, have no trouble letting your anger out. In fact, your tendency to let your anger out *is* the trouble.

From Anger to Action

Want an example of effective anger? Consider Millie Webb.

In 1971, a collision with a drunk driver in Franklin, Tennessee, killed Webb's 4-year-old son and 19-month-old nephew. Webb's husband was horribly burned, as was Webb herself. Worse, she was 7 months pregnant at the time. Her daughter was born premature and permanently blind.

Webb took many years to recover from her injuries, but slowly her body and her mind healed. Fourteen years after the crash, she turned her grief and anger into action. She joined Mothers against Drunk Driving (MADD), which she now leads as president.

To Webb, anger is a normal, natural response to tragedy—not just car accidents, but death, divorce, and other life-altering traumas. But she also believes that anger without action is useless. That is why she takes MADD's motto, "Curse it, then reverse it," for her own.

"When a tragedy happens, we can choose to become bitter or better," she says. "I can't change what happened to me. But I can do everything in my power to keep it from happening to someone else."

If you can learn to moderate the explosiveness of your outbursts, you'll increase the odds that your needs will be heard and met. Here are seven basic anger-management techniques that can help.

1. Don't react—yet. Remember the old adage "Don't just stand there; do something"? Harriet Lerner, Ph.D., clinical psychologist and psychotherapist at the Menninger Clinic in Topeka, Kansas, and author of *The Dance of Anger*, advises Dragon Ladies to reverse it: "Don't just do something; stand there."

The trick is to resist the impulse to react immediately. "Not reacting gives you time to calm down and think about what the real issue is and the best way to approach the problem," Dr. Lerner says. To "stand there" might mean to take a bathroom break in a meeting when you feel yourself about to blow or to tell your partner, "I need some time to sort out my thoughts. Let's set up another time to talk about this."

2. Compose an "anger mantra." Choose a word or phrase to repeat to yourself when your anger threatens to explode. A word or phrase such as *chill* or *think* or *calm down* can become a sort of instant mental cue to turn down the volume on your anger, says Dr. Padesky. Your anger mantra will be more effective, she adds, if you slowly repeat it in rhythm with your breathing.

3. Get rid of the "you." Dragon Ladies tend to use the word *you* a lot, such as "You lazy SOB!" or "You insensitive lout!" Instead, use I-language (see "Learn another language" under "An Assertive Approach," above)

> **NATURAL**FACT
>
> Women who test high for hostility also tend to eat more fat and cholesterol than women who don't test high.

and start your message with "I think," "I feel," or "I want."

"A true I-statement conveys how you feel without criticizing another person or holding that person responsible for your feelings or reactions," says Dr. Lerner. Your mother, for example, may react quite differently if you say, "I feel angry when you tell me how I should raise my child. I want you to stop" rather than "Mind your own business, you meddling control freak!"

4. Make like Spock. Not the baby doctor but the pointy-eared stoic on *Star Trek*. Cold, hard logic is the enemy of anger, says Dr. Lerner. Thinking rationally helps you focus on solving the problem rather than on giving vent to your intense emotions.

To help you think logically about an anger-provoking situation, force yourself to answer the following questions.

- What is it about this situation that's making me angry?
- What is the real issue here?
- What do I want to accomplish?
- What, specifically, do I want to change?

5. Take a Zen-minute break. Anger pumps up your system in all sorts of damaging ways, and 10 minutes' worth of deep breathing can calm it back down. This is the modern version of counting to 10, and it works.

Dr. Thomas suggests this breathing technique: Inhale slowly and deeply while counting, "One, two, three, four." Then, exhale on the same count. Let your body go limp and hollow.

Allow each breath to fill the hollowness with relaxation. Continue inhaling and exhaling for 10 minutes.

If it will help, try seeing your breath as a soft, relaxing color that gently floods your being, washing away the tension and stress.

6. Look in a mirror. "Typically, we get angry at people over things that we have probably done ourselves," says Dr. Padesky. (Perhaps scooting into that parking space when it was clearly the other driver's spot sounds familiar?) Before you lose it, ask yourself if you've ever done to someone else what this person is doing to you. If the answer is yes, you may decide that your "adversary" isn't deliberately being unfair or insensitive.

7. Get physical. Taking a 10- to 15-minute walk can help you shed the physical tension that anger often creates, says Dr. Thomas. At work, take a quick trip around the block or up and down a flight of stairs. At home, try cleaning out that closet you've been meaning to straighten up for months, or let your rug have it with the vacuum.

Chapter 20

Has Stress Stolen Your Sex Life?

Take steps to keep passion burning between you and your mate

In the hurricane of daily life, great sex should be the eye of the storm, the calm in which a couple can draw comfort and satisfaction from each other. But all too often, when stress mounts, sex is the first thing to go. In these harried times, if you ask people, "When was the last time you made love?" many will have to think for a few minutes before they can come up with an answer.

What's more, sex itself can become a source of stress. Simply finding the time and energy is part of the problem. Stress effects the sex drives of men and women differently too. In general, guys consider sex a source of relief from stress, while women's passions tend to cool when they're stressed.

Don't despair. Sex can survive stress, if you know the right moves to make.

Stress Squared

It's true what they've always said: The most important sex organ is the brain. This causes a problem when you live the sort of stressful life that so many people live today.

Emotional stress unbalances brain chemicals that govern sexual desire and arousal, says Mona Lisa Schulz, M.D., Ph.D., a neuropsychiatrist in Yarmouth, Maine. "You need a certain amount of 'juice' in your brain to want sex," she says.

That "juice" comes from brain chemicals collectively known as neuropeptides. These include norepinephrine, epinephrine, dopamine, and oxytocin. "Sex requires all of your neurochemistry to be balanced," Dr. Schulz says. "Stress can unhinge any of the four phases of the sexual-response cycle—appetite, arousal, orgasm, or resolution—causing neuropeptide imbalances at each phase."

Stress affects a woman's sexual response early in the cycle, dampening appetite and arousal, says Nancy Gambescia, Ph.D., a marriage and family therapist in Bryn Mawr, Pennsylvania, who teaches at the Penn Council for Relationships in Philadelphia. As for reaching orgasm, forget it: Stress hijacks a woman's brain, often making her unable to concentrate on physical pleasure.

Women Need Sugar; Men Need Sex

He's stressed; he reaches for you. You're stressed; you reach for the chocolate bar on your nightstand.

Why do women tend to soothe stress with food, while men seek release with sex? The answer may lie within a tiny portion of the brain called the hypothalamus, says neuropsychiatrist Mona Lisa Schulz, M.D., Ph.D.

The hypothalamus is a part of the limbic system, a group of brain structures that govern food, fighting, fear—and sex. In most women, the part of the hypothalamus that rules sexual desire is extremely close to the part that controls feeding, says Dr. Schulz. In most men's brains, these two portions of the hypothalamus are farther apart.

That doesn't mean that some women don't get lusty when they're under stress or that anxious men don't turn to jelly doughnuts. We all have unique ways of soothing ourselves, says Dr. Schulz. "But there's no question that more women than men eat under stress, and there are neuroanatomical differences in how men and women are programmed for sex—at least, in the hypothalamus."

This disinterest in sex might not be a problem if both partners were content to kiss, hug, and go to sleep. All too often, it doesn't work out that way, though, for the simple reason that men often see sex as a stress reliever. That's a dilemma when the woman is too tense for sex, says certified sex therapist Judith L. Silverstein, Ph.D., professor of psychology at Harvard Medical School, since her partner may take her disinterest as a personal rejection. Still, feeling pressured to relieve his tension with a session of sexual aerobics when she's not in the mood is just as stressful on the woman.

Sometimes, stress is a sexual turnoff for men, just as it is for women. Typically, the impact is most dramatic during the arousal phase, which means men have trouble getting or keeping erections. This can trigger performance anxiety, which equals more stress and more erection problems, Dr. Gambescia says.

The longer stress keeps a couple from connecting sexually, the more damage it can cause in a relationship, says Allen Elkin, Ph.D., a certified sex therapist and author of *Stress Management for Dummies*. Just as a man's performance anxiety is a form of stress that creates more stress and more performance anxiety, so, too, does a lack of intimacy between partners build on itself. The level of stress between a couple can build, which can increase the lack of intimacy, and so on.

It sounds grim and often is, but there are solutions.

NATURAL FACT

An international survey found that Americans were more satisfied with their sex lives than citizens of most countries. Only Brazilians and Venezuelans were happier.

Short-Circuit Stress

When we're under stress, it's easy to neglect our health. But the way we treat our bodies can either ease stress or aggravate it. So if you're in a stress-induced sexual slump, try these strategies first.

Ease up on caffeine. Avoid consuming large amounts of coffee, tea, cola, and other caffeinated substances. A stimulant, caffeine may reduce your brain's stores of norepinephrine and epinephrine, says Dr. Schulz. And it may boost your levels of cortisol, a hormone that increases your body's stress response.

Hold the liquor. Limit your intake to one glass of wine before you make love, or avoid drinking completely. Alcohol shunts blood to the vital organs and away from your genitals.

Sweat out tension. Exercise boosts desire by boosting endorphins, hormones that produce sensations of euphoria. "Taking a brisk walk together a few times a week might facilitate closeness and also relieve some of the stress," says Dr. Silverstein.

Check your medications. If you've been stressed out, your doctor may have prescribed an antidepressant or other medication. But some prescription drugs, including antidepressants and blood pressure drugs, can affect arousal, lubrication, and orgasm, according to Dr. Schulz.

Ask your doctor if any of the medications you're taking have sexual side effects. If they do,

Too Old for Sex?

When it comes to sex and aging, studies show that sexual satisfaction depends more on our beliefs about sex than on our bodies' physical changes. Here are three common myths about aging and sexuality. Don't buy into them.

Myth #1: The older we get, the less important sex becomes. "Sexuality is from birth to death," says Wendy Kyman, Ph.D., a certified sex therapist and assistant professor of health education at Baruch College in New York City. "Broaden your definition of sexuality away from just intercourse. Think of it as holding, kissing, touching, intimacy, and sharing, in addition to intercourse."

Myth #2: If we can't have intercourse, we're not having sex. Intercourse is wonderful, but so are oral sex, mutual masturbation, kissing, and holding hands, says Dr. Kyman. It helps to broaden your definition of what constitutes sex, especially if intercourse is a problem for you and your partner for any reason.

Myth #3: It's unseemly for older people to make love. This is the most damaging myth of all. "We never outgrow our need for love and affection," says Dr. Kyman. "Sex is an expression of intimacy between two people who love and care for each other, regardless of their ages."

---

ask him or her if you could take an alternative medication that does not have the sexual side effects, Dr. Schulz advises.

For Mutual Enjoyment

With the right approach, sex can be an antidote to stress—for women as well as men, Dr. Elkin says. So if your libido has been hijacked by stress, try these practical strategies to help liberate it.

Provide adequate ventilation. If you know that your partner is under stress, be a sounding board while he vents. Resist the temptation to offer advice; simply listen sympathetically.

Schedule sex dates. Planning for romance can actually stir up some anticipatory excitement, says Dr. Elkin. You may begin to look forward to these times and prepare for them like your high school self would have prepared for a Saturday night date.

Wake up smiling. Most of us are in the habit of making love at night. But biologically, that may not be the best time. You may be too wiped out by the demands of the day to be able to give or receive pleasure, says Dr. Elkin.

The solution is daytime sex. Try setting your alarm clock a bit earlier in the morning and ease into the day with a roll in the hay. Or indulge in some afternoon delight, if you can fit it into your schedules.

Use the magic touch. "Touching is a form of physical intimacy that promotes psychological intimacy," explains Dr. Elkin. So give each other a lingering hug, a loving caress, a back massage. Or take a warm bath together. You may find that the tension melts away and you're in the mood after all.

"If you're willing to just cuddle, you may find that it's a transition to sex," says Dr. Silver-

NATURALFACT

One study found that having sex once or twice a week boosts a person's immunity. Having more sex than that was said to lower immunity.

stein. Even if it doesn't lead to sexual intercourse, cuddling is nice in and of itself, she adds.

Say yes. If stress has seriously curtailed your lovemaking and you know your partner is frustrated, consider making love anyway—for the relationship. "Just jump in and see what happens," says Dr. Elkin. You may be glad you did. Of course, never make love if doing so would make you resent your partner or if you would feel used, he stresses. This option works only if you give sex wholeheartedly, as a gift.

THE PREVENTION LIST

Stress Busters

Stress is so ubiquitous these days that you can get stressed out by simply reading about how to get rid of stress. That's why these suggestions are short.

We scoured a library of health books to find some quick, effective, and out-of-the-ordinary stress-busting techniques. Here are our five favorites.

1. **Lie down for 5 minutes.** Imagine that your body weighs 600 pounds. Feel that weight press into the floor. The more you allow your body to plaster itself to the floor, the more stress will sink away. In yoga, they call this *savasana*, which means "corpse pose."

2. **Spray yourself.** Is stress keeping you awake at night? Try some aromatherapy. Neroli oil comes from the flower of the exotic bitter-orange plant. Petitgrain oil, which comes from the same plant, is similar but less expensive.

Add five to eight drops of either essential oil to a 2- to 3-ounce spray bottle of water, mist your face and body, and drift off to never-never land.

3. **Go portable.** For stress relief in transit, take aromatherapy with you. Place a few pieces of rock salt in a small vial. Add a few drops of the oil of your choice—basil, chamomile, eucalyptus, lavender, and peppermint are all good options. The rock salt absorbs the oil so the oil doesn't splash out when you open the vial. When-

ever you feel stressed, uncap the vial and inhale deeply.

4. **Go to the gate.** If you're stressed, you probably feel some anxiety too. Try applying acupressure to the point that the Chinese call the spirit gate. It's located on the outside of your wrist, below the fist crease and in line with your pinkie. Press on that spot until you get an aching sensation similar to when you hit your funny bone. Maintain this pressure for 15 to 30 seconds, then release. For optimum results, don't work the same spot more than two or three times a day.

5. **Schedule it.** Fretting can become obsessive, filling up every spare minute of time. Don't let that happen. Keep worry localized by scheduling 20 to 30 minutes each day to brood. Stress experts say that it's best to find a quiet place in which to do this worrying; you don't want to be interrupted. Another tip: Don't schedule your worry session right before bedtime.

Part Eight

No Fat, No Fuss

Lose weight the easy way.

Chapter 21

To Win at Weight Loss, Start at the Top

Your most effective weapon for shedding pounds sits on your shoulders

If you're having trouble losing weight, you may identify with Carla Linder–Mayer. No matter how much she dieted, no matter how much she worked out, something—someone—stood between Carla and her dreams of a slimmer self.

It was her contempt for Carla Linder–Mayer. "I felt so bad about myself, all I would do was eat," she recalls. "I didn't believe I could do anything else."

That changed. After losing 120 pounds, Carla ran the Chicago Marathon, finishing in a respectable 4 hours and 31 minutes.

How did she do it? By setting small, manageable goals that didn't overwhelm her. Her goals and her belief in herself built from there. "It's all positive momentum," she says. "Anyone can do it."

Stop Hating Yourself

Carla's experience proves one of the most fundamental—and yet most overlooked—truths about weight loss: What's in your head is as important as what's on your plate. It may even be more important. Hating your body, a common reason for wanting to lose weight in the first place, can actually sabotage your weight-loss attempts.

The good news is that you can learn to like your body and more than double your chances of getting slimmer. Researchers at Stanford University School of Medicine found that people who started a weight-loss program feeling happiest with their bodies were more than twice as likely to lose weight as their counterparts who were least satisfied with their bodies.

But how do you get happy with your body before you lose weight? Contrary to what you might think, it can be done. We rounded up advice from top body-image professionals, weight-loss experts, and regular folks who found that feeling good about their bodies made losing weight easier. Their advice and examples will show you how learning to like yourself can be the route to weight loss that you've been looking for.

Take a Good Look

"People who worry about how their bodies look often avoid the very things that can help them look and feel better, such as exercising and developing better coping skills," explains Elena Ramirez, Ph.D., research fellow in weight management in the department of nutrition and food sciences at the University of Vermont in Burlington. "Once women improve the way they feel about their bodies, they take better care of themselves, which helps them lose weight."

The following tips can help you learn how to befriend your body.

Look in the mirror. If you're overweight, you probably cringe every time you see

Lose by Giving

A good way to get inspiration for exercise is to sign up for one of those charity walkathons, run-a-thons, or bike-a-thons. Friends and colleagues agree to donate a certain amount of money depending on how much distance you cover in a given sport. These events benefit a wide range of charities and provide a great source of inspiration for staying in shape, says Ann Marie Miller, exercise physiologist and fitness-training manager at New York Sports Clubs in New York City.

Miller has discovered that helping out a favorite charity and getting exercise are not the only benefits to be gained from participating in one of these events. "It also makes you grateful that you have a healthy body that can exercise," she says.

yourself in the mirror. Accepting yourself as you are is a key first step in changing your negative self-image.

Start by slowly acclimating yourself to the image in the mirror. Do that by spending a few seconds a day looking at your clothed body. Slowly wear less and less, working up to viewing yourself unclothed for a few minutes.

"In a few weeks, you'll become comfortable with your reflection and realize that you have some positive physical qualities," says Kimberly Lavoi, 30, who has lost 22 pounds since beginning these body-image exercises. "You also begin to realize that you got yourself into the shape you're in, so you can also get yourself out of it."

Face your fears. It's common to avoid situations that make you feel worse about yourself, such as shopping for clothes or going to parties, says Dr. Ramirez. Feeling better about yourself requires facing those situations.

"Pick one thing you avoid, such as wearing a bathing suit, and take small steps to conquer that fear," she says. "First, just buy the suit. The next day, wear it around the house for 10 minutes. Later, wear it in front of a friend. Soon, you'll feel comfortable enough to swim laps or take part in an aqua aerobics class."

Honor yourself. "If you had a friend who said, 'What a big butt you have!' every time you saw her, you wouldn't remain her friend," says Thomas F. Cash, Ph.D., professor of psychology at Old Dominion University in Norfolk, Virginia, and author of *The Body-Image Workbook*. "Don't tolerate that treatment from yourself either. Every time you start putting

> **NATURAL**FACT
>
> A 150-pound person will burn 400 calories in an hour dancing the jitterbug, as compared to only 200 calories dancing a waltz.

yourself down, stop cold. Instead, encourage yourself as you would a friend. Say, 'Yeah, my shape isn't what I would like, but I'm taking steps to change it. And that's a positive thing.'"

Ditch the magic number. Some people have their whole body images wrapped up in a number on the scale, says Joni E. Johnston, Psy.D., a clinical psychologist in Del Mar, California, and author of *Appearance Obsession*. "If they're just a couple of pounds off, they feel horrible about themselves," she says. "Give yourself an acceptable weight range between 5 and 10 pounds so you can have healthy, normal weight fluctuations and still feel good about your body."

Hold your head high. When you're busy thinking that your thighs are too big, you assume that everyone else is thinking that, too, so you feel self-conscious, says Dr. Cash. "People never judge us as harshly as we judge ourselves. If you hold your head up, smile, and project a healthy, confident person, that's what they'll see—and that's how you'll feel."

Accept Your Power

Poor body image often comes with a little sound track in your head, says Dr. Ramirez. It repeats the same tune over and over, and that tune goes something like this: My weight-loss efforts have never worked before, and they won't work now. I'm a failure.

If you keep that negative sound track

playing, you probably will fail. Consider this: In one study, beginning tennis players who were told that, by trying hard and practicing, they could improve their games scored consistently better than those who were told that poor performance meant that they lacked innate ability.

"If you believe you have bad genes, you're less likely to succeed than if you believe you have the power to control your actions, your attitude, and, consequently, your weight," says study leader Robert Singer, Ph.D., chairman of the exercise and sport science department at the University of Florida in Gainesville.

It's all about developing what psychologists call self-efficacy—a fancy word for believing in yourself and your power to do what needs to be done. Here are tips to help boost your self-efficacy.

Dress for Success

If it's true that your mental attitude has everything to do with losing weight successfully—and it is—dressing well can set the right tone. Here are some simple tips from fashion pros that will help you feel better about yourself when you look in the mirror.

Buy a good bra. "Too often, overweight women wear bras that let their breasts fall too low, making them look older, heavier, and short-waisted," says Jan Larkey, a Pittsburgh-based image consultant and author of *Flatter Your Figure*. "Get fitted for and invest in a good support bra."

Use color strategically. "Wear bright colors on your good features and dark colors on problem areas," advises Harriette Cole, president and creative director of Profundities, an image-development company in New York City. "This lets you show off your best while camouflaging trouble spots."

Sidestep sizes. "Squeezing into clothes that are too small can actually make you look larger," says Cole. If you can't stand to wear larger sizes, cut out the tags.

Try the boot cut. To slim your hips, try boot-cut pants, suggests Cole. "Instead of being tight at the ankles, these pants flare slightly from the knees, making you look more balanced and slimmer in the hips."

Pump up accessories. "It's hard to focus on any figure problems when a woman's wearing unusual, dangling earrings," says Larkey. "Pick up some eye-catching accessories—scarves, pins, handbags, shoes. They'll help you look great before, during, and after you lose weight."

Talk back. One quick way to stop the negative voices in your head is to simply tell them to quiet down, says Dr. Johnston. "Most people walk around putting themselves down without even realizing it. Pay attention when those self-defeating thoughts pop up. Every time your internal voice starts saying, 'I'm too fat; I'm too uncoordinated; I can't do it,' answer back, 'That's enough. I can do whatever I put my mind to.' "

Write your résumé. Your confidence changes from situation to situation, says Edward McAuley, Ph.D., professor of kinesiology at the University of Illinois at Urbana-Champaign. "It might be high in the office yet low at the gym. You want to transfer all the assurance you can from one situation to the other," he says.

Think of it as writing your résumé. You don't always have the experience that a job calls for, but you do have the skills. "Write down the skills that you have to succeed at a fitness plan," Dr. McAuley says. "List attributes such as 'I'm a hard worker; I manage my time well; I'm a fast learner.' Then, use these skills to succeed at your fitness program."

Be a builder. Developing confidence is like building a house with a strong foundation, brick by brick. "Each little success is a brick," says Joyce Nash, Ph.D., clinical psychologist in Menlo Park, California, and author of *The New Maximize Your Body Potential*. "Calling a gym that interests you is one brick. Going to observe an aerobics class is another. Don't disregard all these little steps: Applaud yourself for making progress."

Share success. Mutual support can keep you moving in a positive direction. Find a friend who's trying to lose weight, too, and buddy up. If you can find several weight-loss buddies, so much the better. "The more like-minded people you have to support you," says

Dr. Singer, "the more confident you feel, and the more likely you are to succeed."

Get Moving

There's no getting around it: If you're going to build your confidence and get a better body, physical activity is required. "It's essential for both looking and feeling your best," says Dr. Nash.

That doesn't mean you have to become a gym rat. When a group of middle-age men and women started walking three times a week, they improved not only their heart health but also their self-esteem, confidence, and body image. "It's positive momentum," says Dr. McAuley.

Here's some advice that will help get you started.

Begin at home. Community gyms aren't for everyone. Some overweight people may feel more comfortable starting with a home-based fitness program, such as walking, says Michaela Kiernan, Ph.D., research associate at Stanford University School of Medicine. That way, they don't have to face the stress or embarrassment of a group setting. (For a list of exercise methods you can practice without entering a gym, see "Exercise without Squirming.")

Start in first gear. A common mistake when starting a fitness program is setting your expectations too high. Then you become discouraged and quit when you don't reach those goals.

A better idea, says Dr. Singer, is to picture a ladder with your big goal at the top. Develop short-term goals for each rung on that ladder. Each small success that you achieve builds your confidence about reaching the big one.

This is the strategy that worked so well for Carla Linder-Mayer. Her initial exercise goal was to walk for a half-hour a week; eventually, she ran a marathon. Her initial exercise goal was to lose 10 pounds; ultimately, she lost 120.

Appreciate all of the benefits. Exercise's benefits go way beyond cosmetic ones, says Dr. Nash. "When you establish a goal to lower your blood pressure or your cholesterol, for example, you have something besides your clothing size to measure your progress, and you'll feel better about your body on another level."

Seize those seconds. Just because you don't have 45 minutes to work out doesn't mean you should skip exercising entirely, says Dr. Johnston. "Doing something is always better than nothing. It all adds up in the long run." Even if you exercise for only 10 minutes, mark it on your calendar as a day that you worked out. Being consistent will make you feel better about yourself and help you lose weight.

Exercise without Squirming

If you're insecure about your body, jumping around in an aerobics class or weight room may not be your idea of a good time. Don't let that stop you from exercising. Simply choose an activity that lets you enjoy moving without being self-conscious.

Here are some suggestions.

Go for a walk. "Feel your arms swing and your legs move," says psychology professor Dr. Thomas F. Cash. "Enjoy the fresh air and how good it feels to be alive."

Seek the hills. "Hiking is wonderful for your body, mind, and spirit," says Rebecca Gorrell, director of movement therapy at Canyon Ranch Health Resort in Tucson, Arizona. "No woman gets to the top of a mountain and still hates her thighs."

Find focus. "It's hard to dwell on how your body looks when you're concentrating on breathing and moving in yoga," says Dr. Joni E. Johnston, author of *Appearance Obsession*. "Plus, you can do yoga no matter what your size."

Consider tai chi. This ancient form of exercise, which is still widely practiced in China, emphasizes gentle, fluid movements. The soothing rhythm of tai chi allows you to move without worrying about your body, says Dr. Johnston. "It's relaxing and beautiful."

Dance, dance, dance. Even if you don't care for Richard Simmons, you can still have a ball by dancing for exercise. Pop in your favorite CD and boogie through the house. "When you move with music for fun, you forget about dance steps or how you look," says Dr. Cash.

Chapter 22

Could Losing Weight Actually Be Fun?

Definitely, says the physician who designed the comprehensive CHEF program

Thirty pounds and three chins ago, John La Puma, M.D., was a frustrated Chicago internist treating patients with high blood pressure, heart disease, diabetes, and colon cancer. His own fat was an annoyance. His patients' fat was killing them.

He told them to eat healthier meals and to exercise. They didn't. Neither did he.

Fed up, Dr. La Puma took a leave of absence. He went to culinary school to study how to make healthy food taste delicious. He also discovered that there are ways to exercise that you can actually enjoy.

Dr. La Puma lost 30 pounds and promptly compiled what he'd learned into the easiest, most enjoyable weight-loss program you've ever seen. The name of the program is CHEF.

A Complete Package

CHEF stands for Cooking, Healthy Eating, and Fitness, and it's based on two fundamental principles: 1) lower-fat food can taste great and 2) exercise can be fun.

Dr. La Puma knew that if he could design a program with those principles in mind, people who love to eat and hate to exercise might stick with it. He was right. When the CHEF plan was tested on a group of overweight people, they dropped an average of 24 pounds in 22 weeks without counting a calorie, banning a single food, or avoiding their favorite restaurants.

They also lost 10 percent of their body fat, lowered their systolic blood pressures (the top number that indicates how hard the heart is pumping) by 17 points, decreased their triglyceride levels by 56 points, whittled more than 2 inches off their waistlines, and cut their saturated fat intakes from nearly 24 grams a day to less than 8 grams. The best part was that they had fun doing it—and so can you.

CHEF Cooking

Dr. La Puma's philosophy of food is simple: He loves it. "Food is beautiful, and eating is fun," he says. "No food by itself is 'bad'—how and how often you eat it is what gets you into trouble."

How can you eat joyfully and still lose weight? Easy. Follow the CHEF approach to food shopping and cooking.

Buy fresh. Fruits and vegetables at their peak taste sweeter and juicier. To find the best, look for produce that feels heavy for its size, is

The Basics

The CHEF program, designed by John La Puma, M.D., is designed to teach you how to achieve the following goals, while having fun at the same time.

- Eat a low-fat (15 to 20 percent of calories), high-fiber (35 to 40 grams a day) diet.
- Cook new and familiar foods with little fat but a lot of flavor.
- Shop for the freshest, best-tasting whole and prepared foods.
- Dine out without overeating.
- Fit in 30- to 60-minute workouts 4 or 5 days a week.

deep in color, smells fragrant, and is not wilted, brown, or bruised. Choose loose produce instead of packaged so that you can easily examine it.

Buy quality. Use oils and cheeses, but choose the highest-flavor, highest-quality ones, such as sesame and olive oils and Greek or Bulgarian feta cheese, to get the most flavor. That way, you'll use less, but you won't feel deprived.

Change your palate. Once you have the juiciest, brightest, and freshest foods, savor their natural sweetness—minus butter, salt, and heavy sauces. Eventually, you'll actually prefer clear, natural flavors over oily, rich, heavy ones.

Add taste without fat. Toss a few spicy peppers into soups and sauces. Splash balsamic or fruit-flavored vinegars over salads and veggies. Mix concentrated anchovy, sun-dried tomato, onion, or wasabi paste into stir-fries or marinades.

Don't waste calories. If it doesn't taste good, don't eat it. Otherwise, you're likely to overeat, trying to satisfy your tastebuds.

Expand your flavor universe. Every time you go to the grocery store, buy a vegetable, fruit, or seasoning you've never tried before. Try broccoli sprouts, fennel, jicama, kale, Hubbard squash, sweet potatoes, Swiss chard, or tomatillos. Use the ones you like to add more variety to meals.

Condition your tastebuds. Whole-wheat pasta is a whole lot better for you than regular pasta, but give yourself a chance to get used to it, suggests CHEF nutritionist Linda Braam, R.D. Substituting whole-wheat pasta for your favorite spaghetti all at once is a setup for disappointment. "You're changing dramatically from your expectation," Braam says. "Introduce it slowly, in small portions." One way to ease into it is to use half whole-wheat pasta, half white in your next dish.

Go international. Mediterranean and Asian cuisines offer new flavors and a variety of textures and are traditionally low-fat. To infuse your meals with an ethnic flair, visit authentic, true-to-culture restaurants, or pick up a cook-book that features a particular cuisine.

Successful Eating

There are tricks to avoiding high-fat pitfalls, and they can save you from blowing your weekly calorie count on one unconsidered splurge. Here

> **NATURALFACT**
>
> A loss of as little as 5 pounds maintained for 2 years reduces a woman's risk of developing high blood pressure.

are some ways to make self-discipline easy.

Plan ahead. Fast-food drive-thrus look appealing when you don't know what to make for dinner. Instead, look at your weekly schedule and plan your meals. For hectic nights, be sure to have something handy that's quick and easy—or, better yet, already made.

Start by writing down all the foods you like, then focus on those that minimize meat while maximizing plants. Build your meals around them.

Stock up. When you're cooking, make lots of extra and freeze it for quick meals later. If Dr. La Puma has to roast one eggplant for a recipe, he'll roast two or three, or double or triple the recipe. He freezes the extra for instant duty later.

Be equipped. You'll abandon bulk cooking if you have to repeat a recipe three times because your saucepan is too puny to make one big batch, Braam says. For the indispensable healthy-kitchen tools, see "30 Essentials of a Thin Kitchen."

Take a cooking class. Learning how to mince, roast, and blend like a pro makes cooking quicker, easier, and more fun. It worked for Dr. La Puma.

Get a good cookbook. Here are a few of Dr. La Puma's favorites.

- *Vegetarian Cooking for Everyone*, by Deborah Madison (Broadway Books, 1997)
- *Rick Bayless's Mexican Kitchen*, by Rick Bayless (Scribner, 1996)
- *Steven Raichlen's High-Flavor, Low-Fat Vegetarian Cooking*, by Steven Raichlen (Viking, 1995)

30 Essentials of a Thin Kitchen

In the Cupboard

1. Chef's knife
2. Good-quality cutting board
3. Six- and 8-quart stock pots
4. Large wok or skillet
5. Lemon zester
6. Blender or food processor
7. Long-handled tongs (for broiler-roasting vegetables)
8. Parchment paper (for roasting vegetables)
9. Freezerproof storage containers and bags
10. Mortar and pestle or coffee grinder (for grinding spices)

In the Pantry

11. Canned or dried beans: pinto, black, cannellini, kidney
12. Whole-wheat pasta and couscous
13. Brown rice
14. Onions
15. Canned tomatoes
16. Reduced-sodium, reduced-fat stocks or broths
17. Dried spices and herbs: basil, oregano, dill, black peppercorns, cumin seeds, aniseed, rosemary
18. Vinegars: balsamic, Chinese black, herb, fruit-flavored
19. Olive or canola oil
20. Cooking spray

In the Fridge and Freezer

21. Light silken tofu
22. Fat-free milk
23. Lemons, limes, oranges, other citrus fruits
24. Feta cheese
25. Nonfat sour cream
26. Nonfat plain yogurt
27. Peppers: red, green, spicy, sweet
28. Scallions
29. Cilantro
30. Mustards: spicy brown, onion, other gourmet flavors

Brain Training

The CHEF program puts a big emphasis on joyful living and joyful eating. Here are tips for adding a little zest to your kitchen from Julie Griffis, R.N., a holistically trained nurse who taught the CHEF participants mind/body techniques.

Motivate with music. "Music changes your mood," Griffis says. "What affects your eating? Mood. So it seems logical to use music to change your mood and eating habits."

If you're angry and heading for the cookie jar, stop at the stereo first. Try Pachelbel's Canon in D to soothe stress, anxiety, and a desire to eat. If you're having trouble getting off the couch, try Chuck Berry's "Johnny B. Goode" or some equally rockin' tune to get a move on.

Cooking? Make it a celebration. Pop in the Temptations' "Ain't Too Proud to Beg" or another Motown classic. When Griffis forgot her portable stereo one evening, her cooking students were crushed. "How can we cook without music?" they cried.

Embrace food. Instead of looking at food as good or bad, think of it as fuel for your body. "Focus on nourishing your body, not 'dieting,'" says Griffis. Considering what your body does for you, feeding it healthy food and exercising it isn't a lot to ask.

Redesign your plate. Fill your plate with grains, fruits, and vegetables, placing smaller portions of cheeses and meats on smaller, separate plates off to the side.

Move Joyfully

After Dr. La Puma and his friend Jeanne returned from a 2-mile walk one evening, she crowed, "That was 200 calories burned!"

He said, "And we had a great time!"

Dr. La Puma's priorities are the same in the CHEF program. The key to successful weight loss, he feels, is to focus on fun first, rather than on calories. Here's how to follow his prescription.

Do cool stuff. There are plenty of fun activities—square dancing, walking in the woods, ice skating, and bowling, to name a few examples—that also happen to be great exercise. Pick one that appeals to you and get busy.

Focus on your likes. Plenty of people like treadmills; plenty of people like bicycling. You may hate both. If so, do something else. Otherwise, you'll be back on the couch in no time.

Establish good habits. When Dr. La Puma was overweight, climbing stairs was so inconceivable that using the elevator became a habit. But today, he regularly sprints up the 12 flights of stairs in his building.

Count all activity. Tracking your activity can motivate you to stick with it. But don't count only traditional exercises such as walking, jogging, and lifting weights. Give yourself points for that half-hour spent giving the kids "airplane" rides, the 2 hours devoted to scrubbing the bathrooms, or the morning devoted to shoveling snow—anything that gets and keeps you moving.

Set the right goals. Don't set a big one ("I want to run a marathon") without building lots of little ones ("I want to run around the block without needing CPR"), or you may feel overwhelmed. Here are some other goal-setting pointers.

- If you jogged 2 miles yesterday but only 1 mile today, you haven't failed to hit the mark—you've jogged 3 miles.
- Keep a record of your progress. In a daily calendar or activity journal, write down what you do and every day you do it.
- Reward yourself; it will keep you motivated and spur you to the next level.
- Celebrate victories such as a drop in blood pressure or cholesterol, or feeling less stressed. Treat yourself to a pedicure, a night at the theater, or a weekend at a country inn.

Don't make excuses. Considering that the CHEF participants got more active in Chicago during January, you can become active too. Just get up and get moving.

Talk it up. Let friends know about your efforts. Ask them to review your activity journal. Feeling accountable helps you stick with it.

Don't overdo it. Being overly ambitious at the start is the biggest reason that people fail at fitness programs. Exercise doesn't have to be hard to be effective. Go slow at first; don't go for the "burn."

Be realistic. If you have a full-time job, a nasty commute, and night school on top of that, it's probably not the right time for a fitness overhaul. Do what you can (take the stairs; park farther away from the store), and resolve to put your body first the next chance you get.

Visit the CHEF

Based on the success of the CHEF research, John La Puma, M.D., opened the CHEF Clinic, which offers personal and group programs. For more information, visit the CHEF Clinic Web site at www.CHEFClinic.com, e-mail them at info@CHEFClinic.com, or write to 800 Biesterfield Road, Elk Grove Village, IL 60007.

Chapter 23

Want to Eat Less? Don't Worry about It

When it comes to dieting, willpower is an overrated virtue

You're at the mall, receiving signals from the bakery across the way. The chocolate chip cookies are sweet-talking you. But because you're trying to lose 10 pounds, you can't, you won't, you simply *mustn't*.

"Why don't I have more willpower?" you think. And then you go ahead and succumb to sweet temptation.

If you've been through the temptation-resistance-surrender cycle all too often, we have some wonderful news. Willpower, that elusive quality that you think you lack, is *not* the answer to your weight-loss problems.

In fact, going ahead and eating that delicious chocolate chip cookie may be exactly what you need to do in order to successfully slim down.

Goodbye Bad Habits

"Weight loss is not about gritting your teeth and saying no," says Gary McClain, Ph.D., psychologist and coauthor of *The Complete Idiot's Guide to Breaking Bad Habits*. In truth, weight loss doesn't have much to do with willpower at all, which is great news if you're unable to say no to your favorite indulgences.

Here are easy, proven solutions to the most common weight-loss stumbling blocks.

Choice Is Allowed

Successful weight loss allows—even encourages—you to plan for an occasional indulgence of your favorites. In one study, researchers assigned 24 obese women to one of two treatment groups. The first group stuck to a traditional diet that restricted calories; the second group joined a behavioral-choice program that taught them how to deal with foods they considered a problem. Although the traditional group initially lost weight, they tended to regain it. The behavioral-choice group continued a slow but steady weight loss. A year later, the behavioral-choice group had lost twice as many pounds as the traditional group.

"Instead of saying to themselves, 'I can't have potato chips,' we asked participants to decide if they really wanted them, to determine a reasonable portion if the answer was yes, and then to have them," explains study author Tracy Sbrocco, Ph.D., clinical psychologist at the

The Sensual Meal

It's easy to gulp down a meal without enjoying it, then end up still feeling unsatisfied. If you focus more intensely on your food, a little will go a long way. "You'll satisfy all your senses and realize that you don't need to eat as much food to get the enjoyment out of it," says Melanie Polk, R.D., director of nutrition education at the American Institute for Cancer Research.

Here's how to eat a sensual meal.

- Look at the plate and soak in the colors and textures. "Get the visual enjoyment," Polk says.
- Close your eyes and smell the aroma of the meal.
- As you put a small bite into your mouth, pay attention to the texture, and taste each and every morsel.
- Slowly chew and savor the food before swallowing.

Uniformed Services University of the Health Sciences in Bethesda, Maryland. "Because nothing is forbidden, the seduction and struggle of resisting certain foods is eliminated. Eventually, you say no—and with less effort."

When you eat more like you want to and don't feel deprived, you're happier and more motivated. You'll be much more willing to pass up the popcorn and candy at the movies when you've enjoyed your favorite cookie at the mall the day before.

Timing Is Everything

What time you eat, rather than any lack of willpower, may be the source of your problem, says John De Castro, Ph.D., professor of psychology at Georgia State University in Atlanta, who has looked at how our bodies' natural circadian rhythms affect appetite. "People are particularly vulnerable to overeating in the evening because it seems that they don't get the same degree of satisfaction from food then as they do earlier in the day," he says. It's not that you're actually hungrier, but the same amount of food that satisfied you for breakfast doesn't do the trick at dinner. "The development of artificial lighting has prolonged eating into the time when we're at the low-end of our daily satiation cycle," he suggests.

NATURALFACT

Don't be fooled by restaurant serving sizes, which can be up to four times what a regular serving size should be.

The solution? "Go to bed earlier and get up earlier to take advantage of the times when you get the most satisfaction from your food." This could be as simple as shifting bedtime from 11:00 P.M. to 10:00 P.M. Another option is curbing TV watching and kitchen prowling during the snack-attack time zone.

Bending Is Better

When it comes to losing weight for the long term, calorie counting and restrictive meal plans don't work. "Flexible dieting," on the other hand, is linked to slimmer figures, fewer binges, and less depression and anxiety, according to a study at Pennington Biomedical Research Center at Louisiana State University in Baton Rouge led by clinical psychologist Cheryl Smith, Ph.D.

"A flexible eater is very deliberate in her choices," says Dr. Smith. "She remains conscious of what she's eating throughout the day, either by recording her meals in a diary or keeping mental notes. She tries to balance her meals throughout the day and week without adhering to a stringent plan that feels restrictive and could set her up to blow it. If she has a cheeseburger and fries at lunch, she'll plan to have soup and salad for a light dinner."

So before you eat lunch, grab a snack, or order dinner, review what you've eaten up to that point and adjust your choices accordingly. If

HEALING SPOTLIGHT
Rush Limbaugh

Radio superstar Rush Limbaugh knows all the jokes about how easy it is to lose weight. Like plenty of other people, he's done it dozens of times. "I've tried every diet there is," Limbaugh says. "I've probably lost 90 pounds three times, 60 pounds three or four times, 40 pounds four times. It's been a constant battle."

A couple of years ago, Limbaugh found himself weighing 320 pounds and flirting with a case of diabetes type 2. He quickly dropped 20 pounds, and his blood sugar levels stabilized. But this time, he was determined to get off the diet merry-go-round once and for all.

"My challenge was to find a way to reorder my food priority and my diet so it was a way of life," he recalls. After consulting with doctors, "I took elements of many diets I've tried and combined them into one." The result was a low-fat diet with about 15 grams of fat a day and plenty of proteins and selected carbohydrates. Some staples were salmon, swordfish, and faux fried chicken that is actually baked.

"I didn't care about losing it fast, and it just came off"—some 110 pounds of it, Limbaugh says. And it has stayed off for several years now.

Limbaugh doesn't pretend that he isn't thrilled. "I can't tell you how fantastic it is hearing people say, 'You look great,'" he chuckles. "That never happened to me in my life."

you ate a healthy breakfast but have a party tonight, choose the grilled chicken salad with light dressing rather than the steak sandwich for lunch.

‖ Stay ‖ in Balance

Meals that balance the right amounts of protein and carbohydrates throughout the day may ward off hunger. When 12 overweight participants were fed test meals by researchers at Tufts University in Boston, they ate 81 percent more food in the 5 hours following a high-carbohydrate breakfast of instant oatmeal than when they ate a veggie-omelette-and-fruit breakfast that was equal in calories but included more protein.

Although researchers consider these findings preliminary, they suspect that, once eaten, high-glycemic (high-sugar) foods like oatmeal and other high-carbohydrate foods, such as white

Balance Every Meal

You can keep your appetite on an even keel by including a small amount of a high-protein food at every meal and substituting high-fiber carbohydrates for low-fiber ones. (We've italicized the high-protein foods in these sample meal plans.)

Breakfast	Lunch	Dinner	Snack
DAY 1			
Quiche made with 4 oz tomato, mushroom, and bell pepper; 2 slices whole-grain toast with 1 Tbsp jam; 6 oz grapefruit juice	5 oz bean and *cheese* burrito with ½ cup extra-chunky salsa and 2 Tbsp light *sour cream*; apple with 1 Tbsp *cashew butter*	2 oz grilled *chicken*; 2 cups mixed-greens salad with 2 Tbsp low-cal Italian dressing; baked sweet potato with 1 pat butter; whole-grain roll	¼ cup pineapple with 2 Tbsp 1% *cottage cheese*; 1 graham cracker
DAY 2			
Peach smoothie made with ½ cup fat-free *milk*, 1 banana, 1 peach, and 1 Tbsp sugar; small low-fat bran muffin with 1 Tbsp jam	1 slice of tomato and 1 slice of 2% *cheese* melted on a whole-wheat English muffin; 1 fig bar	3 oz broiled *salmon* with 1 tsp honey-mustard sauce; ½ cup whole-wheat couscous; ½ cup asparagus with 1 pat butter; 1 cup strawberries	1 cup red grapes dunked in ½ cup fat-free plain *yogurt*, topped with ⅓ cup low-fat granola
DAY 3			
Plain bagel with 1 Tbsp *peanut butter* and 1 Tbsp jam; orange	1 slice whole-wheat pizza topped with extra broccoli and 1 cup veggie pepperoni (made with soy), light on the *cheese*; carrot sticks dipped in 3 Tbsp fat-free ranch dressing	1 stuffed pepper made with 2 oz ground *turkey* and 1 cup brown rice; sliced plum	½ oz mixed *nuts*; 5 rye wafer crackers

rice, potatoes, and baked goods, get broken down quickly, released into the bloodstream as glucose, and then stored away almost immediately. This sudden rise and fall of blood sugar levels feels like a roller-coaster ride to your body, explains study author Susan Roberts, Ph.D., professor of nutrition and psychiatry at Tufts: It's over before you know it, and you want to go again.

Foods that are low on the glycemic index, on the other hand, get digested slowly, and their nutrients are released into the bloodstream more steadily, delaying the return of hunger. These include whole-food carbohydrates such as whole-grain breads, pasta, and cereals; as well as fruits and vegetables; and proteins such as lean meats, fish, eggs, beans, nuts, and low-fat dairy products.

"The difficulty that people have with hunger when they're trying to lose weight has probably more to do with what they're not eating than what they are eating," says Dr. Roberts. For example, if you add to your stir-fry high-fiber carbohydrates such as steamed vegetables, plus protein-packed chicken, and subtract some of the white rice, you may feel full longer—so you'll eat less later. (For more meal ideas that serve up the right blend, see "Balance Every Meal.")

This is also why a small handful of fat-packed peanuts may be a better snack choice than low-fat cookies: The protein helps curb your eating later in the day, and it's more nutritious. The fact that the salt and crunch of peanuts enhance the psychological satisfaction you receive is an additional bonus.

"Fad diets come and go. Over and over, we see that the only thing that really works is a balanced, healthy diet with moderation."

—Nutrition coordinator Lorna Pascal, R.D., of Hackensack University Medical Center in New Jersey

Dodge the Low-Fat Trap

If you can satisfy a craving with a low-fat product—meaning that you can control your portions—that helps you to cut calories effortlessly. But be careful: If a low-fat product isn't as satisfying as the regular version, you may eat more to compensate. The result? Your total calorie count is as high as or even higher than it would be with a more fattening treat.

Flavor plays a big part in why some low-fat foods satisfy you while others don't. In a taste test at the University of Missouri in Columbia, participants liked low-fat and regular chocolate ice creams equally, but they didn't like low-fat vanilla as much as regular vanilla.

Why would that be? Probably because many compounds combine to "carry" chocolate flavor, so it's easier to mask any alterations that occur when the fat is reduced, explains Ingolf Gruen, Ph.D., assistant professor of food chemistry at the university and flavor expert on the study. Lovers of dark chocolate, especially, will find this a satisfying switch. "We found that the low-fat chocolate ice creams had more of the bitter or semisweet aspects of the chocolate flavor," says Dr. Gruen.

Vanilla, by contrast, has just one chemical compound responsible for flavor, so vanilla doesn't mask fat reduction as well. Ditto for strawberry. That means you're less likely to be satisfied by low-fat vanilla or low-fat strawberry than by low-fat chocolate. If vanilla or strawberry treats are your passion, you may want to indulge in the real thing in order to avoid gorging yourself on a less-satisfying substitute.

Another key factor in intelligent eating is personal preference. For example, a group of *Pre-*

vention magazine staffers sampled a selection of low-fat treats: shakes, muffins, granola, popcorn, cream cheese, and cheesecake. The consensus was that they tasted as flavorful as their high-fat counterparts, despite having fewer calories. Other low-fat foods, however, didn't pass muster. These included blue cheese dressing, fettuccine Alfredo, and butter. And in those cases, the temptation was to keep eating more.

Wield the Double-Powered Weapon

Physical activity boosts your calorie burn so that you don't have to obsess about every bite you take. Exercise can also keep your appetite in check, naturally. You can literally walk away from cravings.

To make exercise a natural part of your day, use other commitments or tasks as a way of get-

ting and staying active. Setting up a tennis date (instead of a lunch date) with your best friend works just as well for keeping the two of you in touch but makes exercise part of the habit too. Busy with kids? Don't just supervise; play with them. Set out on your next trail walk in search of beautiful views and fresh air.

Try to combine multiple benefits in one activity. "Coaching your daughter's soccer team allows you to spend time with your child, serve your community, socialize, have fun, and exercise too," explains James Prochaska, Ph.D., psychologist at the University of Rhode Island in Kingston.

Appreciate how your body moves—how it feels to whirl your legs on a bicycle, for example. Rhythmic activities such as walking and dancing can also ease you into a stress-relieving meditation or the pleasure of flowing energy. When you're doing activities that you love, exercise becomes automatic. "You get to the point where

The Opportunist's Guide to Exercise

Look how easy it is to fit in a pleasurable 300-calorie burn.

Time	Activity	Min Spent	Cal Burned
6:30 A.M.	Go for Rover's friskiest walk of the day	15	70
12:00 P.M.	Head to the deli to get lunch, 5 minutes away on foot	10	45
3:00 P.M.	Take afternoon break; do light stretches at desk	5	15
5:30 P.M.	Weed and cut flowers before everyone else gets home	15	85
7:00 P.M.	Play after-dinner game of tag with the kids	15	85
TOTALS	AH, WHAT A DAY	60	300

the first thing you do when you open your calendar is write down Wednesday-evening tennis. There's no question; you just do it," says Dr. Prochaska.

Bounce Back

When you've eaten the snack mix . . . and the nachos . . . and the brownies at a party, the tendency is to throw in the towel. But temptations and setbacks are a normal part of weight loss. It's what you do afterward that determines how quickly you get back on track.

Think back to what stimulated you to overeat. Ask yourself what the food represented. If it was comfort food because you were feeling overwhelmed at work, talk with someone about your feelings instead.

If you back up another step to even before the episode that triggered your overindulgence occurred, the situation that caused the trigger may itself emerge, adds Dr. McClain. For example, perhaps you ate because you were frustrated and angry. You were frustrated and angry because you had to stay late at the office and miss your workout. You had to stay late because your boss overwhelmed you with requests. But you let yourself get overwhelmed because you didn't want to say no, even though you were already doing as much work as possible. "You might see that you're actually setting yourself up for those slips," Dr. McClain says.

Once you've thought it through, you can discuss your responsibilities and career goals with your boss—not with the food. Choose a relationship with people over a relationship with food, and you won't be dialing for takeout after hours. You'll be heading home, relishing a job well-done that day.

Become a matter-of-degree (MAT) thinker. In a different study led by Dr. Smith, those who learned MAT thinking reported significantly fewer problems with overeating than did rigid, all-or-nothing thinkers.

Here's how it works: If a MAT thinker eats a small plateful of nachos at a party, she quantifies it by actually attaching a number to it, such as 200 calories. "And that is exactly all she really had," says Dr. Smith. She then accommodates it by cutting back on her drinks for the evening or walking an extra 20 minutes over each of the next 2 days.

If you slip up by skipping your regular evening walking routine for a week, employ some of these strategies: Substitute an apple and string cheese for a less-than-healthy afternoon snack for a while, or fit in a few extra lunchtime strolls or early-morning swims.

Don't forget to examine why you missed your after-work exercise in the first place. Maybe your schedule has changed and now your son needs a ride to karate lessons in the evenings. In that case, a midday walk or before-work swim would fit better into your life and keep you committed to your exercise routine.

Chapter 24

Walk to the Beat of Your Own Drummer

Choose the walker's profile that fits you best

Finding the right weight-loss program can be like choosing a friend or mate: Those that aren't a good fit fade out of the picture, while a great match can last a lifetime.

For more than 75 percent of the people in the National Weight Control Registry who have successfully lost weight and kept it off, walking is the answer. Walking is simple. You already know how, you can do it anywhere, and you don't need special equipment. What you might not have known is that there are different types of walking personalities.

We all have our own styles, tastes, and strengths. Why, then, should we all have to follow the same walking program? Customizing your walks to fit you will help you enjoy and stick to your workouts. Best of all, you'll drop pounds and get firm, faster and easier.

Who Are You?

To help you uncover what type of walker you are, *Prevention* magazine's walking editor, Maggie Spilner, worked with leading walking coaches to develop a "walker's profile" quiz. Take the quiz below to identify your own walking style, then try the specially designed programs that Spilner and her team developed to take maximum weight-loss advantage of that style.

If you're a beginning walker or just coming back to the sport after a break, we've designed special programs for you too. See "The Beginner" on page 216 and "Perfect Your Posture" on page 222.

The *Prevention* Walker's Profile Quiz

So what's your walking personality? Take this quiz to find out. Read the following list of statements, and check one response for each that best describes *you* (not your current walking program).

1. I enjoy walking most when . . .
____ a. It's challenging
____ b. It gets me somewhere
____ c. It's with other people
____ d. It's in a beautiful place

2. If I were on a group hike, I would be . . .
____ a. Out in front
____ b. Wondering, "Are we done yet?"
____ c. In the middle of the pack
____ d. Focusing on my surroundings

3. In an ideal world, the place I'd most like to walk would be . . .
____ a. On a track
____ b. At the mall

____ c. At the park with a friend
____ d. In the woods

4. Others often describe me as . . .
____ a. Determined
____ b. Organized
____ c. Outgoing
____ d. Idealistic

5. The thing I'm most likely to take on a vacation is . . .
____ a. A pair of sneakers
____ b. A watch
____ c. My address book
____ d. A camera

6. If I were a coach, my style would include . . .
____ a. Advising on technique
____ b. Getting the most out of each practice session
____ c. Recruiting others
____ d. Offering inspiration

7. My calendar/date book . . .
____ a. Doubles as my exercise log
____ b. Is filled with appointments
____ c. Includes birthdays and anniversaries
____ d. Contains inspirational quotes

8. The clothes I most enjoy wearing are . . .
____ a. Shorts, a T-shirt, and sneakers
____ b. Whatever is clean and comfortable
____ c. Jeans and loafers
____ d. Loose-fitting and flowing

Count up the number of A's, Bs, Cs, and Ds that you've marked as responses. The letter that you've marked the most number of times indicates your walking personality. Read on for a description of each personality and a personalized plan for each that will send pounds packing.

If you come up with a tie, read the descriptions under both categories to see which fits you best. If you score similarly in more than two, check them out and try whichever you like best. Even if you have one type written all over you, don't overlook the option of also experimenting with another program, or all four, to keep walks interesting.

The individual walker profiles follow.

A: The Athlete

Your walking profile: You get satisfaction from passing others. You're always trying to beat your own time. You know what it takes to hit your target heart rate.

Your weight-loss advantage: Speed. Picking up your pace is the easiest way to increase intensity so that you burn more calories and blast away pounds.

Your best walking program: If you're a competitive type, you need a challenge to stay motivated and committed. Training for and participating in races is a perfect way to do that. Start with a 5-K (5 kilometers, or 3.1 miles). Check your local paper, gym, walking association, or athletic store for announcements. Then, try the "4 Weeks to Your First 5-K" training program, page 220, developed by Elaine Ward, managing director of the North American Racewalking Foundation. It'll help you get ready—and walk faster.

B: The Pragmatic

Your walking profile: You're hurried at work and at home, so your walks are

The Beginner

Walking is one thing; fitness walking is another. But the distance between the two is not as great as you might think. Add a little technique, a little speed, and a little distance to your average after-dinner stroll, and you're on your way.

Whether you're a brand-new fitness walker or back from a hiatus, we have a basic get-started walking plan that will get you up to speed safely, courtesy of Elaine Ward, managing director of the North American Racewalking Foundation.

See the chart at right for your step-by-step start-up plan. Plan to do at least 5 minutes of easy walking and a few minutes of stretching to warm up and cool down. At the end of your walk, you should feel mildly tired, not exhausted. Rest at least 2 days during each week, and if you need to, skip a day or scale back on the number of minutes.

The workout calls for three basic walking speeds. They are moderate pace, bump it up, and 1-minute count.

usually no-frills affairs: the same route at the same time every day, or squeezed in between errands. You walk more for exercise than for pleasure.

Your weight-loss advantage: Frequency. Studies show that doing several daily

Moderate pace. Walk at a pace that is brisk enough to get your heart pumping but that doesn't leave you out of breath.

Bump it up. Walk for 5 minutes at moderate pace, then speed up for 1 minute. Repeat this 5-to-1 moderate/fast mix for as long as the workout specifies.

One-minute count. Walk for 5 minutes at moderate pace, then count the number of steps you take for 1 minute. Repeat for the specified time. (As you get faster, the number of steps will increase.)

Week 1

Day 1: Moderate pace for 15 minutes
Day 2: Bump it up for 20 minutes
Day 3: Moderate pace for 30 minutes
Day 4: Moderate pace for 15 minutes
Day 5: 1-minute count for 20 minutes

Week 2

Day 1: Moderate pace for 20 minutes
Day 2: Bump it up for 25 minutes
Day 3: Moderate pace for 30 minutes
Day 4: Moderate pace for 20 minutes
Day 5: 1-minute count for 25 minutes

Week 3

Day 1: Moderate pace for 15 minutes
Day 2: Bump it up for 25 minutes
Day 3: Moderate pace for 30 minutes
Day 4: Moderate pace for 15 minutes
Day 5: 1-minute count for 25 minutes

Week 4

Day 1: Moderate pace for 20 minutes
Day 2: Bump it up for 25 minutes
Day 3: Moderate pace for 35 minutes
Day 4: Moderate pace for 20 minutes
Day 5: 1-minute count for 25 minutes

workouts of 10 to 15 minutes can be as effective for losing weight as exercising all in one chunk of time. You tend to effortlessly rack up more total minutes by week's end than do single-session folks, who tend to skip entire sessions when time is crunched.

Your best walking program: You can get an exciting, effective workout in just minutes. "There's a huge difference in calorie burn between strolling around and walking fast while tucking your rear end and tightening your abdominals," says Katie LoPresti, assistant pro-

10-Minute Interval Workouts

Do the workouts separately (or combine all three for a full 30-minute walk when you have the time). Warm up with at least 2 minutes of walking at a slow to moderate pace before you begin, and cool down with at least 1 minute of easy walking. Mix 3 days of intervals with 2 days of regular walks each week.

Interval 1

Pushups: Do 15 to 20 reps with your arms wider than your shoulders. Easier move: Begin on your knees before working up to doing them on your toes.

Curb taps: Standing in front of a curb or step, alternate tapping each foot up on the curb. Repeat as quickly as you can for 30 to 45 seconds, working up to a speed where you switch your feet in midair.

Speedwalk: Go for 3 minutes.

Pushups: Do 15 to 20 reps with your arms directly under your shoulders. Keep your elbows tucked in at your sides and pointing toward your feet.

Curb-ups: Standing in front of a curb or step, step up with your right foot. Then, lift your left knee. Put your left foot back on the ground, and step back down with your right foot, as in step aerobics. Repeat, stepping up with your left foot. Repeat as quickly as you can for 30 to 45 seconds.

Interval 2

Jumping jacks: Do them for 45 seconds.

Powerwalk or jog: Go for 5 minutes.

Walking lunges: As you step with your right leg, bend it, keeping your right knee over your ankle and dropping your left knee toward the ground. Pressing off with your right foot, come up and bring your left foot next to your right. Repeat, stepping with your left leg. Do 10 to 15 lunges on each leg.

Interval 3

Walking squats: Step your right leg out to your side about 2 feet, then sit back in a squat. (Keep your knees behind your toes.) Stand up, bringing your left leg next to your right. Do 10 to 15 squats, leading with your right leg.

Side slide: Quickly shuffle your right leg out to your side, followed by your left leg, bringing them together. Repeat for 60 seconds.

Walking squats: Do 10 to 15 squats, this time leading with your left leg.

Side slide: Repeat for 60 seconds, this time leading with your left leg.

March or jog, bringing your knees toward your chest: Go for 2 minutes.

gram director at the University Wellness Center at the University of Medicine and Dentistry School of Osteopathic Medicine in Stratford, New Jersey.

LoPresti has designed three workouts that will add both variety and intensity to your walks (see "10-Minute Interval Workouts"). By coupling higher cardio bursts of energy with whole-body-toning moves, you'll burn more calories as you firm up.

C: The Socializer

Your walking profile: You don't mind exercise but hate to go it alone. Your ideal partner could be your best friend, your neighbor, or a stranger you've just met—as long as she's by your side.

Your weight-loss advantage: Support. "When people are counting on you to show up, you're more likely to," says Ellen Abbott, walking director at the Boston Athletic Club. The more positive reinforcement and fun you have, the more you'll walk—and the more weight you'll lose.

Your best walking program: Here's how to make your walks more social and boost your workouts when you're with a group, in four easy steps.

1. **Find a partner.**

Just ask. That's usually all it takes to find someone to walk with you.

Make it routine. Choose the best days and times that will work for both you and your partner; write them in your weekly planner.

2. **Find more partners.** Two partners are better than one: more lively conversa-tion, and, if one can't make it, you have a backup. Try joining a club, or start your own. Abbott once posted an ad in her apartment building and found several "on call" buddies for neighborhood walks.

3. **Make it challenging.** Choose a long, steep trail so that you can catch up on the past week's happenings as you blast extra calories.

You can also alternate taking responsibility for planning your course. You may lead a speed session one week, while your partner chooses a hilly loop the next.

4. **Keep it fun.** Get a group at work to commit to training for a charity walk. Or create a walking book club. Read a book, then meet your group on Saturday morning to discuss or trade titles while you walk.

If you don't feel like making conversation during your walk, take your dog instead of your human partner. If you don't have your own, volunteer to walk a dog from your local humane society. You may make a new (four-legged) friend.

D: The Romantic

Your walking profile: You love exploring wooded trails or interesting streets. Although your walks are often times for self-reflection, you also enjoy strolls with your loved one at sunset.

Your weight-loss advantage: Distance. When you're interested in your surroundings or in tune with your thoughts, you're likely to walk longer and sustain a brisker pace, explains Carolyn Scott Kortge, author of *The Spirited Walker.*

Your best walking program:
Don't wait for weekends to discover inspiring
places to walk. Here are three ways to make your
everyday route more fulfilling.

1. **Locate interesting places.**
Check out local Rails-to-Trails paths or canal
towpaths. These flat, long routes give the
feeling of being far away even when you're
close to home. For a shorter jaunt, venture
down side streets that you usually zip by
on your way to somewhere else. Notice in-
tricate landscapes, beautiful gardens, and
unique decorations—and steal a few ideas for
your home.

If you're a history buff, seek out an old
neighborhood that has some interesting archi-
tecture. Call your local chamber of commerce
for a walking tour of a historical site, or learn to
be a guide yourself.

2. **Find harmony.** On walks with
your significant other, follow his lead, mimic-
king his every move: pace, stride, and arm swing.
(You can still walk side by side.) Then switch,
and lead him. "This is a great way for couples to
get in step with each other mentally and physically," Kortge says.

"You can use your steps and words to create
a rhythm and energetic pace similar to what
music provides."

A romantic walk doesn't have to be slow,
Kortge points out. By reciting, "One, two, three.
One, two, three" as she walks, she imagines
briskly waltzing to the "Blue Danube."

When you can't walk any farther than your
treadmill, listen to beach, forest, or other nature
sounds on tapes or CDs. "Re-creating the tranquillity of a special place quiets your mind,"
Kortge says. Or "get away" with any kind of
music that transports you.

4 Weeks to Your First 5-K

Warm up and cool down with 5 to
10 minutes of easy walking and light
stretching. Allow 2 days of rest each
week.

Week 1

Day 1: Moderate pace for 2 to 3 miles
Day 2: Superfast for 6 minutes, two
or three times
Day 3: Moderate pace for 4 to 6 miles
Day 4: Moderate pace for 2 to 3 miles
Day 5: Blast off for 25 to 30 minutes

Week 2

Day 1: Moderate pace for 2.5 to 3.5
miles
Day 2: Superfast for 5 minutes,
three or four times
Day 3: Moderate pace for 4.5 to 6
miles
Day 4: Moderate pace for 2.5 to 3.5
miles
Day 5: Up/down for 22 to 29 minutes

Week 3

Day 1: Moderate pace for 3 to 4 miles
Day 2: Superfast for 8 minutes, two
or three times
Day 3: Moderate pace for 5 to 6 miles

3. **Plan a perfect ending.** Carry a
camera to capture a splendid landscape, a cluster
of wildflowers, or a marble water fountain. Your
photos will remind you of walking's pleasures.

Day 4: Moderate pace for 3 to 4 miles
Day 5: 40/20s, five to eight times

Week 4

Day 1: Moderate pace for 3.5 to 4.5 miles
Day 2: Superfast for 6 minutes, three or four times
Day 3: Moderate pace for 5 to 7 miles
Day 4: Moderate pace for 3 to 4 miles
Day 5: Blast off for 25 to 30 minutes

Rest for 2 days before the 5-K. (Skip the last workout if necessary.) The day before, stretch for 15 to 20 minutes, and walk 1 easy mile with two or three 30-second sprints.

On race day, have fun!

A moderate pace is brisk enough to get your heart pumping without leaving you out of breath.

Superfast means walk as fast as you can for 5, 6, or 8 minutes (as specified for particular days), then rest, stretching and drinking some water, for 3 to 5 minutes.

To blast off, walk at a fast pace for 5-, 4-, 3-, 2-, and 1-minute intervals. Between each fast interval, walk at a slow or moderate pace for 2 to 3 minutes.

Up/down means walk at a fast pace for 2-, 3-, 2-, 3-, and 2-minute intervals. Between each fast interval, walk at a slow or moderate pace for 2 to 3 minutes. (Also try 2-, 3-, 4-, 3-, and 2-minute fast intervals.)

For 40/20s, walk at a fast pace for 40 seconds, followed by 20 seconds of slow walking.

You can also keep a record of your walk by jotting down your thoughts and feelings in a journal after a walk. Reviewing it later will make you want to repeat it.

After a long walk, enjoy a soothing bubble bath. Create a relaxing atmosphere by lighting some scented candles and softly playing your favorite music.

Perfect Your Posture

Here are the key points for good walking posture. To check your form, have a friend watch you walk, or walk on a treadmill in front of a mirror.

Eyes: Look 6 feet in front of you.

Head: Keep your chin up and your ears in line with your shoulders.

Chest: Lift it up.

Shoulders: Keep them relaxed and down.

Arms: Relax them and let them swing from the shoulders.

Elbows: Bend them at 85- to 90-degree angles.

Hands: Loosely cup them; pump forward, not across your body.

Back: Stand straight; don't arch.

Abdominals: Keep them firm.

Hips: Swivel them.

Pelvis: Tuck it slightly by pulling your belly button back toward your spine.

Knees: Keep them soft and pointing forward.

Front foot: Plant your heel first; don't let your foot fall inward or outward.

Back foot: Roll it forward, pushing off with your toes.

Both feet: Point your toes forward, keeping your feet parallel. (You will cover ground faster if you keep your stride short— the farther you extend your leg, the more it acts as a brake.)

THE PREVENTION LIST

Real-Life Weight-Loss Secrets

Some of the best weight-loss advice you'll ever get doesn't come from big-shot doctors or hard-body exercise gurus. It comes from regular folks who fought the weight-loss battle and won.

That's the basic principle behind the best-selling book *Win the Fat War* by *Prevention* magazine's former editor-in-chief, Anne Alexander. The book is packed with specific, often surprising techniques that helped dozens of real people shed hundreds of real pounds—without starving themselves to death or chaining themselves to their treadmills.

The inventiveness of the people in the book is inspiring, as is the fact that they've *kept* off the weight they lost. Here are five of our favorite suggestions.

1. **Draw the line.** Barbara Vaughan learned a very direct way to practice portion control: She uses a knife to draw a line down the middle of her plate, neatly dividing all the food in half. She eats whatever is on one side of the line and saves the rest for later. This is part of the reason why she's 25 pounds lighter today than she was when she started.

2. **Wield the brush.** Lisa Gardiner's toothbrush helped her lose 25 pounds. She curbed late-night noshing by brushing her teeth right after dinner. That brushing became her mental signal that she was through eating for the day.

3. **Set for success.** Part of the strategy that helped Toni Willis lose five dress sizes was resetting her table: She ate her meals from a salad plate instead of a dinner plate, so it looked full even with smaller portions.

4. **Picture the pounds.** Whenever Pat Beyer gets the urge to splurge, she picks up a 5-pound bag of sugar. "Five pounds of sugar is *heavy*," she says. "When I think that I lost the equivalent of five of those bags, it's easy for me to resist temptation."

5. **Don't buy the myth.** At age 50, Connie Bissonnette didn't believe she would ever be slim again: Getting fat, she told herself, was a normal part of the aging process. Fortunately, her son, who was studying human performance at the University of Wisconsin, knew otherwise. He helped her embark on a gentle exercise program and reform her meat-and-potatoes diet. At age 54, Connie weighed 41 pounds less than she did at 50.

Safe Use Guide

Emerging Supplements

Reports of adverse effects from emerging supplements are rare, especially when compared to prescription drugs. Supplement manufacturers are required by law to provide information on labels about reasonably safe recommended dosages for healthy individuals. For this reason, you'll find that many experts in this book advise you to follow the label directions for specific supplements.

You should be aware, however, that little scientific research exists to assess the safety or long-term effects of many emerging supplements, and some supplements can complicate existing conditions or cause allergic reactions in some people. For these reasons, you should always check with your doctor before taking any supplements.

We recommend that you take supplements with food to avoid stomach irritation. Never take them as a substitute for a healthy diet, since they do not provide all the nutritional benefits of whole foods. And, if you are pregnant, nursing, or attempting to conceive, do not supplement without the supervision of your doctor.

Alpha-lipoic acid: Experimental; do not take more than 800 milligrams a day, and do not take for longer than 4 months; dosages of as much as 600 milligrams a day have been used for treatment of diabetic neuropathy and have had no serious side effects

Bioflavonoids: Doses above label recommendations may cause blood thinning and increased bleeding time

Calcium d-glucarate: Generally regarded as safe

Choline: Daily doses exceeding 3.5 grams should be taken only under medical supervision; excess choline can cause low blood pressure and a fishy body odor in some people

Chondroitin: Generally regarded as safe

Coenzyme Q$_{10}$: Supplementation for more than 20 days at a daily dose of 120 milligrams or more should be taken only with medical supervision; side effects are rare but may include heartburn, nausea, and stomachache, which can be prevented by taking the supplement with a meal; rarely, a slight decrease in the effectiveness of the blood-thinning medication warfarin (Coumadin) has been reported

Glucosamine: May cause upset stomach, heartburn, or diarrhea

Glutamine: If you have problems with your kidneys or liver, check with your physician before supplementing

Inositol hexaphosphate: Generally regarded as safe

Lactobacillus acidophilus: If you have any serious gastrointestinal problems that require medical attention, check with your doctor before supplementing; amounts exceeding 10 billion viable organisms daily may cause mild gastrointestinal distress; if you are taking antibiotics, take them at least 2 hours before supplementing

Lecithin: Doses exceeding 23 grams a day should be taken only with medical supervision; doses close to 5 grams may cause upset stomach, nausea, and diarrhea; high doses may cause sweating, salivation, and loss of appetite; some people report a fishy body odor after taking high daily doses

Melatonin: Use only under the supervision of a knowledgeable medical doctor; long-term effects are unknown; causes drowsiness—take only at bedtime and never before driving; may cause headaches, nausea, morning dizziness, depression, giddiness, difficulty concentrating, and upset stomach; may interact with prescription medications, including hormone replacement therapy; may have adverse effects if you have cardiovascular disease, high blood pressure, an autoimmune disease such as rheumatoid arthritis or lupus, diabetes, epilepsy, migraine, or personal or family history of a hormone-dependent cancer such as breast, testicular, prostate, or endometrial cancers; may cause infertility, reduced sex drive in men, hypothermia, and retinal damage

Phosphatidylserine: Generally considered to be safe

Psyllium: Do not use if you have a bowel obstruction; do not take within 1 hour of taking other drugs; take with at least 8 ounces of water

Resveratrol: Experimental; limited research conducted to date; read label directions carefully before use

SAM-e: May increase blood levels of homocysteine, a significant risk factor for cardiovascular disease

Essential Oils

Essential oils are inhaled or applied topically to the skin, but with few exceptions, they are never taken internally.

Of the most common essential oils, lavender, tea tree, lemon, sandalwood, and rose can be used undiluted. The rest should be diluted in a carrier base, which can be an oil (such as almond), a cream, or a gel, before being applied to the skin.

Many essential oils may cause irritation or allergic reactions in people with sensitive skin. Before applying any new oil to your skin, always do a patch test. Put a few drops of the essential oil, mixed with the carrier, on the back of your wrist and wait for an hour or more. If irritation or redness occurs, wash the area with cold water. In the future, use half the amount of essential oil or avoid it altogether.

Do not use essential oils at home for serious medical problems. During pregnancy, do not use essential oils unless they're approved by your doctor. Essential oils are not appropriate for children of any age.

Store essential oils in dark bottles, away from light and heat and out of the reach of children and pets.

Flower essences are not essential oils, but they are not recommended for use in the eyes, on mucous membranes, or on broken or abraded skin. Most flower essences contain alcohol as a preservative, so if you are sensitive to alcohol, check with your doctor before using them.

Basil: Do not use while nursing; do not use for extended periods of time; do not use more than three drops in bathwater

Bay: Do not use for more than 2 weeks without the guidance of a qualified practitioner

Chamomile: Generally regarded as safe

Eucalyptus: Do not use for more than 2 weeks without the guidance of a qualified practitioner; do not use more than three drops in bathwater; do not use at the same time as homeopathic remedies

Grapefruit: Generally regarded as safe

Lavender: If using undiluted oil, keep away from your eyes

Neroli: Generally regarded as safe

Peppermint: Do not use more than three drops in bathwater; do not use at the same time as homeopathic remedies; keep away from your eyes

Petitgrain: Generally regarded as safe

Sandalwood: May be used undiluted as a perfume, but keep away from your eyes

‖ Herbs

While herbal home remedies are generally safe and cause few, if any, side effects, herbalists are quick to caution that botanical medicines should be used cautiously and knowledgeably.

Most important, if you are under a doctor's care for any health condition or are taking any medication, do not take any herb or alter your medication regimen without informing your doctor. Do not administer herbs to children with-

out consulting a physician. Also, if you are pregnant, nursing, or attempting to conceive, do not self-treat with any natural remedy without the consent of your obstetrician or midwife. Some herbs may cause adverse reactions if you are allergy-prone, have a major health condition, take prescription medication, take an herb for too long, take too much, or use the herb improperly. Homeopathic remedies are generally considered safe.

The guidelines in this chart are intended for adults only and usually refer to internal use. Be aware that some herbs may cause a skin reaction when used topically. If you are applying an herb for the first time, it is always wise to do a patch test. Apply a small amount to your skin and observe the exposed area for 24 hours to be sure that you aren't sensitive. If redness or a rash occurs, discontinue use.

Due to reports that some Chinese-made products contain potentially harmful contaminants, it is recommended that you obtain Chinese herbal remedies from a qualified practitioner of Traditional Chinese Medicine. While Ayurvedic herbs do not pose the same concern, it is best to consult an Ayurvedic practitioner to obtain the highest-quality herbs and receive personalized recommendations regarding their safe use.

Ashwaganda (*Withania somnifera*): Do not use with barbiturates—may intensify their effects

Bilberry (*Vaccinium myrtillus*): Generally regarded as safe

Black cohosh (*Actea racemosa*): Do not use for more than 6 months

Boswellia (*Boswellia serrata*): Generally regarded as safe

Cascara sagrada (*Rhamnus purshianus*): Do not use if you have an inflammatory condition of the intestines, intestinal obstruction, or abdominal pain; may cause laxative dependency and diarrhea; do not use for more than 14 days

Celery (*Apium graveolens*): If you have a kidney disorder, use therapeutic doses with caution; wear sunscreen while taking it—it can make your skin more sensitive to the sun

Chamomile (*Matricaria recutita*): Very rarely, may cause an allergic reaction when ingested; drink the tea with caution if you are allergic to closely related plants, such as ragweed, asters, and chrysanthemums

Cinnamon (*Cinnamomum zeylanicum*): Generally regarded as safe

Cordyceps (*Cordyceps sinensis*): Generally regarded as safe

Echinacea (*Echinacea angustifolia, E. purpurea, E. pallida*): Do not use if you are allergic to closely related plants, such as ragweed, asters, and chrysanthemums; do not use if you have tuberculosis or an autoimmune condition such as lupus or multiple sclerosis; stimulates the immune system

Garlic (*Allium sativum*): Do not use supplements if you are taking anticoagulants (blood thinners) or before undergoing surgery; thins the blood and may increase bleeding; do not use more than two cloves of fresh garlic daily prior to surgery or if you are taking anticoagulants; do not use if you are taking drugs to lower blood sugar

Ginger (*Zingiber officinale*): If you have gallstones, do not use therapeutic amounts of dried root or powder unless under the supervision of a knowledgeable medical doctor; may increase bile secretion

Ginkgo (*Ginkgo biloba*): Do not use with antidepressant MAO inhibitor drugs such as phenelzine sulfate (Nardil) or tranylcypromine (Parnate), aspirin or other nonsteroidal anti-inflammatory medications, or blood-thinning medications such as warfarin (Coumadin); may cause dermatitis, diarrhea, and vomiting in doses exceeding 240 milligrams of concentrated extract

Ginseng (*Panax ginseng, Panax quinquefolius*): May cause irritability if taken with caffeine or other stimulants; do not take if you have high blood pressure

Goldenrod (*Solidago virgaurea*): Do not use if you have a chronic kidney disorder

Gotu kola (*Centella asiatica*): Generally regarded as safe

Grape seed extract (*Vitis vinifera*): Generally regarded as safe

Hawthorn (*Crataegus oxycantha, C. laevigata, C. monogyna*): If you have a cardiovascular condition, do not take regularly for more than a few weeks unless under the supervision of a knowledgeable medical doctor; you may require lower doses of other medications, such as blood pressure drugs; if you have low blood pressure caused by heart valve problems, do not use without medical supervision

Horsetail (*Equisetum spp.*): Do not use tincture if you have heart or kidney problems; may cause a thiamin deficiency; do not take more than 2 grams per day of powdered extract or take for prolonged periods

Kava (*Piper methysticum*): Do not use with alcohol or barbiturates; do not exceed the dosage recommended on the label; use caution when driving or operating equipment—kava is a muscle relaxant

Licorice (*Glycyrrhiza glabra*): Do not use if you have diabetes, high blood pressure, liver or kidney disorders, or low potassium levels; do not use daily for more than 4 to 6 weeks because overuse can lead to water retention, high blood pressure caused by potassium loss, or impaired heart and kidney function

Maitake (*Grifola frondosa*): Generally regarded as safe

Oats (*Avena sativa*): Do not use if you have celiac disease (gluten intolerance)—contains gluten, a grain protein

Oregon grape (*Mahonia aquifolium*): Generally regarded as safe

Rosemary (*Rosmarinus officinalis*): May cause excessive menstrual bleeding in therapeutic amounts; considered safe when used as a spice

Sage (*Salvia officinalis*): In therapeutic amounts, can increase sedative side effects of drugs; do not use if you have low blood sugar or are undergoing anticonvulsant therapy

St. John's wort (*Hypericum perforatum*): Do not use with antidepressants unless under the supervision of a knowledgeable medical doctor; avoid direct sunlight while using; may cause skin sensitivity

Saw palmetto (*Serenoa repens*): Consult your doctor before using to treat enlarged prostate

Siberian ginseng (*Eleutherococcus senticosus*): Generally regarded as safe

Turmeric (*Curcuma domestica*): Do not use medicinally if you have high stomach acid or ulcers, gallstones, or bile duct obstruction

Valerian (*Valeriana officinalis*): May intensify the effects of sleep-enhancing or mood-regulating medications; may cause heart palpitations and nervousness in sensitive individuals—if such stimulant action occurs, discontinue use

Vitamins and Minerals

Although reports of toxicity from vitamins and minerals are rare, they do occur. This guide is designed to help you use vitamins and minerals safely. The doses mentioned below are not recommendations; rather, they are the levels at which harmful side effects can occur. Some people may experience problems at significantly lower levels, however.

For best absorption and minimal stomach irritation, take most supplements with a meal unless otherwise indicated. It's important to realize that supplements should never be taken as substitutes for a healthy diet, since they do not provide all the nutritional benefits of whole foods. If you have a serious chronic illness that requires continual medical supervision, always talk to your doctor before self-treating. And even if you're perfectly healthy, you should always tell your doctor which supplements you're taking. That way, if you need medication for any reason, your doctor can take your supplements into consideration and avoid dangerous drug combinations. If you are pregnant, nursing, or attempting to conceive, do not take supplements without a doctor's supervision.

Vitamin A: Taking more than 10,000 IU a day may cause vomiting, fatigue, dizziness, and blurred vision; do not exceed 10,000 IU daily unless under the supervision of a knowledgeable medical doctor; pregnant women should avoid doses of 5,000 IU or more

B-complex vitamins: Do not exceed the dosage recommended on the label

Vitamin B$_6$: Daily doses of more than 100 milligrams may cause nerve damage, resulting in a tingling sensation in the fingers and toes; other possible side effects include pain, numbness, weakness in the limbs, depression, and fatigue; do not exceed 100 milligrams daily unless under the supervision of a knowledgeable medical doctor

Vitamin B$_{12}$: No known toxicity

Beta-carotene: Doses exceeding 15 milligrams seem to have no benefit and should be taken only under the supervision of a knowledgeable medical doctor; in one study, smokers who received doses of 30 milligrams had an increased risk of lung cancer

Biotin: No known toxicity

Vitamin C: Daily doses exceeding 1,000 milligrams may cause diarrhea

Calcium: (all forms) Do not exceed 2,500 milligrams daily unless under the supervision of a knowledgeable medical doctor; some natural sources of calcium, such as bone meal and dolomite, may be contaminated with lead

Chromium: (all forms) Do not exceed 200 micrograms daily unless under the supervision of a knowledgeable medical doctor

Copper: Do not exceed 9 milligrams daily unless under the supervision of a knowledgeable medical doctor

Vitamin D: Do not exceed 2,000 IU (50 micrograms) daily unless under the supervision of a knowledgeable medical doctor

Vitamin E: Do not exceed 400 IU daily unless under the supervision of a knowledgeable medical doctor; may increase risk of hemorrhagic stroke; because the vitamin acts as a blood thinner, consult your doctor before beginning supplementation in any amount if you're already taking aspirin or a blood-thinning medication such as warfarin (Coumadin), or if you're at high risk for stroke

Folic acid: Do not take more than 1,000 micrograms daily unless under the supervision of a knowledgeable medical doctor

Iron: For most people, doses exceeding 25 milligrams daily must be taken under medical supervision; the maximum daily dose for men and postmenopausal women is 10 milligrams

Vitamin K: Take only under the supervision of a knowledgeable medical doctor

Magnesium: (all forms) Check with your doctor before beginning supplementation if you have heart or kidney problems; doses exceeding 350 milligrams a day may cause diarrhea

Niacin: (all forms) Do not exceed 35 milligrams daily unless under the supervision of a knowledgeable medical doctor

Pantothenic acid: Relatively nontoxic

Potassium: Take only under the supervision of a knowledgeable medical doctor

Riboflavin: No known toxicity

Selenium: Do not exceed 200 micrograms daily unless under the supervision of a knowledgeable medical doctor

Thiamin: No known toxicity

Zinc: Do not exceed 30 milligrams daily unless under the supervision of a knowledgeable medical doctor

Credits

Cover photograph

Rodale Images

Interior photographs

Roderick Angle: page 179

Bettmann/Corbis: page 80

Charles William Bush: page 54

Angelo Caggiano: pages 109, 116, 119, 122, 123

Andrew Eccles/ABC: page 167

Tony Esparza/CBS: page 140

Eyewire: page 61

Mitchell Gerber/Corbis: page 14

Michael Goldman/FPG: page 217

Brian Hagiwara: pages 71, 135, 300

John P. Hamel/Rodale Images: pages 52, 102, 176

Hilmar: pages xiv, 2, 5, 7, 9, 15, 16, 18, 21, 39, 44, 47, 59, 63, 65, 67, 72, 74, 94, 97, 101, 104, 142, 145, 147, 160, 162, 164, 168, 170, 191, 192, 197, 200, 204, 206, 207, 214, 221, 222

Jeff Katz/ABC: page 3

Michael A. Keller Studios: page 149

Graham Kuhn: page 11

Ed Landrock/Rodale Images: pages 40, 98, 138, 143

Catherine Ledner/Corbis Outline: page 172

Mitch Mandel/Rodale Images: pages 136, 146, 174, 186

Don Mason: page 158

Nature's Herbs, a TwinLab Division: page 159

Courtesy of NBC: page 78

Joseph Pluchino: page 178

Stephanie Rausser: page 155

Thomas Renaut/Stone: page 166

Rodale Images: pages 24, 27, 31, 33, 37, 42, 45, 49, 57, 77, 151, 211, 223

Margaret Skrovanek/Rodale Images: page 92

Wendy Smith/Rodale Images: page 87

Kurt Wilson/Rodale Images: pages 50, 66, 107, 108, 110, 111, 113, 114, 115, 117, 120, 121, 125, 126, 127, 128, 129, 131, 132, 133, 134, 182, 187, 194

Courtesy of WPLJ FM Radio: page 209

Victoria Yee/Stone: page 177

INDEX

Boldface page references indicate photographs. <u>Underscored</u> references indicate boxed text.

Conversion Chart

These equivalents have been slightly rounded to make measuring easier.

VOLUME MEASUREMENTS

U.S.	Imperial	Metric
¼ tsp	–	1 ml
½ tsp	–	2 ml
1 tsp	–	5 ml
1 Tbsp	–	15 ml
2 Tbsp (1 oz)	1 fl oz	30 ml
¼ cup (2 oz)	2 fl oz	60 ml
⅓ cup (3 oz)	3 fl oz	80 ml
½ cup (4 oz)	4 fl oz	120 ml
⅔ cup (5 oz)	5 fl oz	160 ml
¾ cup (6 oz)	6 fl oz	180 ml
1 cup (8 oz)	8 fl oz	240 ml

WEIGHT MEASUREMENTS

U.S.	Metric
1 oz	30 g
2 oz	60 g
4 oz (¼ lb)	115 g
5 oz (⅓ lb)	145 g
6 oz	170 g
7 oz	200 g
8 oz (½ lb)	230 g
10 oz	285 g
12 oz (¾ lb)	340 g
14 oz	400 g
16 oz (1 lb)	455 g
2.2 lb	1 kg

LENGTH MEASUREMENTS

U.S.	Metric
¼"	0.6 cm
½"	1.25 cm
1"	2.5 cm
2"	5 cm
4"	11 cm
6"	15 cm
8"	20 cm
10"	25 cm
12" (1')	30 cm

PAN SIZES

U.S.	Metric
8" cake pan	20 × 4 cm sandwich or cake tin
9" cake pan	23 × 3.5 cm sandwich or cake tin
11" × 7" baking pan	28 × 18 cm baking tin
13" × 9" baking pan	32.5 × 23 cm baking tin
15" × 10" baking pan	38 × 25.5 cm baking tin (Swiss roll tin)
1½ qt baking dish	1.5 liter baking dish
2 qt baking dish	2 liter baking dish
2 qt rectangular baking dish	30 × 19 cm baking dish
9" pie plate	22 × 4 or 23 × 4 cm pie plate
7" or 8" springform pan	18 or 20 cm springform or loose-bottom cake tin
9" × 5" loaf pan	23 × 13 cm or 2 lb narrow loaf tin or pâté tin

TEMPERATURES

Fahrenheit	Centigrade	Gas
140°	60°	–
160°	70°	–
180°	80°	–
225°	110°	–
250°	120°	½
300°	150°	2
325°	160°	3
350°	180°	4
375°	190°	5
400°	200°	6
450°	230°	8
500°	260°	–